MIX
Papier aus verantwortungsvollen Quellen
Paper from responsible sources
FSC® C105338

Suresh Mani Tripathi

Fundamental Rights and Directive Principles in India

Anchor Academic
Publishing

Tripathi, Suresh Mani: Fundamental Rights and Directive Principles in India, Hamburg, Anchor Academic Publishing 2016

Buch-ISBN: 978-3-96067-003-2
PDF-eBook-ISBN: 978-3-96067-503-7
Druck/Herstellung: Anchor Academic Publishing, Hamburg, 2016

Bibliografische Information der Deutschen Nationalbibliothek:
Die Deutsche Nationalbibliothek verzeichnet diese Publikation in der Deutschen Nationalbibliografie; detaillierte bibliografische Daten sind im Internet über http://dnb.d-nb.de abrufbar.

Bibliographical Information of the German National Library:
The German National Library lists this publication in the German National Bibliography. Detailed bibliographic data can be found at: http://dnb.d-nb.de

Hermannstal 119k, 22119 Hamburg
http://www.diplomica-verlag.de, Hamburg 2016
Printed in Germany

Preface

The Constitution of India is social document which contains various aspects of ideas of our Founding Father. The preambular promise of socio economic justice has been in corporated by the Founding Father in various provisions of Part 3 and Part 4 of the Constitution which represents Fundamental Rights and Directive Principles of State Policy respectively. This is an humble attempt on the part of a beginner in the field of legal writing. This book contain the meaning,concept and development of Fundamental Rights and Directive Principles of State Policy.An attempt has been made in this book to present in a systematic manner the Fundamental Rights and Directive Principles of State Policy. As embodied in the Constitution of India. The historical aspects of the subject has also been dealt with in a lucid and interesting manner. The changing dimension of Fundamental Rights and Directive Principles of State Policy has also been deal in this book..Every point has been explained with the help of new case law and articles of the Constitution.

I am grateful to my Parents **Sri Roop Narian Tripathi**, Add. District and session Judge (Retd.).Bihar and **Smt Kalawati Tripathi** who inspired me to write this book..I am also thankful to my elder brother **Sri Umesh Mani Tripathi**,JM first class,Bihar who inspired me and gave some valuable suggestions. I am also thankful to my sister **Ms Shashi Tripathi** and **Dr. V.S. Tripathi**, Sr.Lecturer , B N D College, Kanpur University, UP who encourage me to write this book.

I am also grateful to **Prof. R K Mishra**, Ex Dean, Faculty of Law BHU and Vice Chancellor of DDU Gorakhpur University, **Abha Trivedi**, Associate Professor ,Law faculty, BHU and **Dr Bibha Tripathi**, Associate Professor, Faculty of Law.I am also grateful to my supervisor **Dr CP Upadhyay**, Associate Professor,Faculty of Law for his kind guidance and blessings.

I am also thankful to my friends **Mr Shashank Singh**,JM,MP,**Mr Awadh Kishore**,JM, Chhattisgarh, **Mr.Ratneshwar Singh**, **Mr. Sharad Chandra Mishra**, **Mr. Pradeep Kr. Tiwari, Mr. Neeraj singh, Mr. Gazi Saiful Hasan,** Sr.,Lecturer,Metropolitan University, Bangladesh, **Mr.Bibek Kr. Paudel,** Associate professor, Tribhuvan University, Nepal, **Rhem Rick Corpuz** Faculty at Angeles University Foundation, Philippines, **Ambalika Biswas,** Associate Lecturer, Royal Thimphu College, Royal University of Bhutan, **Zelina Sultana**, Lecturer, Department of Law, Jagannath University ,Bangladesh, **David Tushaus,** Missouri Western State University, USA, **Dr.Palollo Michael Lehloenya,** Sr. Lecturer, University of South Africa(UNISA) and Editorial Board of an International Journal **''Indian Journal Of Socio Legal Studies, ISSN 2320-8562.''**

Lastly,I thank to the editorial team of Publication House for their excellent work in bringing out this book in record time. It is hoped that this book will serve the genuine need of the students of law and other persons. Any suggestion for the book shall be highly appreciated and gratefully accepted.

Suresh Mani Tripathi.
Assistant Professor (Law),
Govt. Naveen Law College
Chhattisgarh Higher Education
Chhattisgarh

About the book

This book is fully devoted to the Fundamental Rights and Directive Principles of State Policy under Indian Constitution. In this book the author has described the historical back ground of Fundamental Rights and Directive Principles of State Policy and what were the view of Constituent Assembly about these rights. An attempt has been made to dissect the various parts of these rights. A comparative study of Fundamental rights and Directive Principles of State Policy is also made in this book.A comparative analysis of Fundamental Rights and Directive Principles of State Policy under Indian Constitution has also been made. The most important part of this book is the changing dimension of Directive Principle vis-à-vis Fundamental Rights

Abbreviations

A.P.	:	Andhra Pradesh
AIR	:	All India Reporter
Alld.	:	Allahabad
Art.	:	Article
Bom	:	Bombay
Cl.	:	Clause
CULR	:	Cochine University Law Review
e.g.	:	Example gratia
ed.	:	Edited
etc.	:	etcetra
Ibid	:	Ibidum
JILI	:	Journal of Indian Law Institute
KLT	:	Karnataka Law Times
Pun.	:	Punjab
SC	:	Supreme Court
SCC	:	Supreme Court Cases
SCJ	:	Supreme Court Journal
Supra	:	as above
Viz.	:	Namely
Vol.	:	Volume

List of Cases

List of Cases	*Citation*
A.B.S.K. Singh(Rly.) V. Union of India	*AIR 1981 SC. 298*
Abdul Rahman Antuley Vs. R.S. Nayak	*AIR 1992 SC 1630*
AIIMS Students' Union v. AIIMS	*(2002) 1 SCC 428*
Ajaib Singh V. State of Punjab	*AIR 1952 Pun. 309*
Asstt. Commissioner Vs. B&C Co	*AIR 1970 SC 169*
Bai Tahisa Vs. Ali Hassein Fissali Chotia	*AIR 1979 SC 362*
Bajiban Salambhai Chauhan Vs. UPSRTC	*(1990) Supp SCC 769*
Baldev Raj Guliani v. Punjab and Haryana High Court	*(1976) 4 SCC 201*
Bandhua Mukti Morcha V. Union of India	*AIR 1984 SC 82*
Bandhua Mukti Morcha Vs. Union of India.	*AIR 1984 SC 802*
Bhim Singh V. Union of India,	*AIR 1981 SC 234*
Buddhu V. Municipal Board. Allahabad,	*AIR 1951 Alld. 753*
C. I. Water Transport Corp. Ltd. Vs. Brajonath	*AIR 1986 SC. 1571*
C.B. Boarding and lodging V. State of Mysore	*AIR 1970 SC. 2024*
Consumer Ed. and Research Centre V. U.O.I.	*AIR 1995 SC 923*
Corpn. Vs Sitaram Mills Ltd	*AIR 1986 SC 1234*
Ct Balwant Raj Vs U.O.I	*AIR 1968 ALL 14*
D. Bhuvan Mohan Patnaik v. State of Andhra Pradesh,	*AIR 1974 SC 2092*

D.S. Nakara v. Union of India	*AIR 1983 SC 13*
Daily Casual Labour Employees and P & T Dept., Vs. Union of India	*AIR 1987 SC 2342*
Jacob Vs.Kerala Water Authority	*AIR 1990 SC 2228*
Daryao v. State of U.P	*AIR 1961 SC 1457*
Delhi Domestic Working Women's Forum Vs. Union of India	*(1995)1 SCC 14*
Francis Coralie v. union territory of India	*AIR 1978 SC 597)*
Gaurav Jain Vs. Union of India	*(1997) 8 SCC 114*
Golaknath V. State of Punjab	*AIR 1967 SC 1643*
Grih Kalyan Kendra V. Union of India	*AIR 1991 SC 1173*
Gujarat Electricity Board, Vs. Hind Mazdoor Sabha	*AIR 1995 SC 1893*
Hanif Quareshi Mohd. Vs. State of Bihar	*AIR 1958 SC 731*
In re Kerla Education Bill	*AIR 1958 SC. 956*
Jacob M. Pathuparambi V. Kerla Water Authority	*(1991) 1 SCC. 28*
Jagannath L Vs. LRO Madurai	*AIR 1972 SC 425*
Jagwant Kaur V. State of Bombay	*AIR 1952 Bom. 461*
John Vallamottam V. Union of India	*AIR 2003 SC 2902*
Kapoor Vs. Union of India	*AIR 1990 SC 1923*
Kesavananda Bharati V. State of Kerla,	*AIR 1973 SC 1416*
Kirloskar Brothers Ltd., Vs. E.S. I C	*1996)2 SCC 682*
Kishan Pattanayak V. State of Orrisa 1989	*Supp(1) SCC 258*
Kishen Pattnayak Vs. State of Orrisa,	*1989 Supp (1) SCC 258*
Laxmi Kant Panddy Vs. Union of India .	*AIR 1987 SC 232*
M.C. Mehta v. Union of India	*(1996) 6 SCC 756*

M.C. Mehta V. Union of India	*(1988) 1 SCC 471*
M.C. Mehta v. Union of India,	*AIR 2007 SC 1087*
M.C. Mehta v. Union of India,	*MANU/SC/0271/2003*
M.C. Mehta Vs. Union of India	*AIR 1997 SC 735*
M.H. Hoskot Vs. State of Maharashtra	*AIR 1978 SC 1548*
Mackinon Mackenzie and Co. Ltd Vs. Andry D'costa	*AIR 1987 SC 1281*
Maneka Gandhi V. Union of India	*AIR 1978 SC 597*
Md. Hanif Qureshi V. State of Bihar	*AIR 1958 SC 731*
Minerva Mills Ltd. V. Union of India	*AIR 1980 SC. 1789*
Mohini Jain V. State of Karnataka	*(1992)1 SCC. 28*
Mukesh Advani Vs. State of M.P.	*AIR 1985 SC 1363*
Mumbai Kamgar Sabha V. Abdul Bai,	*AIR 1974 SC 1455*
Mumbai Kamgar Sabha Vs. Abdul Bhai;	*AIR 1976 SC 1455*
Municipal Corporation of Delhi Vs. Female Workers	*AIR 2000 SC 1274*
Narendra Prasadji A P Maharaj Vs. St of Gujarat	*AIR 1974 SC 2008*
Narendrea Prasad V. State of Gujrat	*AIR 1974 SC 2098*
Nashirwar Vs St of M.P	*AIR 1975 SC 360*
Olga Tellis V. Bombay Municipal Coporation	*AIR 1986 SC 180*
Omprakash V. State	*AIR 1951 Pun. 93*
Pareena Swarup Vs. Union of India	*2009 AIR SCW 206*
Peoples Union for civil liberty V. Union of India	*(204) 6 SCC 23*
R L E K & Ors. v. State of Uttar Pradesh & Ors	*1986 (Supp) SCC 517*
R. Chandevarappa v. State of Karnataka	*(1995) 5 SCALE 620*

Ramesh Chandra Kaushal Capt Vs Veena Kaushal *AIR 1978 SC 1807*

Randhir Singh V. Union of India *AIR 1982 SC 879*

Ratlam Municipal Counsil Vs. Vardhichand *AIR 1980 SC 1622*

Razakbai Issukbai Mansuri Vs. State of Gujarat *1993 Supp (2) SCC 659*

Sajjan Singh V. State of Rajsthan, *AIR 1965 SC. 845*

Samantha V. State of A.P. *1997 8 SCC 191*

Sanjeev Coke Manufacturing Co., Vs B C C Ltd. *AIR 1983 SC 239*

Sarla Mugdal V. Union of India *(1995) 3 SCC 635*

Sheela Barse Vs. State of Maharashtra . *AIR 1983 SC 378*

State of Bihar V. Kameshwar Singh *AIR 1952 SC. 292*

State of Gujarat v. Mirzapur Moti Kureshi Kassab Jamat, *AIR 2006 SC 212*

State of Kerala Versus B. Renjith Kumar & Others *CDJ 2008 SC 1101*

State of Kerala Vs. Joseph Antony *AIR 1994 SC 721*

State of Kerala Vs. Thomas *AIR 1976 SC 490*

State of Kerla V. N.M. Thomas, *AIR 1976 SC. 490*

State of Madras V. Champakam Dorairajan *AIR 1951 SC 226.*

State of Punjab Vs. Mohinder Singh Chowla *AIR 1997 SC 1225*

State of T.N. Vs Sri A P Samadhi Adheenakartha, *(1997) 9 SCC 313*

State of TamilNadu C. Abu Kayur Bai *AIR 1984 SC 626*

T.N. Godavarman Thirumalpad v. Union of India & Ors *(2002) 10 SCC 606*

TMA Pai Foundation V. State of Karnataka *(2002) 8 SCC 481*

Union of India v. Dineshan K. *(2008) 1 SCC 586*

Unni Krishnan V. State of A.P. *(1993) 1 SCC. 645*

UPSE Board Vs. Harishankar Jain	*AIR 1979 SC 65*
V. Markandeya v. State of A.P	*AIR 1989 SC 1308*
Vincent Parikurlangara Vs. Union of India ,	*(1987) 2 SCC 165*
Vishaka Vs. State of Rajasthan	*AIR1997 SC 3011*

CONTENTS

(C) Purpose of Directive Principles of State Policy

(D) Characteristics of Directive Principles of State Policy

(E) Status of the Directive Principles of State Policy

(3) Classification of Fundamental Rights and Directive Principles of State Policy in Indian Constitution

(A) Classification of Fundamental Rights

(i) Right to Equality

(ii) Right to Freedom

(iii) Right against Exploitation

(iv) Right to Freedom of Religion

(v) Cultural and Educational Rights

(vi) Right to Constitutional Remedies

(B) Classification of Directive Principles

(i) Social and Economic Charter

(a) Social order based on Justice

(b) Principle of Policy to be followed by the State for securing Economic Justice

(c) Means of livelihood

(d) Distributive Economic system

(e) No concentration of wealth

(f) Equal pay for Equal work.

(g) Welfare of children

(h) Bonded Labour.

i. Freedom of Speech and Expression and its limitations in Indian Constitution and other Constitutions

ii. Freedom of Assembly and its limitations in Indian Constitution and other Constitutions

iii. Freedom of Association and Union and its limitations in Indian Constitution and other Constitutions

iv. Freedom of movement and residence and its limitation in Indian Constitution and other Constitutions

v. Right to Property in Constitutions

(C) Right against Exploitation in Indian Constitution and other Constitutions

i. Prohibition of traffic in human beings and forced labour in Indian Constitution and other Constitutions

ii. Prohibition of employment of Children in factories, etc in Indian Constitution and other Constitutions

(D) Right to Freedom of Religion in Indian Constitution and other Constitutions

i. Freedom of conscience and free profession Practice and Propagation of religion in Indian Constitution and other Constitutions

ii. Freedom to manage religious affairs in Indian Constitution and other Constitutions

iii. Freedom Not to pay Taxes for religious Promotion in Indian Constitution and other Constitutions

iv. Freedom not to attend religious instructions in Indian Constitution and other Constitutions

(E) Cultural and Educational Rights in Indian Constitution and other Constitutions

i. Protection of interest of Minorities in Indian Constitution and other Constitutions

ii. Right to Minorities to Establish and Administer Educational Institutions in Indian Constitution and other Constitutions

(F) Saving of Certain laws in Indian Constitution and other Constitutions

i. Saving to laws Providing for acquisition of estates, etc. (Article 31-A)

ii. Validation of certain Acts and Regulations (Article 31-B)

iii. Saving of laws giving effect to certain Directive Principles (Article 31-C)

(G) Right to Constitutional Remedies in Indian Constitution and other Constitutions

i. India: Article 32

ii. India: Article 33

iii. India: Article 34

iv. India: Article 35

(2) Directive Principles under Indian Constitution and other Constitutions

(A) Social and Economic charter in Indian Constitution and other Constitutions

i. Social order based on Justice in Indian Constitution and other Constitutions

ii. Economic Justice in Indian Constitution and other Constitutions

(B) Social Security charter in Indian Constitution and other Constitutions

i. Equal Justice and Free Legal Aid in Indian Constitution and other Constitutions

ii. Social Services in Indian Constitution and other Constitutions

iii. Condition of work in Indian Constitution and other Constitutions

iv. Living wages in Indian Constitution and other Constitutions

v. Participation of Workers in Management of Industries in Indian Constitution and other Constitutions

vi. Free and Compulsory Education in Indian Constitution and other Constitutions

vii. Promotion of Educational and Economic Interests of weaker section in Indian Constitution and other Constitutions

viii. Raising standard of living in Indian Constitution and other Constitution

(C) Community Welfare Charter in Indian Constitution and other Constitutions

i. Organisation of Village Panchayats in Indian Constitution and other Constitutions

ii. Uniform Civil Code in Indian Constitution and other Constitutions

iii. Organisation of Agriculture and Animal husbandry in Indian Constitution and other Constitutions

iv. Protection of Environment in Indian Constitution and other Constitutions

Chapter I

Introduction

Synopsis

(1) Evolution of Fundamental Right

Idea of Fundamental Rights in India prior to the Constitution

(i) The Constitution of India Bill, 1895

(ii) The commonwealth of India Bill, 1925

(iii) Nehru Report, 1928

(iv) Karachi Revolutions, 1931

(v) Govt. of India Act, 1935

(vi) Sapru Committee Report

(2) Evolution of Directive Principles of State Policy

Idea of Directive Principles of State Policy in India prior to the Constitution

(i) The Constitution of India Bill, 1895

(ii) The commonwealth of India Bill, 1925

(iii) Nehru Report, 1928

(v) Sapru Committee Report

(3) Fundamental Rights and Directive Principles and Constituent Assembly Debate

(A)Fundamental Rights and Directive Principles in Rau's Draft Constitution.

(i) Fundamental Rights in Rau's Draft Constitution

(ii) Directive Principles in Rau's Draft Constitution

(B) Deliberation of Drafting committee and final adoption of Directive Principles.

(4) Sources of Directive Principles in Indian Constitution

The Indian constitution is first and foremost a social document and socio-economic justice is its signature tune. Socio economic justice is the cornerstone emblem of peoples Constituted edifice. The Directive Principles enshrined in Part IV and Fundamental Rights enshrined in Part III of the constitution epitomise the ideals, the aspirations, the sentiments, the Precepts and the goals of our entire freedom movement.

The Fundamental Rights and the Directive Principles of State policy in the constitution of India are the Products of human right movement. Roughly they represent the two stream in the evolution of human right, which divide them into the so-called negative and Positive or Civil and Political and Social and economic rights respectively. More exactly justiciablity in the basis of division between them. The Fundamental Rights are justiciable, while the Directive Principles are not. It is this difference which initially led the Supreme Court to hold that "the Directive Principles........ have to conform to and run as subsidiary to the chapter of Fundamental Rights."[1] The position was disapproved through constitutional changes, juristic writings and subsequent judicial decision. Finally, the court held that "harmony and balance between Fundamental Rights and Directive Principles is an essential feature of the basic structure of the Constitution". Granville Austin rightly pointed out that both "Fundamental Rights" and "Directive Principles" Constitute "Conscience of the constitution" and they were included in the

[1] State of Madras Vs. Champakam Dorairajan AIR 1951 SC. 226

constitution with the hope and expectation that "One day the tree of true liberty world bloom in India." No doubt Fundamental Rights occupy a very important place in the Constitution but for a common man directive Principles enshrined in Part IV comes first and Fundamental Rights later because excellence comes only after existence. Though Directive Principles are not enforceable in the court of law yet they are "fundamental in the governance of the country" and what is fundamental in the governance of the country cannot be less fundamental then the Fundamental Rights of the individual. Directive Principles represent the goals which all the three organs of the state, i.e., executive, legislature and judicature must try to achieve within the shortest possible Span of time.

In evolving the Fundamental Rights and Directive Principles our founding fathers in addition to the experience gathered by from the events that took place in other Part of the world, also largely drew on their own experience in the Past. The Directive in Part IV of the constitution form an organic unit along with the fundamental Rights in Part IV. According to Justice Deshpandey "they were divided into two Parts for the Sake of convenience", because it was thought that the Directive Principles by their very nature cannot be made justiciable through Courts, he said that "Part IV of the Constitution deals with the area of individual freedom and the extent to which the State can restrain the freedom but Part IV deals with the object of the State and are morally binding on the Legislature and the Executive. The Judiciary Stands outside the Government under Part III and IV of the constitution. So that it may be able to enforce not only the Fundamental Rights in Part III of the Constitution but also the legislation enacted in pursuance of Part IV of the Constitution. The Directive Principles of State policy require to be implemented by specific legislation. The goals or direction set out in Part IV cannot be altered by the States. Those who are having a doubtful opinion about the Directive Principles because of its unenforceability should know that this does not make these Principles less important and unworthy of serious consideration, M.C. Setalvad in his thanks-giving speech at the B.N. Rau Memorial lecture, said that "*these are not enforceable in the court of law because it is not for the court of law to legislate, to act executively so as to carry out the various measures laid down in Part IV for the welfare of the people.*" It is for the State to take necessary steps by means of making Proper laws and executing such laws to translate the ideals enshrined in Part IV into reality. Thus, the directive principle of State policy should not be considered as mere pious wishes or Platitudes of no significance. They also act as a catalyst of special revolution and serve as the code of interpretation for the judiciary.

Directive Principles of State policy are fundamental postulates of social revolution, as envisaged by the founding fathers and as reflected in the aspiration of the People. They have been designed as the Prime movers of the dynamics of Social change and have been rightly termed as the *'Conscience o the Constitution'*.

Although the idea for inclusion of Directive Principle of State Policy in the framework of the Indian Constitution was borrowed, primarily, from the Irish Constitution, it had undergone vital changes at the hands of the framers of the Indian Constitution, inter alia, in its scope and applicability. The vital change that the Indian Constitution makers made even, at the outset, while borrowing the idea of the Irish Directives was in respect of its applicability and scope. Whereas in the Irish Constitution the Principle Contained in the "Directives" were intended for the general guidance and Care of the Oireachtas alone, and in the Indian Constitution it was made fundamental in the governance of the country and the "duty of the State" to apply these Principles in framing laws. In other words, the frames of the Indian Constitution not merely enhanced the Stature of the Directive by making it "fundamental" in the governance of the Indian

Union but also broad based it by making it a 'duty' devolving upon the Spite as a whole, which included not only the legislative machinery but also the executive and administrative machinery in the Union, State and local levels to take cognizance of the directive and apply them in framing laws.

The Constitution of India classified the rights into two distinct categories- Justiciable right and non justiciable right as Fundamental Rights and Directive Principles of State Policy. Thus both of these parts being integral components of the same organic Constitutional and system, no conflict between them could have been intended by the founding fathers. The history of Fundamental Rights and Directive Principles and the circumstances of their adoption reveal that there could not possibly be any conflict between them. The Constituent Assembly entrusted its Fundamental Rights Sub Committee with the task of providing of Fundamental Rights. The Fundamental Right sub committee had recommended that the list of Fundamental Rights Should be Prepared in two parts, the first part consisting of rights enforceable by appropriate legal process, and the Second consisting of Directive Principles of State policy, which though not enforceable in courts were nevertheless to be regarded as "fundamental in the governance of the country". With the growth of a ideal of welfare State, it has become a common practice to provide in the Constitution for social and economic policy. Several Constitution stated such 'Directives' to be followed by the States, naturally. In Past Nehru Committee and Sapru Committee was also in favour of Directives and Fundamental Rights.

Hence it is not surprising that the framers Provided for the Directives of State Policy. Novelty was in fact that they made these directives non judiciable. In making then so, the Constitution makers looked more to the Irish Constitution. The transformation of these 'Directive Principles' into justiciable rights would have entailed changes of vast magnitude in the social and economic structure of the country for which the makers of the Indian Constitution were not then Prepared although they aimed at their realisation by a slow and gradual process.

In this book an attempt has been made to dissect the anatomy of various aspects of Directive Principles and Fundamental Rights and Changing dimensions of 'Directive' jurisprudence. In the recent years the judicial activism has provided further impetus to the importance of various Directive Principles. They have been treated as reasonable restrictions in the public interest. Agarian reform legislation aiming of Socio-economic Justice have been upheld by the judiciary from time to time. Today judiciary has recognised many directive i.e., right to health, right to education, right to food, right to free legal aid, right to equal pay for equal work etc. as a Fundamental Rights.

Objective of the Study

Against this background the present study make a humble attempt to discuss the nature, concept and changing dimension of Directive Principles vis-a-vis Fundamental Rights. The aim of the present study is also to discuss and examine the justiciability of Directive Principles and the aim of Judiciary towards the implementation of Directive Principles.

Research Methodology

Keeping in view the nature of the problem analytical, descriptive, informative and evaluative methods have been adopted to draw the necessary interferences and conclusions. Materials for the present study have been collected from the both primary and secondary sources. In general, Constituent Assembly Debates, Legislations, Statutes and Judicial decision of

Supreme Court have been consulted. The study also makes an extensive use of materials available on the websites.

Framework of the Study

In the light of forgoing discussion, the main issues and Problem, which deserve query in the context of Directive Principle Jurisprudence and Fundamental Rights, have been divided into the Seven Chapters. The First chapter deals with the introduction of Directive Principles vis-a-vis Fundamental Rights. It consist introductory highlights of the general scheme of Directive Principle and socio economic justice.

Second Chapter deals with the historical development of Fundamental Rights and Directive Principle of State Policy. In this Chapter, I have attempted to examine that how and why Fundamental Rights and Directive Principles were incorporated in the Constitution of India. Why these Rights and Principles were enunciated into a 'separate Part, that in Part III and Part IV of the Constitution? The evolution of the Fundamental Right and Directive Principles, right from the advent of British Raj to Sapru Committee Report has been discussed in this dissertation. An attempt has also been made to discuss the evolution of Fundamental Right and Directive Principles through constituent assembly from the adoption of the 'objective Resolution' to their final adoption in the Constitution.

Third Chapter deals nature, object and concept of Fundamental Rights and Directive Principles. In this Chapter, I have also attempted to draw a list of Fundamental Rights and Directive Principles.

Fourth Chapter deals with the comparative study of Fundamental Rights, Directive Principles and Fundamental Duties in Indian Constitution and it also deals complete scheme of chapter-III, chapter-IV and chapter IVA of Indian Constitution.

Fifth Chapter deals with the comparative study of Fundamental Rights under Indian Constitution and Fundamental Rights under other Constitutions. This chapter also deals with comparative study of Directive Principles at world level.

Sixth Chapter seeks to evaluate the relationship between Directive Principles and Fundamental Rights. The fundamentalness and bindingness of the Directive Principles has been discussed in this chapter. In this chapter, it has been shown that due to the non-justiciable nature of the Directive Principles, they do not become inferior to Fundamental Rights.

This chapter gives deep insight to the various questions dealing with the Status relationship between Fundamental Rights and Directive Principles. In this chapter I also discussed that how the judiciary has applied the Directive Principles as reasonable restrictions in public interest on Fundamental Rights, so as to achieve the objective of socio-economic justice.

Seventh Chapter is devoted to the changing dimension of Directive Principles vis-a-vis Fundamental Rights. In this chapter, I have tried to focusing on the enforcement of Directive Principles and the approach of legislature and judiciary.

Lastly, chapter Eight deals with concluding observation. In this chapter the panoramic Survey of the whole discussion in summarized and it incorporates suggestions for securing socio economic justice for all by implementing Directive Principles enshrined in the Constitution of India.

Chapter II

Historical Development of Fundamental Rights and Directive Principles of State Policy

---

Synopsis

(1) Evolution of Fundamental Right

Idea of Fundamental Rights in India prior to the Constitution

(i) The Constitution of India Bill, 1895

(ii) The commonwealth of India Bill, 1925

(iii) Nehru Report, 1928

(iv) Karachi Revolutions, 1931

(v) Govt. of India Act, 1935

(vi) Sapru Committee Report

(2) Evolution of Directive Principles of State Policy

Idea of Directive Principles of State Policy in India prior to the Constitution

(i) The Constitution of India Bill, 1895

(ii) The commonwealth of India Bill, 1925

(iii) Nehru Report, 1928

(v) Sapru Committee Report

(3) Fundamental Rights and Directive Principles and Constituent Assembly Debate

(A)Fundamental Rights and Directive Principles in Rau's Draft Constitution.

(i) Fundamental Rights in Rau's Draft Constitution

(ii) Directive Principles in Rau's Draft Constitution

(B) Deliberation of Drafting committee and final adoption of Directive Principles.

(4) Sources of Directive Principles in Indian Constitution

The Constitution of India which, came into force in 1950, incorporated certain Fundamental Rights in Part III and Directive Principle of State Policy in Part IV. These Principles are also known as socio-economic rights. These Fundamental Rights and Directive Principles are not the brain child of any Particular individual or group of individuals. They are mainly the product of history. They are the outcome of class of ideas and ideals and social power. The Philosophy underlying Part III and Part IV was evolved from the experience of momentous events of the world in general, and India in particular, during the last three to four centuries.[2] *Granville Austin* also points out that Fundamental Rights and Directive Principles have their roots deep in the struggle for Independence.[3]

If we study the history, we would come to know that socio-economic rights and principles were recognised since the ancient days. After the French

---

[2] G. Austin, The Indian Constitution: Cornerstone of a Nation, (Bombay: Oxford University Press, 1979),P. 50

[3] Ibid at 49

Revolution in 1789, it was realised that the political freedom would be impaired without the protection of Socio economic right of the people.

In the British Period, our country was economically exploited and the people were deprived of their social and economic rights. Due to the growth of Political consciousness, the national struggle for freedom started in the nineteenth century to free the Country from British empire and to provide the people their due fundamental and socio-economic rights. The heroes of the freedom struggle were convinced that the solution to socio economic ills of the country lay in the Political freedom. Hence they demanded not only Political rights but also socio economic rights.

Throughout the national struggle, the national leaders of India drafted number of socio-economic rights to be given to the people of India. This provided them the training of drafting the future Constitution of India with critical eye. At the time of framing of Indian Constitution, constituent Assembly Separated the Socio-economic rights from the civil and Political rights. The former were made non justiciable but fundamental in the governance of the Country.

In this chapter an attempt has been made to trace, the evolution of Fundamental Rights and Directive Principles in the pre-independent era and to see how they were shaped in the Constituent Assembly.

1. Evolution of Fundamental Right

Fundamental Rights are considered to be essential to the development of human personality and human happiness. The recognition, promotion and protection of these rights are the main justification for the existence of a State and every State is known by the rights it maintain. But the concept of rights are varied widely from generation to generation. In earlier age Peoples demanded mainly civil and Political rights. In the modern age peoples demanded civil and political rights with economic and social rights. The idea of right canvassed as of modern origin and usually traced to the magnacarta of 1215 of Great Britain. An eminent historian U.N. Ghoshal Points out a number of civil rights enjoyed by the individuals in ancient India and they occupied an important place in the literature of Smrities[4]. In the fourth century BC, we find that Kautilya Classified the right in the civil right, economic right and legal rights.[5]

A. Idea of Fundamental Rights in India Prior to the Constitution

Before the enactment of the Indian Constitution in 1950, there was no charter of Fundamental Right of a justiciable nature. Although the demand for such rights and their Constitutional of guarantee had its roots in the nineteenth century.

It was implicit in the formation of the Indian national congress in 1885. in the beginning the INC demanded some civil rights.

According *G. Austin* :

[4] Dr. P.S. Jaiswal, Directive Principles Juris prudence and socio economic Justice in India, (New Delhi: APH Publishing Corporation, 1996), p. 18

[5] Ibid at 17

"Indians wanted the same rights and privileges that British masters enjoyed in India and that Britains had among themselves in England.... And wanted to end the discrimination of colonial regime."

In the era of pre independent India, many resolutions were passed for political and socio economic rights by freedom fighters. Here I am mentioning some resolutions.

(i) The Constitution of India Bill, 1895

The first implicit demand for Fundamental Rights appeared in the Constitution of India Bill 1895. This bill was issued under the inspiration of Lokmanya Bal Gangadhar Tilak. This bill was described as 'Home-rule' by Mrs. Annie Beasant. A glimpse of the rights may be found in the provisions. Article 16 of the Bill contained the right of free speech and imprisonment only by competent authority. This bill also contained the right of property, equality before the law, equality to admission to public offices and right to petitions for redress of grievances.[6]

After publication of Montangu-Chelmsford Report, the Indian National Congress demanded a new Constitution for India in August 1918 which contains "a declaration of the right of the people of India as British Citizens guaranteeing the equality before the law, Freedom of speech and Press and Protection in respect of liberty, life and Property.

---

[6] B. shiva Rao, The framing of India Constitution : selected documents, vol I (New Delhi: IIPA, 1966),P.5

(ii) The Commonwealth of India Bill, 1925

The commonwealth of India Bill was drafted by Annie Beasant and it was adopted at National Convention. This bill sought to achieve for India a self governing Dominion status except for defence and foreign affairs. For the first time it contained an article relating to the grant of Fundamental Rights. Article-4 of this bill was called as "Declaration of Rights". It contained the following provision: inviolability of the liberty of the person and of his dwelling and property, Freedom of conscience and the free practice of religion subject to public order or morality. Free expression of opinion and right of assemble peacefully and without arms and of forming associations or unions subject to public order or morality and equality before law.

Within two years of the publication of the commonwealth of the Indian bill, the commission headed by Sir John Simon was adopted to study the possibility of Constitutional reform in India.

(iii) Nehru Report, 1928

After the Bombay Session of the Congress Motilal Nehru moved a resolution for framing a Swaraj Constitution. A swaraj Constitution was mainly based upon the declaration of rights and the preamble of this Constitution declared swaraj as the inherent and inalienable right of people of India. Nehru committee was constituted to determine the principle of the Constitution for India. This committee was constituted by seven members and chairman M.L.

Nehru. The report of the committee is known Nehru Report and it was based on the principle of Dominion Status with full responsible government on the parliamentary Pattern. This report recommended number of Fundamental Rights. The report, inter alia, contained right of personal liberty, freedom of conscience and the freedom to profess and practice any religion subject to public order and morality, right of free expression of opinion, right to assemble peacefully without arms and right of equality. The Fundamental Rights of the Nehru report were reminiscent of the American and post war European Constitutions and in same cases they were word for word from the rights listed in the commonwealth of India bill. The rights laid down by the Nehru report were close precursor of the Fundamental Rights of the Constitution. British Indian legislature appointed a committee which supported the inclusion of Fundamental Rights in the proposed Government of India Act. But commission did not recommend any declaration of Fundamental Rights to be included in the Constitution of India. Subsequently in all the three sessions of the Indian Round Table Conference, efforts for the inclusion of a chapter on Fundamental Rights in the Constitutional documental for India were made. At the first round table conference N.M. Joshi, a representative of the Indian Labour Organisation, emphasised the need for incorporating certain Fundamental Rights including economic rights also. B. Shiva Rao also represented a draft of the ten rights. B.R. Ambedkar also drew attention of the British government towards the urgency of incorporating adequate provisions for the enforcement of Fundamental Rights in the Constitution.[7] He also supported for inclusion of a

[7] K.C. Markandan, *Directive Principles in the Indian Constitution,* (Jalandhar : A.B.S. Publishers, 1987) P.23

right of redress for the violation of any Fundamental Right. Despite various efforts of the Indian delegates, the attitude of the British Government towards the grant of fundamental rights to the people of India remained unchanged and the demand was rejected at the first round table conference.[8]

(iv)Karachi Resolution: 1931

The Indian National Congress passed a historic resolution on the declaration of Fundamental Rights at its forty fifth session held at Karachi on 29th March 1931.

(v) Government of India Act : 1935

The Government of India Act, 1935 did not enumerate any guaranteed rights except to a very limited extent." It provided that" no person shall be disqualified by sex for being appointed to any Civil Service or Post under the crown, except a service or post specified by order made by the Governor General, Governor or Secretary of state. Another provision declared that no British subject domiciled in India shall be ineligible for office under the crown or be prohibited from acquiring, holding or disposing of property or carrying on any occupation, trade, business in British India on grounds only of religion, place of birth, descent colour or any of them.A third provision provided that no

[8] N.V. Paranjape, *Role of Directive Principles under Indian Constitution,* (Allahabad: Central Law Agency 1975) , P. 11

person shall be deprived of his property in British India save by the authority of law.[9]

(vi). Sapru Committee Report, 1945

The subject of fundamental rights figured prominently in the deliberation of the Sapru Committee appointed by the all Parties conference during the years 1944-45. The Committee expressed the view that Fundamental Rights were necessary not only as assurance and guarantees to the minorities, but also for prescribing a standard of conduct for the legislatures governments and the courts. Finally the Sapru Committee in its Constitutional proposals recommended that a declaration of Fundamental Rights in an Indian Constitution was absolute necessary. It envisaged two set of Fundamental Rights one justiciable and the other non justiciable.

The proposals of the Sapru committee were definitely a significant achievement and advancement on the earlier proposals because it made distinction between Fundamental Rights as justiciable and non justiciable and recommended the inclusion of latter also in the Constitution.

2. Evolution Directive Principle of State Policy

---

[9] H.R. Khanna, *Making of India,s Constitution,* (Lucknow: Eastern Book Company 1981) P. 26

Directive Principles of state policy provides one of the most novel and Striking features of modern Constitutional government. It seems that the framers of the Constitution were in this respect influenced most by the Constitution of Irish Republic which embodies a chapter on Directive Principles of State policy. The Irish themselves had, however taken this idea from the Constitution of republican Spain which was first ever to incorporate such principles as part of a Constitution. But the idea of such principles can be traced back to the ' Declaration of Rights of Man and citizen' Proclaimed by revolutionary France and the declaration of Independence by American colonies.[10]

The leaders of India's freedom movement visualized that in the new dispensation following political freedom, the people should have the fullest opportunities for advancement in the social and economic spheres and that the state should make suitable provisions for ensuring progress.[11] The Directive Principles of State Policy, embodied in Part IV of the constitution, are directions given to the central and state governments to guide the establishment of a just society in the country. The Directive Principles commit the State to promote the welfare of the people by affirming social, economic and political justice, as well as to fight economic inequality. According to the constitution, the government should keep them in mind while framing laws, even though they are non-justiciable in nature. The idea of Directive Principles of State Policy has been taken from the Irish Republic. They were incorporated in our Constitution in order to provide economic justice and to avoid concentration of wealth in the hands of a few people. Therefore, no government can afford to ignore them. They are infact, the directives to the future governments to incorporate them in the decisions and policies to be formulated by them. The

---

[10] M.V. Pylee, *Constitutional Government in India,* (Bombay : Asia Publishing House, 1965), P. 326

[11] Subhas C. Kashyap, The Framing of India's Constitution 320 (2nd Ed. ,Universal Law Publishing Co. Pvt. Ltd).

directives were meant to be the fundamental principles which should necessarily be made the basis of all executive and legislative actions that might be taken in future in the governance of the country. If directives is not obeyed or implemented by the state, its obedience or implementation cannot be secured through judicial proceedings.[12]Directive Principles mean that they will not be binding on the State; in any case, they would not be enforceable in a court of law.[13]It was the intention of the Constituent Assembly that in future both the legislature and the executive should not merely pay lip service to these principles enacted but they should be made the basis of all executive and legislative action that may be taken in the matter of governance of the country. The Directive Principles commit the State to raise the standard of living and improve public health. It should also organize agriculture and animal husbandry on modern and scientific lines by improving breeds and prohibiting slaughter of cows, calves, other milch and draught cattle.[14] The State must safeguard the environment and wildlife of the country.[15]The Directive Principles exhort the state to ensure that citizens have an adequate means of livelihood, that the operation of the economic system and the ownership and control of the material resources of the country sub serve the common good, that the health of the workers, including children is not abused, and that special consideration be given to the pregnant women. Among the primary duties of the state is the raising of the level of nutrition and the general standard of living of the people. The Principles expressed the hope that within ten years of the adoption of the Constitution there will be compulsory primary education for children up to the age of fourteen years. The other provisions of the Principles seek equally to secure the renovation of

---

[12] V.N. Shukla, Constitution Of India 298 (10th Ed, Eastern Book Company).
[13] Constituent Assembly Debates; Vol. VII; P. 473.
[14] ibid.
[15] Granville Austin, The Indian Constitution Corner Stone of A Nation ,52 (Oxford University Press).

Indian society by improving the techniques of agriculture, husbandry, cottage industry, etc. The core of the commitment lies in the fundamental rights and the directive principles of state policy.

Idea of Directive Principles in India, Prior to the Constitution

Before the independence, there was no charter of Directive Principles of State Policy. Although the demand for such rights and Constitutional guarantee had its root in the nineteenth centuries. Some social rights were demanded by our Political leaders but they were rejected by Britishers. In the era of Pre-independent India, many revolutions were passed for socio-economic rights by own freedom fighters. Here I am going to mention some resolutions.

(i) The Constitution of India Bill, 1895

The first implicit demand for Fundamental Rights appeared in the Constitution of India Bill 1895. This bill was issued under the inspiration of Lokmanya Bal Gangadhar Tilak and described as the Home-rule by Smt. Annie Beasant. This bill contained some rights and Directive Principles. The bill had also a provisions guaranteeing free State education and compulsory Primary education. After enactment of our Constitution in 1950 a provision is also included for providing a free and compulsory education for children.

(ii) The Commonwealth of India Bill, 1925

The commonwealth of India Bill, 1925 was drafted by Mrs. Annei Beasant and it was adopted at National Convention. This bill contained some Directive Principles. Article 8 of the Bill, which was approved by the Indian National Congress, enumerated, inter alia, provision for education Stating that "all persons in commonwealth of India have the right to free elementary education and such right shall be enforceable as soon as due arrangements shall have been made by the Competent authority.

(iii) Nehru Report, 1928

Indian nationalist leaders constitute a small committee with Motilal Nehru as its chairman and seven other members. This committee was constituted to determine the principles of the Constitution for India. It contains certain social and economic rights. It contained following rights: right of free elementary education without any distinction of caste or creed in the matter of admission in to any educational institutions, maintained or aided by the state and such right shall be enforceable as soon as due arrangements shall have been made by competent authority; freedom of combination and association for the maintenance and improvement of labour and economic conditions was guaranteed to everyone and of all corporations; maintenance of health and fitness for work of all citizens, securing a living wage for every workers; Protection of motherhood infirmity and unemployment. This Constitution was hailed by the congress as great Contribution towards the solution of India's Political and communal problem. These social rights reappears materially unchanged as the Directive Principles. Subsequently in all the three sessions of Indian Round Table Conference, efforts for the inclusion of a chapter on Fundamental Rights and socio economic rights in the Constitutional document for India were made.

(iv) Sapru Committee Report, 1945

Sapru committee report was prepared by Tej Bahadur Sapru. In this Report, for the first time, an attempt was made to separate civil and justiciable rights on the one hand and the Socio-economic non justiciable rights on the other hand. But in this report it could not be said that these non justiciable socio economic rights were inferior to justiciable rights.

3. Fundamental Rights and Directive Principles and Constituent Assembly Debate

The constituent Assembly was mainly an elected body and represented almost all shades of Public opinion. Its deliberations began on December 9, 1946. It became a sovereign body on 15th August 1947 when India gained independence. Its broad ideological spectrum provided by the Indian national congress was enlarged by the inclusion of non-congress specialists from various disciplines and walks of life. On December 13, 1946, Jawaharlal Nehru moved a resolution for Fundamental Rights and Directive Principles. This resolution formed the basis not only of various provisions of the Constitution but also its preamble. The relevant parts of resolution are:[16]

(a) This constituent assembly declares its firm and solemn resolve to proclaim India as an Independent Sovereign Republic and to draw up for her future governance a Constitution.

(b) Wherein shall be guaranteed and secured to all the people of India justice, social and political,

(c) Wherein adequate safeguards shall be provided for backward and tribal areas and depressed and other backward classes.

(d) This ancient land attains its rightful and honoured place in the world and make its full and willing contribution to the Promotion of world peace and the welfare of mankind.

Nehru in his speech on the resolution emphasized that the house should not consider this resolution in its literal meaning but should look at its spirit. Many members of the constituent Assembly Participated in the discussion on the objectives resolution. There was great emphasis on what we call Fundamental Rights under the Present Constitution. The emphasis on the socio-economic rights also did not lag behind. The majority of the members considered the incorporation of Social Policy in the Constitution without undermining the importance of Fundamental Rights. M.R. Jayakar also highlighted the economic and socialistic importance of the resolution and observed that it envisaged far reaching social changes – Social Justice in the fullest sense of the term S. Radha Krishnan visualising the importance of

19 Constituent Assembly Debate, Vol. I., P. 57

Fundamental Rights, emphasized that the State regulation for socio-economic revolution was necessary. It should not have been done at the expense of the human spirit.

After studying the objectives Resolution, B.N. Rau, the Constitutional advisor to the Government of India, Suggested that the best way of embodying the assurances contained in paras (5), (6) and (8) of the Resolution was to spilt two sets of assurance in the following manner: First Fundamental Rights relating the personal liberty and Political Freedom and unenforceable in the court of law. Second Fundamental Principles of State Policy relating to social, economic and other matters and unenforceable in the courts. According to Rau there was difference in both the classes of rights, that is, Fundamental Rights imposed a negative duty on the State while the others required a positive action on its part. He found this difference clearly in Irish Constitution and Lauterpacht's "International Bill of the Rights of Man".

(A) Fundamental Rights and Directive Principles in Rau's Draft Constitution

The constituent Assembly, after a brief discussion on the supplementary report of the advisory committee on the Fundamental Rights, Minorities etc. on August 30, 1947 sent it to the Constitutional Advisor B.N. Rau for being adopted in the Draft Constitution and for further Consideration by the Drafting committee.

In the Drafting Constitution of October 7, 1947 Prepared by the Constitutional Advisor, B.N. Rau, all the Provisions regarding Fundamental Rights and Directive Principles were included in Part III which was entitled as "Fundamental Rights including Directive Principles of the State Policy". This part was divided into three chapters, the first containing general Provisions, the second Fundamental Rights and the third Directive Principles of State Policy.

(i) Fundamental Rights in Rau's Draft Constitution[17]

Constitutional Advisor B.N. Rau drafted Fundamental Rights in Chapter II of the Part III of Draft Constitution. Clauses 11 to 30 was related to Fundamental Rights. The Fundamental Rights, which in framed by Sri B.N.Rau, read as follows:

Cl. 11(1): The States shall not discriminate against any citizen on grounds only of religion, race, caste, sex or any of them.

In particular, no citizen shall, on grounds only of religion, race, caste, sex or any of them, be subject to any disability, liability, restriction or condition with regard to

(a) access to shops, public restaurants, hotels and places of public entertainment, or

(b) the use of wells, tanks, roads and places of public resort maintained wholly or partly out of revenues of the State or dedicated to the use of the general public.

[17] B. Shiva Rao, The Framing of India's Constitution: Selected Documents, Vol. III (New Delhi: IIPA, 1968) P. 7-12

(2) Nothing in this section shall prevent the State from making any special provision for women and children.

Cl. 12(1): There shall be equality of opportunity for all citizens in matters of employment under the State.

(2) No citizen shall, on grounds only of religion, race, caste, sex, descent, place of birth or any of them, be ineligible for any office under the State.

(3) Nothing in this section shall prevent the State from making any provision for the reservation of appointments or posts in favour of any particular classes of citizens who, in the opinion of the State, are not adequately represented in the services under the State.

(4) Nothing in this section shall affect the operation of any law which provides that the incumbent of an office in connection with the affairs of any religious or denominational institution or any member of the governing body thereof shall be a person professing a particular religion or belonging to a particular denomination.

Cl. 13:"Untouchability" in any form is abolished and the imposition of any disability on that account shall be an offence which shall be punishable in accordance with law.

Cl. 14(1): No title shall be conferred by the Federation.

(2) No citizen of the Federation shall accept any title from any foreign State.

(3) No person holding any offence of profit or trust under the State shall, without the consent of the Federal Government, accept any present, emolument, title or offence of any kind from or under any foreign State.

Rights of Freedom

Cl. 15 (1): There shall be liberty for the exercise of the following rights subject to public order and morality, namely:

(a) the right of every citizen to freedom of speech and expression;

(b) the right of citizens to assemble peaceably and without arms;

(c) the right of citizens to form associations or unions;

(d) the right of every citizen to move freely throughout the territories of the Federation;

(e) the right of every citizen to reside and settle in any part of the territories of the Federation, to acquire, hold and dispose of property and to practice any profession or to carry on any occupation, trade or business.

(2) Nothing in this section shall restrict the power of the State to make any law or to take any executive action which under this Constitution it has power to make or to take, during the period when a Proclamation of Emergency issued under sub-section (1) of section 182 is in force, or, in the case of a unit during the period of any grave emergency declared by the Government of the unit whereby the security of the unit is threatened.

(3) Nothing in this section shall affect the operation of any law which in the interests of the public including the interests of minorities and special tribes imposes restrictions on the exercise of any of the rights conferred by this section.

Cl. 16: No person shall be deprived of his life or personal liberty without due process of law, nor shall any person be denied equality before the law within the territories of the Federation.

Cl. 17: Subject to the provisions of any Federal law, trade, commerce and intercourse among the units shall, if between the citizens of the Federation, be free: provided that nothing in this section shall prevent any unit from imposing on goods imported from others units any tax to which similar goods manufactured or produced in that unit are subject so, however, as not to discriminate between goods to imported and goods so manufactures or produced

Provided further that no preference shall be given by any regulation of trade, commerce or revenue to one unit over another

Provided also that nothing in this section shall preclude the Federal Parliament from imposing b Act restrictions on the freedom of trade, commerce and intercourse among the units in the intersects of public order, morality or health or in cases of emergency.

Cl. 18: Traffic in human beings and begar and other similar forms of forced labour are prohibited and any contravention of this provision shall be an offence punishable in accordance with law.

Provided that nothing in this section shall prevent the State from imposing compulsory service for public purposes without any discrimination on the ground of race, religion, caste or class.

Cl. 19: No child below the age of fourteen years shall be employed to work in any factory or mine or engaged in any other hazardous employment.

Rights relating to Religion

Cl. 20(1): Subject to public order, morality and health and to the other provisions of this Part, are persons are equally entitled to freedom of conscience and the right freely to profess, practise and propagate religion.

Explanation I: The wearing and carrying of *Kirpans* shall be deemed to be included in the profession of the Sikh religion.

Explanation II: The rights conferred by this sub-section shall not be include any economic, financial, political or other secular activities which may be associated with religious practice.

(2) Nothing in this section shall preclude the State from making laws for social welfare and reform and for throwing open Hindu religious institutions of a public character to any class or section of Hindus.

Cl. 21: Every religious denomination or any section thereof shall have the right to manage its own affairs in matters of religion and, in accordance with the provisions of law, to own, acquire and administer property, movable or immovable, and to establish and maintain institutions for religious or charitable purposes.

Cl. 22: No person may be compelled to pay taxes, the proceeds of which specifically appropriated in payment of expenses for the promotion or maintenance of any particular religion or religious denomination.

Cl. 23: No person attending any school maintained or receiving aid out of public funds shall be compelled to take part in any religious instruction that may be imported in the school or to attend any religious worship that may be conducted in the school or in any premises attached thereto.

Cultural and Educational Rights

Cl. 24(1) : The interests of minorities in the territories the Federation in respect of their language, script and culture shall be protected and no law shall be passed or executive action taken by the State which may affect prejudicially the right conferred by this sub-section.

(2) No minority whether based on religion, community or language shall be discriminated against in regard to the admission of any person belonging to such minority into any educational institution maintained by the State.

(3) (a) All minorities whether based on religion, community or language shall be free to establish and administer educational institutions of their choice.

(b) The State shall not, in granting aid to schools, discriminate against schools which are under the management of minorities whether based on religion, community or language.

Miscellaneous Rights

Cl. 25(1): No person shall be deprived of his property save by authority of law.

(2) No property, movable or immovable, including any interest in, or in any company owning, any commercial or industrial undertaking, shall be taken possession or such acquisition unless the law provides for the payment of compensation for the property taken possession of or acquired and either fixes the amount of the compensation or specifies the principles on which and the manner in which the compensation is to be determined.

Cl. 26(1): No person shall be convicted of any offence except for violation of a law in force at the time of the commission of the act charged as an offence, nor be subjected to a penalty greater than that which might have been inflicted under the law at the time of the commission of the offence.

(2) No person shall be punished for the same offence more than once nor, save as provided in section 132 of the Indian Evidence Act, 1872 as in force at the commencement of this Constitution, shall any person be compelled in any criminal case to be a witness against himself.

Cl. 27(1): Full faith and credit shall be given throughout the territories of the Federation to public acts, records and judicial proceedings of the Federation and of every unit. And the manner in which and the conditions under which such acts, records, and proceedings shall be proved and the effect thereof determined shall be as provided by law.

(2) Final judgments or orders delivered or passed by civil courts in any part of the territories of the Federation shall be capable of execution anywhere within those territories according to law.

Rights to Constitutional Remedies

Cl. 28(1): The right to move the Supreme Court by appropriate proceedings for the enforcement of the rights provided for in this chapter is guaranteed.

(2) Such right shall not be suspended except when a proclamation of Emergency issued under sub-section (1) of section 182 is in force, or a grave emergency, declared by the Government of any unit whereby the security of the unit is threatened, exists.

Cl. 29: The Federal parliament may be Act determine to what extent any of the rights guaranteed in this chapter shall in their application to the members of the armed forces or the forces charged with the maintenance of public order be restricted or abrogated so as to ensure the proper discharge of their duties and the maintenance of discipline among them.

Cl. 30: As soon as may be after the commencement of this Constitution provision shall be made by Act of the Federal Parliament –

(a) for those matters which under this chapter are required to be provided for by legislation in so far as provision with respect to such matters has not been made in any existing law; and

(b) for prescribing punishments for those acts which are declared to be offences under this chapter and are not punishable under any existing law.

(ii) Directive Principles in Rau's Draft Constitution

The 'Preamble' of the 'Fundamental Principles of governance' found its place in Rau's draft in Chapter I as clause 10 and the principles in Chapter III as Clause 31 to 41. The preamble of Part III and Directive Principles of State Policy, which is framed by B.N. Rau, read as follow:

Clause-10

Preamble

The principles of policy set forth in chapter III of this part are intended for the guidance of the state. While these principles are not cognizable by any court, they are nevertheless fundamental in the governance of the country and it shall be the duty of the state to apply these principles in making laws.

Chapter III

Directive principal of state policy

Cl. 31-: The state shall strive to promote the welfare of the whole people by securing and protecting as effectively as it.May by a social order in which justice, social. Economic and Political shall inform all the institutions of the national life.

Cl. 32: The state shall in particular, direct its policy towards securing-

(i) that the citizens, man and women equally, have the right to an adequate means of livelihood,

(ii) that the ownership and control of material resources of the community are so distributed as best to sub serve the common good,

(iii) that the operation of free competition does not result in the concentration of the ownership or control of essential commodities in a few individuals to the common detriment.

(iv) that there is equal pay for equal work for both man and woman,

(v) that the strength and health of workers, men and women, and the tender age of children are not abused and the citizens are not forced by economic necessity to enter avocations unsuited to their age or strength.

(vi) the childhood and youth are protected against exploitation and against moral and material abandonment.

Cl. 33: The state shall, within the limits of its economic capacity and development make effective provision for securing the right to work, to education and to public assistance in cases of unemployment, old age sickness, disablement, and other cases of undeserved want.

Cl.34: The state shall make provision for securing of work and for maternity relief for workers.

Cl.35: The state shall endeavors to secure, a suitable legislation or economic organisation or in any other way to all workers, industrial or otherwise, work a living wage conditions of work ensuring a decent standard of life and full enjoyment of leisure and social and cultural opportunities.

Cl.36: The state shall endeavor to secure for the citizens a Uniform Civil Code.

Cl.37: Every citizens is entitled to free primary education and it shall be the duty of the state to provide, within a period of ten years from the commencement of this constitution, for free and compulsory primary education for all children until they complete the age of fourteen years.

Cl.38: The state shall promote with special care the educational and economic interests of the weaker sections of people an in particular of scheduled castes and the schednled tribes and shall protect them from social injustice and all forms of exploitation.

Cl.39: The state regard the raising of the level of nutrition and the standard of living of its people and the improvement of public health as among its primary duties.

Cl.40: It shall be the obligation of the state to protect every monument or place or object of artistic or historic interest declared by federal law to be of national importance from spoilation, destruction, removal, disposal or export as the case may be and to preserve and maintain according to federal law all such monument or places or objects.

Cl.41: The State shall promote international peace and security by the prescription of open, just honourable relations between nations, by the firm establishment of understandings of international law as the actual role of conduct among Government and by the maintenance of justice and the scrupulous respect for treaty obligations in the dealings of organised people with one another.

On the completion of the draft of the Constitution for consideration by the Drafting committee, the Constitutional advisor, Sir B.N. Rau visited the United States of America, Canada, Ireland and the United Kingdom for personal discussion with some of the leading personalities and Constitutional experts on important features of India's Draft Constitution. At that time also he had in mind the danger of conflict between Directive Principles and Fundamental Rights. The US Justice Frankfurter agreed with Rau that there should be an express provision in the Constitution that when a law made by the state in the discharge of one of the Fundamental Duties imposed upon it by the Constitution happens to conflict with one of the Fundamental Rights guaranteed to the individual, the former should prevail over the latter. John Hearne also expressed the similar view. But Justice Hand held a different view and said that it would be mistake to have any justiciable, Fundamental Rights at all in the Constitution. He preferred to retain all Fundamental Rights as word precepts rather than as legal fetters in the Constitution.

It is clear from the above observations that the conflict between the Fundamental Rights and Directive Principles was visualised by Rau at the time of the presentation of the Draft Constitution and he wanted to give more importance to the social welfare rather than to the individual right. Certain modification in clauses 9(2) and 10 of his Draft Constitution prepared on October 7, 1947 are clear proof his intention. The modified clauses read as follows:

Cl. 9(2): Subject to the provisions of Section 10, nothing in this Constitution shall be taken to empower the state to make any law which curtails or takes away or which has the effect of curtailing or taking away any of the rights conferred by Chapter II of this Past except by way of amendment of this Constitution under section 232 and any law made in contravention of this sub section shall, to the except of the contravention be void.

The following new paragraph was added to clause10: "No law which may be made by the state in the discharge of its duty under the first paragraph of this section and no law which may have been made by the state in pursuance of the principles of policy set forth in chapter III of this part shall be void merely on the ground that it contravenes the provisions of section 9, or is inconsistent with the provision of Chapter II of this part."

According to Rau, the object of these amendments was to clarify that in case of conflict between Chapter II which included Fundamental Rights and chapter III containing Principles of State Policy, the general welfare should prevail over the individual rights. Thus the only purpose of the amendment was to give binding effect to the principles which the state could apply irrespective of the fact that they might contravene Fundamental Rights. The proposed amendment of Rau was not incorporated in the body of Constitution but it was realised that in case of conflict between Fundamental Rights and Directive Principles of State Policy, the latter were to prevail. Ambedkar also pointed out that by virtue of the Directive Principles, the state could enact laws for the general welfare of the community was which might ever contravene Fundamental Rights.

(B) Deliberations of Drafting Committee and Final adoption of Directive Principles

Rau's Draft Constitution was considered by the Drafting committee on October 27, 1947 and it was decided that the Directive Principles of the state policy should be transferred from Part III to a new Part. It was further decided that the clause 10 of Chapter I entitled 'General' relating to the principles of policy set forth in Chapter III should also be transferred to a new part containing the Directive Principles of state policy.

At the meeting of the drafting committee on November 1, 1947 Directives were transferred to a new Part, namely, III-A and the new clauses namely, 30-A and 30-B were also introduced in this part. The Drafting committee in the subsequent meeting held on November 3, 1947 affected further changes in clause 36 and 40 of this newly introduced Part III-A of the Draft Constitution. Clause 30-B, 34 and 37 of the Directive Principles were further modified by the drafting committee in the meeting held on 20 January 1948.

The new clauses 30-A, 30-B and 36 and modified clause 40 read as follows:

Cl. 30-A: "In this Part unless the context otherwise requires, the state has the same meaning as in Part II of the Constitution."

Cl. 30-B: "The Principles of the policy set forth in this Part are intended for the guidance of the state, while these principles are not cognizable by any court, they are nevertheless fundamental in the governance of the country and it shall be the duty of the state to apply these principles in making laws."

Cl. 40: "It shall be the obligation of the state to protect every monument or place or object of artistic or historic interest, declared by parliament by law to be of national importance, from spoilation, destruction, removal, disposal or export, as the case may be and to Preserve and maintain according to law made by parliament, such monuments or Places or Objects."

The final Draft Constitution was prepared by the Drafting committee. Subsequently, a number of suggestions were received and the drafting committee held meetings on March, 23, 24 and 27, 1948 to consider these recommendations and certain Amendment were made in the original Draft. The original Draft Constitution together with the proposed amendments was considered by a special committee in its meetings on April, 10, 11, 1948 and the final Draft was prepared for being approved by the constituent assembly.[18]

The second stage in the framing of the principles took place in the assembly in November and December 1948 during the debate on the Draft Constitution. The assembly's reaction to the draft principles revealed two major opinions. One was that the Directive did not go far enough towards establishing a socialistic state, and the other was that they should have placed greater emphasis on certain institutions and principles central to Indian Practice and to Hindu thought, particularly those glorified by Gandhiji's teaching.

At the time of circulation of Draft Constitution for comments and opinion there was again Criticism of the unenforceable chapter of the Directive Principles and of the external source from which the idea of a declaration of state policy was borrowed. Dealing with first criticism that the Constitution was not the place for moral precepts or sermons, Rau observed in an article published in the Hindu that many Constitutions contained such moral precepts and it can not be denied that they had an educative value. According to Rau, it might be occasionally essential for the state to invade private rights in order to raise the nation's standard of health, of living etc.

[18] K.C. Markandan, Directive Principles in the Indian Constitution, (New Delhi: Allied Publishers, 1966) P. 87

Rau also responded to the second criticism that the Directive Principles were borrowed from the other Constitution. He pointed out how some of the ancient Indians shastras contained references to injunctions to Kings similar to the Directive Principles of state policy. On November 4, 1948, Ambedkar introduced the Draft Constitution in the Assembly and stated that though the Directive Principles had no legal force behind them, but he was not prepared to concede that they were useless simply because they had no binding force in law. According to him, the Draft Constitution does not install any particular part in power and who- so-ever comes in power has to respect this instrument of instructions that is the Directive Principles.[19]

The consideration of the Draft articles commenced on November 19, 1948 lasted for the days. The discussion on the Directive began with an amendment moved by Sayaid Karimuddin that in the heading under Part IV, the word 'Directive' be deleted and substituted by the word 'fundamental' as the provisions contained in Part IV' were important and fundamental in nature and the use of the former word would mean that they were not binding on the state. He felt that it was very necessary that all these principles should be made mandatory so that a scheme embodying these principles could be brought into operation within ten years. To support his arguement, he quoted Ambedkar's booklet "State and Minorities' submitted to the Advisory committee on Fundamental Rights and Minorities etc. In the discussion of the title H.V. Kamath also favoured replacement of 'Directive' in the title by the word 'fundamental'. He pointed out that the Advisory committee had given them the title "fundamental Principles of governance" and the chairman of the Advisory committee had stated though not cognizable in any court of law, they 'should be regarded as fundamental in the governance of the country'. This suggestion of replacement was opposed by Ambedkar who said that the object that these principles be treated as fundamental was already achieved by the words of Draft article 29 and that it was

[19] Constituent Assembly Debate, Vol. VII at 42.

necessary to retain the word "Directive' because it showed that by enacting this part of the Constitution, the constituent assembly was giving certain directions to the further legislature and executive, If the word 'Directive' was omitted, the intention of the member of the assembly in enacting this part would fail in its purpose that the Directives were meant to be fundamental principles which should be made the basis of all executive and legislative action that might be taken in future in the governance of country. Finally the assembly rejected the amendment and adopted the title 'Directive Principles of State Policy'.

Five other amendments for the addition of new provisions were proposed in the assembly and finally these were adopted by the assembly.[20] Santhanam moved the first amendment to add a new article.

The state shall take stepes to organise village panchayats and endow them with such power and authority as may be necessary to enable them to function as unit of self government.

The task of the constituent Assembly was to Draft a Constitution that would serve the ultimate goal of social revolution, of national renascence. But this task was a far more complicated than the simple drafting of the Fundamental Rights or the moral precepts of preamble. The amendment was accepted by Ambedkar without any comment. The aim of the draft article has long been generally accepted, "If India is to progress, it must do so through reawakened Village life."

Thus at last the 'Assembly incorporated the amendment of Santhanam in to Constitution under draft articles 40 and it has been proved to have been less a gesture to romantic sentiments that how to realist insight.

The second amendment was moved by T.A. Ramalingam chethiar, he proposed the addition of clause providing.:

[20] B. Shiva Rao, The Framing of India's Constitution : A Study, (New Delhi : I.I.P.A., 1968) P.330.

"The state shall endeavor to promote cottage industries on co-operative lines in rural areas."

This amendment was made keeping in mind the support given by Gandhiji to cottage industries during independence movement. This amendment was supported by several members. Ambedkar was also prepared to accept the amendment after some changes and add it to the article which dealt with the state's obligation to secure to all workers a living wage, good condition of work and decent standard of life etc. The change which he proposed included the use of the Phase: "On an individual or co-operative basis", to satisfy the two schools of thought in the assembly, one of which believed in the organisation of cottage industries solely on the co-operative basis, and the other which held that there should not be any such limitation.The assemble accepted the amendment as suggested by Ambedkar and placed the promotion of cottage industries in the Directive Principles."

The third amendment, relating to the prohibitions of intoxicating drinks and injurious drugs was moved by Mahavir Tyagi and modified by Saxena to make their use for medical purposes permissible. This amendment was adopted by the assembly.

The fourth amendment, which was proposed by Thakurdas Bhargava, sought the addition of the following article:-

Article38-A" the state shall endeavour to organise agriculture and animal husbandry on modern and scientific lines and shall in particular take steps for preserving and improving the breeds of Cattle and prohibit the slaughter of cows and other useful cattle, specially milch and draught cattle and their young stock."

This provisions was adopted to the Directive Principles for number or reasons. The need to improve agriculture was obvious and cattle generally, the cow particularly, held a special place of reverence in Hindu thought.

The fifth amendment was moved by Ambedkar. It sought the addition of a new article enjoining the state to take steps to secure the separation of judiciary from executive within the period of three years from the commencement of the Constitution. During the Constituent Assembly debate, Ambedkar agreed to drop three years time limit on the suggestion of T.T. Krishnamachari who stated that no useful purpose could be served by imposing three years limit when the provisions of the article themselves were not enforceable. The article, as modified, was finally adopted by the Assembly and added to the Constitution of India.

Some other amendments were also introduced to modify one or the other of the directives as formulated in the Draft Constitution. But, Ambedkar, opposing all these amendments, said that the main object of the incorporating the Directive Principles in the Constitution was to lay down that future government should strive for the achievement of the ideal of economic democracy, but not to prescribe any particulars rigid method whether individualistic, socialistic or communist to achieve it.

The article enjoining the state to secure for the citizens a Uniform civil code throughout the territory of India evoked considerable controversy. A number of muslim members opposed it on the ground that its enforcement would impinge on the right of a group of community to follows its own personal law. Replying to this crticism, Munshi said that, "we were in a stage at which we must unify and consolidate the nation by every means without interfering with religious practices.

On November 4, 1948, Ambedkar while introducing the Draft Constitution in Assembly, observed in his speech that the criticism in so far it distinguishes Fundamental Rights from non-fundamental rights is not sound. It is not correct to say that the Fundamental Rights are absolute while non Fundamental Rights are not absolute. The real distinction between the two is that non fundamental rights are created by the agreement of the parties while fundamental rights are the gift of the state it does not follow that the state cannot qualify them.

The clause by clause consideration of the draft Constitution was taken up by the Constituent assembly on November 15,1948 and was concluded on October 17, 1949. The Draft Constitution, with several amendments adopted by the assembly was then referred again to the Drafting Committee with instructions to carry out such renumbering of the articles, clauses and sub-clauses and such revisions and completion of marginal notes as might be necessary. At last Draft Constitution was submitted to the president of the constituent assembly on November 3, 1949. Part IV of this Draft contained Directive Principles of State Policy and were enumerated in Articles 36 to 51 of the Constitution as adopted on November 26, 1949[21].

The whole scheme of Directive Principles of this Part IV although the 'Fundamental Rights', which are enunciated in Part III, form an integrated scheme to accomplish the objectives pronounced in the Preamble. In other words both 'Directives' and Fundamental Rights in the light of the preamble are intended to improve the social and economic conditions of the people in a democratic manner.

(4) Sources of Directive Principles in Indian Constitution

[21] B. Shiva Rao, The Framing of India's Constitution : Selected Documents, Vol. IV (New Delhi : IIPA, 1969), P. 762.

The concept of Directive Principles of State Policy was borrowed from the Irish Constitution. The makers of the Constitution of India were influenced by the Irish nationalist movement. Hence, the Directive Principles of the Indian constitution have been greatly influenced by the Directive Principles of State Policy. The idea of such policies "can be traced to the Declaration of the Rights of Man proclaimed Revolutionary France and the Declaration of Independence by the American Colonies." The Indian constitution was also influenced by the United Nations Universal Declaration of Human Rights. Though the makers of our Constitution drew the inspiration for including in the Constitution non-justiciable provisions in the shape of Directive Principles of State Policy from Constitution of Eire, in the text of provisions as well as their working, certain differences may be noted.

Art. 45 of the Constitution of Eire, 1937 says:

"The principle of social policy set forth in this article are intended for the for the general guidance of the Oireachtas. The application of those principles in making laws shall be the care of the Oireachtas exclusively, and shall not be cognizable by any court under any of the provisions of this constitution."

While, Art. 45 of the Irish Constitution addresses the Directives to the legislature only, Art. 36 of the Indian Constitution issues the Directives to the State as defined in Part III, which obviously comprehends all the organs of the State.[22] While, Art. 45 of the Irish Constitution says that the Directive 'shall not be cognizable' by any court, 'under any provision of this Constitution', Art. 37 of Indian Constitution use the words 'shall not be enforceable' by any court.[23] The result is that so far as the courts in Eire are concerned, the Directive provisions of the Constitution are a closed chapter. But so far as the Indian courts are concerned, though they

---

[22] Kesavananda Bharati V. State Of Kerala, (1973) 4 Scc 225: Air 1973 Sc 1461 (Para. 1802).

[23] D D Basu. Commentary On The Constitution Of India ,4016 (8th Ed. Lexis Nexis, Nagpur 2008).

cannot legally enforce the Directives or the rights or duties arising there from, they are not debarred from taking cognizance of the Directives, as a part of Constitution, for other purposes, e.g., for the purpose of interpreting other provisions of the Constitution or laws made by the Legislature.

The duty of the State to implement the Directives has also been laid down in the Constitution of India in stronger terms: while the Irish Constitution says that the Directives "are intended for the general guidance of the Oireachtas", Art. 37 of the Indian Constitution provides that the Directives are to be "fundamental in the governance of the country and it shall be the duty of the State to apply these principles in making laws."[24]

The idea of incorporating in the Constitution non-justiciable Directives was, of course, taken from the Constitution of Eire. As Dr. Ambedkar explained the precedent under the Government of India Act, 1935, of issuing Instruments of Instructions to the Governor General also influenced the makers of the Constitution:

"The Directive Principles are like the Instrument of Instructions which were issued to the Governor General and the Governors of Colonies, and to those of India by the British Government under the 1935 Government of India Act. What is called 'Directive Principles' is merely another name or the Instrument of Instructions. The only difference that they are instructions to the legislature and the executive. Whoever captures power will not be free to do what he likes with it. In the exercise of it he will have to respect these instruments of instructions which are called Directive Principles."[25] The sanction behind the Directives is of course political not juridical. Though these are not cognizable by the court and, if the Government of the day

[24] .Ibid.

[25] Constituent Assembly Debates; Vol. Vii; P. 41.

fails to carry out these objectives, no court can make the Government implement them, yet, these principles have been declared to be "fundamental in the governance of the country."

Chapter III

Nature, Object and Concept of Fundamental Rights and Directive Principle of State Policy

---

Synopsis

(1) Nature, Object and Concept of Fundamental Rights

(A) Nature and Concept of Fundamental Rights

(B) Object behind Fundamental Rights

(C) Need of Fundamental Rights

(2) Nature, Object and Concept of Directive Principles of State Policy

(A) Nature and Concept of Directive Principles of State Policy

(B) Object behind Directive Principles of State Policy

(C) Purpose of Directive Principles of State Policy

(D) Characteristics of Directive Principles of State Policy

(E) Status of the Directive Principles of State Policy

(3) Classification of Fundamental Rights and Directive Principles of State Policy in Indian Constitution

(A) Classification of Fundamental Rights

(i) Right to Equality

(ii) Right to Freedom

(iii)Right against Exploitation

(iv) Right to Freedom of Religion

(v) Cultural and Educational Rights

(vi) Right to Constitutional Remedies

(B) Classification of Directive Principles

(i) Social and Economic Charter

(a) Social order based on Justice

(b) Principle of Policy to be followed by the State for securing Economic Justice

(c) Means of livelihood

(d) Distributive Economic system

(e) No concentration of wealth

(f) Equal pay for Equal work.

(g) Welfare of children

(h) Bonded Labour.

(ii) Social security charter

(a) Equal Justice and free legal aid

(b) Social services

(c) Condition of work

(d) Living wages

(e) Participation of workers in management of industries

(f) Free and compulsory education

(g) Promotion of educational and economic interest of weaker section

(h) Raising standard of living

(iii) Community welfare charter

(a)Uniform civil code

(b)Organisation of agriculture and animal husbandry

(c) Protection of environment

(d) Protection of monuments

(e) Separation of judiciary from executive

(f) Promotion of International peace

(g) Organisation of village Panchayats

Constitution is the fundamental law of the nation. An important feature of the constitution is the Fundamental Rights and Directive Principles of State Policy incorporated in the Constitution. Although the Directive Principles are asserted to be "fundamental in the governance of the country," they are not legally enforceable. Instead, they are guidelines for creating a social order characterized by social, economic, and political justice, liberty, equality, and fraternity as enunciated in the constitution's preamble. Judiciary as being the protector and promoter of rights of the individual to perform the balancing act in an unbiased and fair manner has immense role to play in these days to interpret the directive principles as enforceable in order to establish welfare based society. The Directive Principles and state policies therefore offer the state an opportunity for use of the constitution as an instrument for change in definite social directions. The courts can even give directives to the state organs regarding what the state is required to achieve through legislative process. The author has tried to focus on the nature of Fundamental Rights and Directive Principle of state policy.

(1) Nature object and Concept of Fundamental Rights

(A) Nature and Concept of Fundamental Rights

Fundamental Rights are the modern name of what have been traditionally known as natural right. They are moral rights, which every human being everywhere at all times ought to have simply because of the fact that in contradistinction with other being, he is rational and moral. They are the primordial rights necessary for the development for the human personality. They are the right, which enable a man to chalk out his own life in the manner he likes best[26]. Supreme Court, some eminent jurist and few prominent publics men considered the rights contained in the chapter on Fundamental Rights as immutable and transcendental. In a series of judgments Supreme Court described them as 'paramount 'sacrosanct', rights reserved by the people, inalienable and inviolable, transcendental. The immutability and permanence of the Fundamental Rights were sought to be established first on the reasoning that there rights are rooted in the doctrine of natural law. But the Fundamental Rights contained in part III of the constitution, are neither rooted in the doctrine of natural law nor are they based on the theory of the reserved rights. Speaking in the importance of Fundamental Rights in the historic judgments of the ***Maneka Gandhi Vs. UOI.,*** Justice Bhagawati observed:

"*These Fundamental Rights represent the basic value cherished by the people of this country since the Vedic times and they are calculated to protect the dignity of the individual and create condition in which every human being can develop can his personality to the fullest extract. They weave a pattern of guarantee on the basic structure of human rights and impose negative obligations on the state not to encroach on individual liberty in its various dimensions*".[27]

(B) Object behind Fundamental Rights

[26] Golaknath Vs. State of Punjab, AIR 1967 SC. 1643

[27] AIR 1978 SC 597 at 619

The object behind the inclusion of chapter of Fundamental Rights in India, constitution is to establish a government of law and not of man, a government system where the tyranny of the majority does not oppress the minority. In other words the object of declaration of Fundamental Rights in the Indian constitution "was not merely to provide security to and equality of citizenship of the people living in the land and there by helping the process of nation building but also and not less importantly to provide certain standards of conduct citizenship, justice and fair play. The object it to ensure the inviolability of certain basic rights against the political changes inevitable in any democratic form of government and to achieve the high ideal of establishing a society founded on the principle of social economic and political justice, liberty of thought, expression, belief faith and worship equality of status and opportunity, and of fraternity assuring the dignity of the individual and the unity of the nation.[28]

(C) Need of Fundamental Rights

Fundamental rights were deemed essential to protect the rights and liberties of the people against the encroachment of the power delegated by them to their government. They are limitations upon all the powers of the government, legislative as well as executive and they are essential for the preservation of public and private rights. These rights are regarded as fundamental because they are most essential for the attainment by the individual his full intellectual, moral and spiritual status. The negation of these rights will keep the moral and spiritual rights stunted and his potentialities underdeveloped. Part III of the Constitution serves as remainder to the government in power that certain liberties assured to the people by the Constitution are to be respected. The object behind the inclusion of Part III in the Constitution is

[28] A.S. Chaudhari, Constitutional Rights and Limitations, Second edition, (Allahabad : The Law Book Pvt. Co., Ltd. 1997), P. 68

to establish a government of law and not of man. In ***Daryao V. State of U.P.***[29], the SC observed that, "the fundamental rights are intended not only to protect individual's rights but they are based on high public policy. Liberty of the individual and the protection of his fundamental rights are the very essence of the democratic way of life adopted by the Constitution......" In ***Golak Nath V. State of Punjab***[30], the SC held that, Part III of the Constitution of India guarantees certain fundamental rights because they are considered necessary for the development of human personality. These rights enable a man to chalk out his own life in the manner he likes best. In ***Maneka Gandhi V. Union of India***[31], SC observed that, fundamental rights are calculated to protect the dignity of the individual and creates conditions in which every human being can develop his personality to the fullest extent.

Fundamental Rights-to whom available

Part III of the Constitution of India deals with various fundamental rights in its Articles 12-35. The fundamental rights in Articles 15, 16, 19, 29 and 30 are available only to citizens, while the rights guaranteed by other Articles are available to the citizens and non-citizens alike.

Fundamental Rights- against whom available

Most of the Fundamental Rights in Part III of the Constitution of India are available against the State only but some of them are also available against the private individuals. For example- the Fundamental Rights guaranteed in Articles 14, 15(1), 16, 18(1), 19, 20, 21, 22, 25, 26, 27, 28, 29 and 30 are available against the State only. While the Fundamental Rights

---

[29] AIR 1961 SC 1457
[30] AIR 1967 SC 1643
[31] AIR 1978 SC 597

guaranteed in Articles 15(2), 17, 23(1) and 24 are available against the State as well as against the private individuals.

(2) Nature, Object and Concept of Directive principles of state policy

(A) Nature, and concept of Directive Principles

The Directive Principle of state policy in chapter IV of the constitution of India is not platitude as observed by critic rather, it is the mirror of Indian polity through which one can make an estimate of the expectation of the people of India. They are, the embodiment of the ideals and goals towards which the State in expected to govern the country. The renowned author in Indian Constitutional law Mr. M.P. Jain has lucidly observed on this matter and said that "*the directive principle seeks to give certain directives t the legislature and government ..... as to how, and in what matter and for what purposes, they are to exercise their power. The reason behind the legal non-enforceability and non-justifiability of these principles is that they impose positive obligations on the state.*[32] So Directive reinforces and elaborates what has been stated in the preamble to the constitution. India's concept of welfare state has been envisaged in the Directive Principles[33]. These have been added in the Constitution to infuse a democratic sense and prepare grounds for justice and liberty and to instill confidence in the minds of people that the future state would govern only for their welfare. Directive Principle engagingly elaborates the welfare concept which the government shall have to take into consideration while administering the country. There was a good debate on the nature and significance of directive principle in the constituent assembly. Some members considered them as just pious wishes

[32] K.S Hedge, Directive principle of the state policy in the constitution of India, SC Journal India. (1971) 63

[33] S.I. Laskar, Directive Principles of State Policy in Indian Constitution, (New Delhi : Deep and Deep Publications, 1988), P. 33

devoid of any constitutional value. Others assigned them a place of real significance in the constitution. In order to evaluate the nature and significance of Directive Principles, it is necessary to analyse the view expressed on them by the members of the constituent's assembly. Naziruddin Ahmad opined that these were pious expression pious superfluities. Shah regarded the chapter on Directives as "One of the most cardinal, important and creative chapter of the constitution. Some of the members criticised the distinction made between justiciable and non justiciable and proposed to make these principles justiciable. The nature and significance of the Directives can be well found in the word of **Ambedkar**:

"Directive principle are nothing but obligation imposed by the constitution upon the various government in the country that they shall do certain things although it says that if they fail to them, no one will have the right to call for specific performance but the fact that they are the obligation of the government. I think stands unimpeached"[34].

Following conclusion can be drawn from the above discussion, which took place in the constituent assembly: First the directives are like the instrument of instructions to the Legislatures and Executive. Directives were the guidelines on which the government is to frame laws and conduct its administrative activities. Second, the Directives cannot and will not be ignored by any responsible government because the sanction behind them is not the court but the electorate. Third, the directives wedded to the ideal of economic and social democracy, represent a dynamic move towards certain objectives. Fourth, non justiciability of the directives do not mean that they are non-cognizable. The courts take cognizance of the Directives Principle in the determining the responsibility of restriction imposed by the legislative enactment on any of the Fundamental Rights of the citizen or to adjudge whether a particular state action was for public

[34] K.C. Markandan, Directive Principles in the Indian Constitution, (New Delhi: Allied Publisher, 1966) P 143.

purpose or otherwise[35]. Thus we says that the sole aim of the Directives Principles specified in part IV of the constitution is to achieve the socio economic justice and real equality in the country by peaceful revolution.

(B) Object behind Directives Principles

The Directives Principle of State Policy contained in part IV of the Constitution set out the aims and objectives to be taken up by the state in the governance of the country. The idea of welfare state envisaged by our constitution can only be achieved if the states endeavour to implement them with a high sense of moral duty. The Directive Principles are the ideals, which the Union and State Government must keep in mind while they formulate policy or pass a law. They lay down the certain social, economic and political principles, a suitable to peculiar conditions prevailing in India. In the words of **Sri G.N. Joshi** "they constitute a very Comprehensive political, socials and economic programme for a modern democratic State." The underlying objectives of the directives principle can better be understood from the speech of **Dr. Ambedkar** in the constituent assembly. He said:

"Our constitution lays down a parliamentary democratic system. By parliamentary democracy we mean "one man, one vote." If any government ignores them, they will certainly have to answer for them before electorate at election time.[36]*"*

The object of Directive principle is to embody the concept of welfare state and ideal of a welfare state is political, social and economic democracy.[37]Every government in power ought to

---

[35] N.V. Paranjape, Role of Directive Principles under the Indian Constitution (Allahabad: Central Law Agency, 1975) P 28
[36] Constituent Assembly Debates, Vol. VII, P. 41

achieve these ideas[38].The main object of Directive principles is to create such social and economic conditions which favours a good life for all the citizens. They also aim at building an economic and social democracy though a welfare state. They are a kind of yardstick in the hands of people to check the performance of government and if they do not full fill their commitments, to throw them out of the power. DPSP"S though are non-justifiable rights of citizens but the states have to give considerable importance to their essence while making any laws. Apart from the state all other executive wings have to understand the very importance of DPSP"S and even Judiciary is under a duty to give a notable effect to these principles while deciding on social, economic and other fundamental issues. The directive principles make certain that the state shall endeavour to promote a welfare state in which social, economic and political justice is given due consideration in all the institutions of life. They also compel the state to reduce the economic and other inequalities like in status and opportunities not only among the individuals but also among various groups putting up in different areas and engaged in diverse working fields.

Thus it is clear that the main object in enacting the Directive Principle appears to have been to set standards of achievement before the legislature and the executive, the local and other authorities, by which their success of failure can be judged. They lay down the goals, which may be achieved through various means, which have to be devises from time to time.

(C) Purpose of Directive Principles.

The Directives lay down the lines on which the State of India should work under this Constitution. Their contents may be divided into several groups:

1. Certain ideals, particularly economic, which the framers of the Constitution wished that the State should strive for.

---

[37] S.L.A Khan , Justice Bhagwati on Fundamental Rights and Directive principle, (New Delhi : Deep and Deep Publications,2003) 199.

[38] Ibid , 202.

2. Certain directions to the future Legislature and the future Executive to show in what manner they should exercise their legislative and executive powers.
3. Certain rights of citizens should not be enforceable by the courts like the 'Fundamental Rights' but which the State shall nevertheless aim at securing, by regulation of its legislative and administrative policy.

If the Preamble is the key to understanding of the Constitution or to open the mind of its makers, the Directive Principles of State Policy as enshrined in part IV, are its basic ideal. It is here that the Constitution makers poured their mind by setting forth the humanitarian socialist principles which epitomized the hopes and aspirations of the people and declared them as fundamental in the governance of the country. They are affirmative instructions from the ultimate sovereign to the State authorities, which are creatures of the Constitution established by them, to secure to all citizens justice, social, economic and political; liberty of thought, expression, belief, faith and worship; equality of status opportunity; and to promote among them all fraternity, assuring dignity of the individual and unity and integrity of the nation.

B. R Ambedkar told the Constituent Assembly that every government, Central, State and local "shall be on the avail, both in the daily affairs and at the end of a certain period when the voters and the electorate will be given an opportunity to assess the work done by the Government. While we have established political democracy, it is also the desire that we should lay down our ideal economic democracy. There are various ways in which people believe that economic democracy can be brought about, we have deliberately not introduced in the language that we have used in the Directive Principles something which is fixed or rigid. We have left enough room for the people of different ways of thinking, with regard to the reacting of the ideal of economic democracy. [39]The Indian Constitution is the first and foremost social document. The majority of its provisions are either directly aimed at furthering the goals of the social revolution or attempt to foster this revolution by establishing the conditions necessary for its achievements. Yet, despite the permeation of the entire Constitution by the aim of national renaissance, the core of the commitment to the social revolution lies in parts III and IV, in the Fundamental Rights and Directive Principles of State Policy. These are the conscience of the Constitution. [40] The Directive Principles had their roots deep in the struggle for independence. And they are included in the Constitution in the hope and expectation that one day the tree of true liberty would bloom in India. The Rights and Principles thus connect India's future, present, and giving strength to the pursuit of the social revolution in India. In the Directive Principles, however, one finds an even clear statement of social revolution. They aim at making the Indian masses free in the positive sense, free from the passivity engendered by centuries of coercion by society and by nature, and free from the object physical conditions that had prevented them from fulfilling their best selves. By establishing these positive obligations of the State, the members of the Constituent Assembly made it the responsibility of the future of the Indian governments to find a middle way between individual liberty and the public good between preserving the property and the privilege of the few and bestowing benefits on the many in order to liberate "the powers of all men equally for contribution to the common good."[41] The leaders of India's freedom movement visualized that in the new dispensation following political freedom, the people should have the fullest opportunities for advancement in the social and economic spheres and that the State should make suitable provisions for ensuring such progress. Among the Fundamental Rights adapted by All Parties conference was a provision entitling every citizen to free elementary education and

[39] .Constituent Assembly Debates; Vol. VII; P. 494 - 495.
[40] Granville Austin, The Indian Constitution Corner Stone Of A Nation 50 (Ninth Ed. Oxford University Press).
[41] .Ibid.

another which required the enactment of suitable laws for the maintenance of health and fitness for work of all citizens, a living wage for every worker, the protection of motherhood, the welfare of children and provisions for assistance in old age, infirmity and unemployment.[42] Similar provisions were also contained in the Declaration of Fundamental Rights, adopted by the Indian National Congress in 1931, which, in addition, specifically declared that "in order to end the exploitation of the masses, political freedom must include real economic freedom of the starving millions", and that the organization of economic life must confront to the principles of justice.[43] The 1937 Constitution of Ireland made a distinction between the "fundamental rights" strictly so called, and the "directive principles of social policy", the latter being expressly excluded from the purview of the courts. A similar distinction was also recognized by Lauterpacht in his "International Bill of Rights" published in 1945. In India, the idea of the division of rights to be incorporated in the Constitution into justiciable and non-justiciable rights was for the first time envisaged in the report of Sapru Committee in 1944-1945.[44]

(D)Characteristics of Directive Principles of State Policy

The Directive Principles of State Policy possess two characteristics. Firstly, they are not enforceable in a court of law and therefore, if a Directive is not obeyed or implemented by the State, its obedience or implementation cannot be secured through judicial proceedings. The reason behind the legal non-enforceability and non-justifiability of these principles is that they impose positive obligation on the state. While taking positive action, government functions under several restraints, the most crucial of these being that of financial resources. The Constitution

[42] .Subhas C. Kashyap, The Framing Of India's Constitution 59 (1st Ed, Universal Law Publishing Co. Pvt. Ltd).
[43] B. Pattabhi Sitaramayya, The History Of Indian National Congress 463, Vol. I.
[44] .Constitutional Proposals Of The Sapru Committee, Appendix II (Recommendation No. 17 And Chapter Vii, P. 256-72.

makers therefore taking a pragmatic view refrained from giving teeth to these principles. They believed more in an awakened public opinion, rather than in court proceedings, as the ultimate sanction for the fulfillment of these principles.[45] This characteristic has been diluted in practice by court decisions which have enforced some the directive principles in support of the fundamental rights. Secondly, they are fundamental in the governance of the state and it shall be the duty of the state to apply these principles in making laws. The expression 'laws' must be construed in a generic sense and should include all normative exercise of power including the decision making.[46] Directive Principles of State Policy aim to create social and economic conditions under which the citizens can lead a good life. They also aim to establish social and economic democracy through a welfare state. They act as a check on government, theorized as a yardstick in the hands of the people to measure the performance of the government and vote it out of power if it does not fulfill the promises made during the elections. Directive Principles mean that they will not be binding on the State in any case; they would not be enforceable in a court of law. Since the Directive Principles are not enforceable by court, it has been advocated that they are not law and therefore their non-observance by the state does not entail any legal consequences. Directive Principles of State Policy direct to work for an egalitarian society, where there is no concentration of wealth, where there is plenty, where there is equal opportunity for all, to education, to work, to livelihood and where there is social justice.[47] The Directive Principles Emphasizes, in amplification of the Preamble, that the goal of the Indian polity is not laissez, faire, but a Welfare State, where the State has a positive duty to ensure to its citizens social and economic justice and dignity of the individual. It would serve as an "Instrument of

[45] .M. P. Jain, Indian Constitutional Law. (Fifth Ed. Wadhwa Nagpur).p1366
[46] .V. N. Shukla, Constitution Of India (Eleventh Ed. Eastern Book Company).p342.
[47] Golak Nath V. State Of Punjab, AIR 1967 Sc 1643: (1967) 2 SCR 762.

Instruction" upon all future governments irrespective of their party creeds.[48] Part IV of the Constitution aims to end poverty, ignorance, disease and inequality of opportunity.[49] Though the provisions of part IV are not enforceable by the courts, the principles therein laid down are nevertheless fundamental in the governance of the country. It shall be the duty of State to apply these principles in making laws.[50] Whenever action is taken by the State in consonance with the provisions laid down in the Directive Principles of State Policy, as envisaged in Part IV of the Constitution, the same is considered as to be reasonable action. However, this does not amount to saying that any action which is not in consonance with the provision of Part IV will be ultra vires. There cannot be any doubt whatsoever that the principles contained in Part IV would form a relevant consideration for determining a question in regard to price fixation of an essential commodity. Directive Principles of State Policy provides for guidance to interpretation of fundamental rights of a citizen is also the statutory rights.[51]

Merely because the Directive Principles of State Policy are not enforceable in a court of law, it does not mean that they cannot create obligation or duties binding on the State. The crucial test which has to be applied is, whether the Directive Principles impose any obligations or duties on the State; if they do, the State would be bound by Constitutional mandate to carry out such obligations or duties, even though no corresponding right is created in any one which can be enforced in a court of law. The state is under a Constitutional mandate to carry out the mandate in Art. 37.[52]

(E) Status of the Directive Principles

---

[48] .Bhim Singhji V. Union Of India, AIR 1981 SC 234: (1981) 1 SCC 166.

[49] .G.B. Pant University Of Agriculture & Technology V. State of U.P., AIR 2000 Sc 2695

[50] Jacob M. Puthuparambil V. Kerala Water Authority,AIR 1990 SC 2228

[51] .Ashoka Smokeless Coal India Ltd. V. Union Of India, (2007) 2 SCC 640

[52] .Minerva Mills Ltd. V. Union Of India, Air 1980 SC 1789: (1980) 3 SCC 625

Directive Principles of State Policy, or Directive Principles as generally known, or DPSPs form one of the basic and an important part of the Indian Constitution. These principles have been embodied under Part IV of the Constitution. The socio-economic condition of India at the time of the independence was in shambles. The agricultural land belonged to the zamindars, banks and industries were controlled by the capitalists, labours were exploited. And, there was no proper legislation or provision which can make sure that these activities can be stopped. Most of the population was illiterate, and it was the aim of framers of the Indian Constitution to make India a literate and a prosperous nation. And for this purpose, there were several rights which the framers of the Indian Constitution were keen to include in the list of Fundamental Rights, but they were aware of the fact that the resources available in the Country are very limited and it would not be possible for them to include each and every such right in the list of the Indian Constitution. So, these rights were included in the Indian Constitution as "Directive Principles of State Policy" which are not justifiable, but forms a fundamental part in the governance of the country and it is the duty of the State to enforce such rights. These are the basic guidelines which have been mentioned in the Indian Constitution to have a ordered society characterized by social, economic and political justice accompanied by Liberty, Equality and Fraternity. These principles have been borrowed from the Irish Constitution

These principles are specific policies which are to be fulfilled by the State in distant future, and provide a much-desired philosophy to the Government and a set of instructions which are to be complied with. After analyzing these principles, it can be seen that these principles can be classified into various categories viz. Social, Gandhian and Liberal ideas. But, there have been various issues regarding the applicability of these provisions which have been laid down under the Indian Constitution. These principles cannot be enforced in any court of law in the country, nor is it the duty of the state to comply with these principles mandatorily. Directive Principles are seen as a positive set of principles unlike Fundamental Rights, as it allows State to implement these principles on its own convenience. It has been argued by various political leaders, and even by several members of the Constitution that these principles are superfluous and mere instruction with no agency to enforce it. The same view has been taken by various scholars at several instances, but it has been laid down in various decisions though not enforceable, should not be ignored by the legislature which would be discussed later in this article. But this view has been contradicted by Dr. B.R. Ambedkar stating that these principles are mere guidelines which are issued to the legislature and it would be quite interesting to note that it was never denied by Ambedkar that these principles have no legal force. In other words, it can be concluded that Directives principles are the instruction which have been incorporated under the Indian Constitution so that it can provide directions or guidance to the legislature and the executive as regards the manner in which they should exercise their powers.

Every legal aspect in India is accompanied by a number of case laws which act as precedents which are to be followed by several courts while dealing with the matters similar to such case laws. Also, these case laws provide directions to the state to consider what has been decided by a particular court as the case may be.

These case laws have reiterated at various occasions that state should not overlook the Directive Principles, and it should implement these principles as and when it becomes important to do so. The importance of Directive Principles was enhanced by the 42ndamendment to the Indian Constitution which provided that Directive Principles cannot be declared unconstitutional only on the ground that they have violated any of the fundamental rights. The amendment simultaneously stated that laws prohibiting "antinational activities" or the formation of "antinational associations" could not be invalidated because they infringed on any of the Fundamental Rights. From this amendment, it can be seen that the duty of the state and the importance of Directive principles have been enhanced not only by the Judicial decisions, but also by the legislative actions from time to time. In other words, a state has been achieved wherein the Directive Principles are looked upon as equivalent to Human Rights and the directives have been held to supplement fundamental rights in achieving a welfare state. The main problem which arises while dealing with Directive Principles is the inability of the Indian Courts to implement these principles. There have been various instances when State escapes from implementing these principles on the ground that it is not bound to implement these principles. The power which has been provided to Indian High Courts and Supreme Court is very vast, and it has directed state on various occasions to do or not to do something. The judgment which curtailed the power of the legislature to amend the Indian Constitution to the extent that it should not amend the basic structure of the Indian Constitution and various such judgements indicates that there has always been an active role played by the Indian Judiciary in instructing the state with regard to certain matters.

One of the earliest case law after the Indian Independence which deals with the matter related to State's duty towards the implementation of Directive Principle is ***Keshvananda Bharti Vs. State Of Kerela***[53] in which it was held by the Supreme Court that while imposing the restrictions on fundamental rights, the directive principles are to be kept in mind mandatorily and opined that "In view of the principles adumbrated by this Court it is clear that the directive principles form the fundamental feature and the social conscience of the Constitution and the Constitution enjoins upon the State to implement these directive principles. The directives thus provide the policy, the guidelines and the end of socio-economic freedom and Articles 14 and 16

[53] (1973) 4 SCC 225

are the means to implement the policy to achieve the ends sought to be promoted by the directive principles". The reason behind providing importance to Directive Principles was crucial. There had been a lot of dispute over the distinction between Fundamental Rights and Directive Principles. There is a view which had been taken by various scholars that Fundamental Rights are the end which has to be achieved, and Directive Principles act as a source to that means that has to be achieved. These principles provide a medium or source for the government for implementing the Fundamental Rights.

It can be seen that while implementing the fundamental rights of a citizen, the state should not underestimate or ignore the importance of Directive Principles and there should be a balance between these two sets of principles. The relation between Fundamental Rights and Directive Principles was once again discussed in the case ***Pathumma and Others Vs. State of Kerala and Ors.***[54] where it was held by the Supreme Court that Fundamental Rights and Directive Principles constitute the "conscience" of the Constitution. The purpose of the latter is to fix certain social and economic goals for immediate attainment by bringing about a non-violent social revolution. The Constitution aims at bringing about a synthesis between fundamental rights and directive principles by giving to the former a place of pride and to the latter a place of permanence. It is clear from this decision that even after remaining unenforceable, Directive Principles find a prominent position under the Indian Constitution.

Similar set of principles as that of Directive Principles, which have been included under Chapter IV-A of the Indian Constitution i.e. Fundamental Duties. Though not enforceable in any court of law, this set of duties finds a very important place under the Indian Constitution. In ***AIIMS Students' Union Vs. AIIMS and Ors***[55], it was opined by the Supreme Court that in

---

[54] (1978) 2 SCC 1
[55] (2002) 1 SCC 428,

the era of globalisation, where the nation as a whole has to compete with other nations of the world so as to survive, excellence cannot be given an unreasonable go-by and certainly not compromised in its entirety. Fundamental duties, though not enforceable by a writ of the court, yet provide a valuable guide and aid to interpretation of constitutional and legal issues. In case of doubt or choice, people's wish as manifested through Article 51-A, can serve as a guide not only for resolving the issue but also for constructing or moulding the relief to be given by the courts. Constitutional enactment of fundamental duties, if it has to have any meaning, must be used by courts as a tool to tab, even a taboo, on State action drifting away from constitutional values.

These are the few cases which deal with the importance of Directive Principles as considered by the Supreme Court from time to time. The reason behind providing such importance to the Directive Principles is quite simple, firstly there must have been a motive for including these principles under the Indian Constitution. The framers of the Indian Constitution wanted to create a society where each and every citizen of the country would be able to live a happy and prosperous life. But for achieving this goal, they wanted to include several human rights in the form of fundamental rights in the constitution. But they were also aware of the fact that the amount of resources which were available at the time of independence was limited. And, that was the fundamental reason why these principles were not enforceable in any court of law. In case these principles had been enforceable, then there would have been an extra burden on the government to implement these principles irrespective of the available resources with them. But it is the law of nature that as and when time changes, the economic, political, social scenario change. It would be quite illogical to interpret the provision in the same way as they were interpreted at the time of the independence. The economic condition of India has changed over a period of time, and the resources and means which are now available with them are much greater than ever before. Considering these facts, it now becomes the duty of the state to implement these principles as and when it becomes necessary to implement them. Instead, there have been various provisions which were once parts of these directive principles have been enacted in the form of some legislation, and some have been included in the some other parts of the Indian Legal System. But, still there is a need to understand the basic difference between the provisions and its applicability which are present under the head of Fundamental Rights and Directive Principles of State Policies. The differences can be understood as follows-

1. On one hand where Fundamental Rights are the basic civil rights which are guaranteed to every citizen of India equally and are enforceable in the court of law, Directive Principles are considered as basic human rights which are not enforceable in any court of law.
2. Directive Principles in order to get implemented need a specific legislation passed by the legislature, but fundamental rights do not require any legislation for their enforcement in the court of law.
3. Directive Principles are the guidelines which have been included in the constitution so as to instruct the state to implement these guidelines as and when it is capable to do so taking into account the available resources.

These are some basic differences which are to be kept in mind while dealing with Fundamental Rights and Directive Principles. But as the time has passed, the importance of directive principles has been increasing through various judicial decisions. The Supreme Court and High Courts have started providing importance to these principles more than ever before. This can be seen from various judicial decisions.

Article 39(d) of the Indian Constitution states that *the state shall, in particular, direct its policy towards securing that there is equal pay for equal work for both men and women*. This provision has been considered by Supreme Court from time to time, and finally it was decided in ***Grih Kalyan Kendra Workers" Union Vs. Union Of India And Others***[56] that "Equal pay for equal work is not expressly declared by the Constitution as a Fundamental Right but in view of the Directive Principles of State Policy as contained in Art. 39(d) of the Constitution "equal pay for equal work" has assumed the status of the Fundamental Right in service jurisprudence having regard to the constitutional mandate of equality in Articles 14 and 17 of the Constitution". This view was reiterated by the Supreme Court in ***Randhir Singh Vs. Union of India*** that "equal pay for equal work" is not a mere demagogic slogar but it is a constitutional goal capable of attaining through Constitutional remedies. The Court went on to declare thus: "*Directive Principles as even pointed out in some of the Judgments of this Court, have to be read into the Fundamental Rights as a matter of interpretation*".

Another important section of Part IV of the constitution which has received importance in section 41 which states that the State shall, within the limits of its economic capacity and development, make effective provision for securing the right to work, to education and to public assistance in cases of unemployment, old age, sickness and disablement, and in other cases of undeserved want. Right to Education, as popularly known was included in the list of Fundamental Rights in the year 2002 by 86thAmendment Act, and became functional in the year 2010. The need of making Right to Education a fundamental right was opined by the Supreme Court *in* ***Mohini Jain Vs. State of Karnataka***[57] stating that *the directive principles which are fundamental in the governance of the country cannot be isolated from the Fundamental Rights guaranteed under Part III. These principles have to be sent into the Fundamental Rights. Both are supplementary to each other.* The State is under a constitutional mandate to each other. The

[56] AIR 1991 SC 1773
[57] AIR 1992 SC 1858

State is under a constitutional mandate to create conditions in which the Fundamental Rights guaranteed to the individuals under Part III could be enjoyed by all. Without making "Right to education" under Article 41 of the Constitution a reality, the Fundamental Rights under Chapter III shall remain beyond the reach of large majority which is illiterate. The Fundamental Rights guaranteed under Part III of the Constitution of India including the right to freedom of speech and expression and other rights under Article 19 cannot be appreciated and fully enjoyed unless a citizen is education and is conscious of his individualistic dignity.

Article 44 of the constitution states that the State shall endeavour to secure for the citizens a uniform civil code throughout the territory of India. This provision is very hard to get implement for various reasons. In a country like India where different religious groups are present, it is quite difficult to have a uniform civil code which should be followed by members of every religion in a same way. This instance can be seen in the case of ***Shah Bano Begum Vs. Mohd. Akeel Khan***[58] where a Muslim woman was demanding maintenance from her husband after their divorce. Being a Muslim, husband had paid her maintenance for the period as required by the personal Muslim Law, but it was held by the Supreme Court that Shah Bano would be entitled to get maintenance under section 125 of Cr.PC. This decision was followed by several protests from the Muslims priests and society claiming that this decision would harm their personal law. Soon an action was taken by the then Prime Minister Rajiv Gandhi by passing *the Muslim Women's (Protection of Rights in Divorce) Act in 1986*, a law that essentially provided for maintenance for Muslim women outside the criminal code, thus ensuring that Muslim women were not protected under the constitutional right to equality, and that they could no longer have recourse to section 125 of the Criminal Code. Thus, protection which was provided to Muslim women by Shah Bano judgment was made invalid subsequently due to the pressure from the

[58] 1985 SCC (2) 556

Muslim section. This is just an example which shows that how difficult it is to implement a uniform civil code in India, and this question remains in ambiguity i.e. whether there would be any legislation in India which can be implemented uniformly. Other legislations such as the *Indian Succession Act of 1925*, which dealt with inheritance and succession, specifically exempted Muslims, *the Special Marriage Act of 1872,* which was essentially a secular civil marriage law, also exempted Muslims. Although, some pieces of legislation which don't exempt anyone from its purview e.g. *section 112 of the Indian Evidence Act, 1872* concerning the legitimacy of the children. It was initially not applicable to Muslims, but later it became applicable to them also despite its inconsistency with Muslim Law.

The above discussion throws a light over the changing status of Directive Principles. The time is not the same where state can escape from its duty to implement these principles when resources are available. At the time of independence, India was not in a condition so that it can provide each and every citizen of the country a happy and prosperous life. Poor administrative system, poor political system, unemployment due to lack of opportunities were some of the major problems which were prevalent at the time of independence. These problems have been solved to a great extent on many parts of the country, and in a process to get solved in the other parts of the country. The Indian Judicial system is considered to be the most powerful judicial system in the world. Here, judiciary is empowered to direct the executive to implement the required legal provisions or to work in accordance with the Constitution. And as the time would pass, it seems that more and more Directive Principles would be implemented.

(3) Classification of Fundamental Rights and Directive Principle in the Indian Constitution

The Indian Constitution is first and foremost a social document .The majority of its provisions are either directly aimed at furthering the goal of social revolution or attempt to foster this revolution by establishing condition necessary for its achievement. The core of commitment to the social revolution lies in part III and part IV dealing with Fundamental Rights and Directive Principles respectively. These are the 'conscience of the constitution'[59] In the Indian constitution, the Fundamental Rights and the Directive Principles of State Policy are divided into two separate parts. Part III of the Indian constitution deals with Fundamental Rights and part IV of the Indian constitution deals with directive principle of state policy.

(A) Classification of Fundamental Rights

Chapter III of Indian constitutions which deals with Fundamental Rights is also characterized as the "*Magnacarta of India*". It embodies and sanctifies certain fundamental, individuals, justiciable rights which are primarily meant to protect the individual against the state action by imposing negative obligations[60]. The Fundamental Rights place limitations on all kinds of authority that has either the power to make laws or have discretion vested in it. The Indian constitution defines the state, inclusively, to mean the Government and Parliament of India and Government and legislature of each of the state and all local or other authorities within territory of India or under the control of government of India[61].Ambedkar made this point clear in the constituent assembly. He explained that the object of Fundamental Rights was two fold. First that every citizen must be in position to claim those rights. Secondly, they must be binding upon

[59] Dr. P.S. Jaiswal, Directive Principles Jurisprudence and socio economic justice in India, (New Delhi : APH Publishing Corporation, 1996) P 108
[60] Supra Note 8 at 108
[61] Article 12, The Constitution of India.

every authority ....upon every authority, which has got either the power to make laws or the power to have discretion vested in it. There fore it is quite clear that the Fundamental Rights are to be real then they must be binding not only upon the central government, they must not also be binding upon the provincial government ...... they must also be binding upon district local boards, municipalities even village Panchayat and taluk boards, in fact every authority which has been created by law and which has got certain power to make laws, to make rules or make by laws.[62]

The Fundamental Rights as incorporated in the Indian Constitution is divided into following six groups

(i) Right to Equality (Articles 14-18)

(ii) Right to Freedom (Articles 19-22)

(iii) Right against Exploitation (Articles 23-24)

(iv) Right to Freedom of Religion (Articles 25-28)

(v) Cultural and Educational Rights (Articles 29-30)

(vi) Right to Constitutional Remedies (Articles 32-35)

The 44th amendment has abolished the right to properly as a Fundamental Right as guaranteed by article 19(1)(f) and article 31 of the constitution:

(i) Right to Equality

[62] Constituent Assembly Debate, Voll III, P. 110

Article 14 to 18 of the constitution guaranteed the right to equality to every citizen of India. Article 14 embodies the general principles of equality before law and prohibits unreasonable discrimination between persons. Article 14 embodies the idea of equality expressed in the preamble. Article 14 declare that the state shall not deny to any person equality before the law or the equal protection of the laws within the territory of India. Article 14 uses two expressions "*equality before law*" and "*equal protection of law*". The first expression equality before law has been taken from English constitution and second expression "equal protection of law" has been taken from the American constitution. Both these expressions have been also in used Art.7 of Universal Declaration of Human Rights. Article 7 of UDHR says: "All are the equal before the law and are entitled without any discrimination to equal protection of the law". Both the expression may seem to be identical, but they do not convey the same meaning. "Equality before the law" is a negative concept implying the absence of any special privilege in the favour of individuals and the equal subjects of all classes to the ordinary law. "Equal protection of the law is a more positive concept implying equality of treatment in equal circumstances[63]. According to Dr. Jennings, equality before the law means that "among the law should be equal and should be equally administered, that like should be treated alike. The right to sue and be sued to prosecuted and be prosecuted for the same kind of action should be same for all citizens of full age and understanding without distinctions of race, religion, wealth, social status or political influence"[64]. The succeeding articles 15,16, 17,and 18 lay down specific application of the general rules laid down in the article 14. Article 15 relates to prohibition of discrimination on grounds of religion, race, caste, sex or place of birth. Article 16 guarantees equality of opportunity in matters of public employment. Article 17 abolishes untouchability and Art. 18 abolishes 'title'. Right to

---

[63] Dr. J.N. Pandey, Constitutional law of India, Thirty Ninth Edition, (Allahabad : Central Law Agency, 2003) P.69.
[64] Sir Ivor Jennings, The Law and the Constitution, Third Edition (London : University of London Press, 1953) P.49

equality intended to remove the social and civic disabilities from which the masses of India had suffered all through these ages. Democracy can only exist and flourish amongst a society of equals and the Indian constitution make social and civic equality as the bedrock of Indian polity[65]. The theme of 'equality' is illustrated not only by articles 15 to 18 but also by the several articles in part IV, in a particular, articles 38,39,39 A, 41 and 46 of the constitution.[66]

Some exception are however, inevitable and the constitution set out these exception. A legislature may make laws with special provisions for a women and children. The constitution (first amendments) Act 1951, further provided that "Nothing in this article 15 or in clause (2) of article 29 shall prevent the state from making any special provision for the advancement of any socially and educationally backward classes of citizens or for the scheduled castes and scheduled tribes". In another exception parliament may confine employment under a state or local authority to residents. A State may also provide for the reservation of the appointments or posts for members of backward classes, which in the opinion of the state are not adequately represented in the service under the state.

(ii) Right to freedom

The right to freedom is covered by articles 19 to 22 and embraces the classical liberties of the individual of these Article 19 is the most important as it originally guaranteed six Fundamental Rights, which may be described as six freedoms. These are the right:

(a) to freedom of speech and expression

(b) to assemble Peacefully and without arms

---

65 A.C. Kapur, Constitutional History of India, Third Ed.(New Delhi : S. Chand and Co., 1985)P. 443

66 Supra Note 8 at109

(c) to form association or unions

(d) to move throughout the tertiary of India

(e) to reside and settle in any part of tertiary of India

(f) to practice any profession or to carry out an occupation, Trade or business.

All these freedoms are the most important ingredients of human happiness and progress as without them no individual can rise to the full stature of his personality. The preamble of almost every constitution epitomises these freedoms and declares them as its objectives. For instance, the preamble to the constitution of United States declares, "to secure the blessing of liberty to over selves and to our posterity". The permeable to the India constitution declares that one of its objectives is to secure to all citizens liberty of thoughts, expression, belief, faith and worship".[67]

Article 19 may be divided into two parts. The first is the declaration of rights and second part contains limitations. In other words, Fundamental Rights to freedom are not absolute. Fundamental Rights of freedom provided by article 19(1) (a) to (g) can be enjoyed by the citizens, sub Articles (2) to (6) of Article 19 is specially provide the manner in which the said fundamental freedoms guaranteed by article 19 enables the state to make law in public interests imposing reasonable restrictions on the said freedom. For example the freedom given in article 19 (1) can be restricted in the interest of the sovereignty and integrity of India, the security of the state, friendly relationship with foreign state, public order, decency or morality or in relation to contempt of court, defamation or incitement to an offence. The right guaranteed under Article 19(1)(b) can be restricted in the interest of the sovereignty and integrity of India or Public order. The right guaranteed under Article 19 (1) (c) can be restricted in the interest of sovereignty and integrity of India or public order or morality. The right guaranteed under 19(1) (d) and (e) can be restricted in the interests of the general public or for the protection of the interest of any

[67] Supra Note 14 at 444

scheduled tribe. The right guaranteed under Article 19(1)(g) can be restricted in the interest of the general public and it can also be restricted in respect of matters covered by article 19(6) sub clauses (i) and (ii). The right guaranteed in articles 20,21, and 22 relates to the individuals personal liberty and collectively come under the sub heading "Right to freedom". These rights strengthen the liberties conferred on citizen under the Article 19. Article 20 deals with certain Fundamental Rights of a accused and embodies certain important principles of criminal jurisprudence. Clause (1) of the article embodies the principle that they no one should be made to suffer any punishment for an offence under any law not in force at time of the commission of an offence. Similarly, no person shall be subject to a penalty greater than that which might have been inflicted under the law in force at the time of the commission of the offence. Clause (2) of the same article embodies the fundamental principle that no one should be placed in Jeopardy twice for the same offence. Clause (3) gives effect to the principle that no one should be compelled to give evidence against himself in a criminal case.[68]

Article 21 guarantees to every person the most essential of all right the right to life and liberty. Article 21 clearly points out that right to life and liberty provided by it, can be limited only by the 'procedure established by law'. The procedure so laid down must be in conformity with article 22 of the constitution. Art. 22 deals with two separate matters firstly it deals with person arrested under the ordinary law of Crimes and secondly it deals with Person detained under the ordinary law of Preventive detention.

(iii) Right against Exploitation

[68] Supra Note 14 at 447

Art.23 and Art.24 deals with right against exploitation. Article 23 categorically prohibits all traffic in human beings and begar and other similar forms of forced labour. Traffic in human beings is evidently a very wide expression and would embrace not only the prohibition of slavery and bonded labour but also traffic in women for immoral or other purposes. Any contravention of the same shall be punishable in accordance with the law. But clause (2) of Article 23 enables the state to impose compulsory service for public purpose. This article thus provides right against exploitation and it is characterised a Charter of liberty of the down trodden people of India[69]. But we found that the painful gap between preachment and performance of this article. Constitutional guardian supreme court also quoted ' Tolstay' in ***'Peoples Union for Democratic Rights Vs. Union of India'***[70] in the following words:

"*The abolition of slavery has gone on for a long time. Rome abolished slavery, America abolished it and we did but only the words were abolished, not the things.*'"

Articles 24 prohibit the employment of children (boys as well as girls) below the age of fourteen years to any work or factory of hazardous nature. The genesis of this article is that the children below the age of fourteen years should not work in hazardous employment.

(iv) Right of freedom of religion

Article 25 to 28 of the constitution guarantees to all persons freedom of conscience, and to profess, practice and propagate any religion subject to the prescribed limitation of the public order, morality and health an other provisions of part III. The constitution, as such, does not only guarantee the freedom of religious faith and belief but it protects also acts done in pursuance of religion and this is made clear by the use of the expression "Practice of religion". But religious

---

[69] Supra Note 8 at 116

[70] AIR 1982 SC 1473 at 1489

freedom and freedom of conscience do not diminish in any manner the regulatory power of the state given to it by the provision of the constitution.

(v) Cultural and Educational Rights

The constitution recognizes and guarantees certain non-political rights of religious, cultural and linguistic minorities, groups or section of the people. Article 29 guarantees to every minority or section of the people to preserve its language, script and culture. Clause (2) of the same article provides that no citizen may be denied admission to state and state - aided educational institutions on the ground only of religion, race, caste or language. Art. 30 guarantees to all minorities whether based on religion or language the right to establish and administer their educational institutions and the state shall not discriminate against them in making grants on grounds of religion, race of language.

(vi) Right to Constitutional Remedies

Article 32 guarantees to every citizen the right to move the Supreme Court by appropriate proceedings for the enforcement of Fundamental Rights, and for that purpose the Supreme Court is given general powers to safeguard the Fundamental Right as well as the power to issue direction or orders or writs in the nature of Habeas Corpus, Mandamus, Prohibition, Quo-warranto and Certiorari whichever writes which ever may be appropriate' for the enforcement of any of the Fundamental Right . A right without a remedy is a meaningless formality.

(B) Classification of Directive Principle of State Policy

The Directive Principles of state policy contained in part IV of the Constitution set out the aims and objectives to be taken up by the states in the governance of the country. This novel feature of the constitution is borrowed from the constitution of Ireland which had copied it from the Spanish constitution[71]. The Directive Principles of state policy set forth the humanitarian socialist percepts that were and are the aims of the Indian social revolution. The Directive Principles lay down certain economic and social policies to be pursued by the various governments in India and they impose certain obligation on the state to take positive action in certain directions in order to promote the welfare of the people and achieve economic democracy.

The Directive principle of state policy may be classified in to the following groups:

(i) Social and Economic Charter

Art 38 and Article 39 jointly known as social and economic charter. It divided in eight subgroups.

(a) Social order based on Justice

Article 38 (1) provides that the state shall strive to promote the welfare of the people by securing and protecting as effectively as it may, a social order in which justice, social, economic and political shall inform all the institutions of national life.

Art 38 (2) provides that the state shall in particular strive to minimise the inequalities in income and endeavour to eliminate inequalities in status, facilities and opportunities not amongst individuals but also amongst people residing in different areas or engaged in different vocations.

---

[71] Supra Note 12 at 353

In ***Air India Statutory Corp. Vs. United Labour Union***[72] the court envisages not only legal justice but socio-economic justice as well. The Supreme Court has observed: "*The Constitution commands justice, liberty, equality and fraternity as supreme value to usher in the egalitarian social, economic and political democracy. Social justice, equality and dignity of person are cornerstone of social democracy.*" Thus social justice is an integral part of justice in the generic sense. Justice is the genus of which social justice is one of its species."

(b) Principle of policy to be followed by the state for securing Economic Justice

Article 39 visualises a new social order in which high social values will change according to the changing socio-economic condition of the society. It lays down certain specific policies to achieve the much-covered goal of socio-economic justice.

(c) Means of livelihood

Article 39 (a) says that the state shall direct its policy towards securing the equal right of men and women to adequate means of livelihood.

(d) Distributive Economic system

Article 39 (b) and 39 (c) is related with distributive economic system. Article 39 (b) says that the state shall direct its policy towards securing a proper distribution of the material resources of the community for the common good.

---

[72] MANU/SC/0163/1997 : AIR 1997 SC 645: 1997 AIR SCW 430: (1997) 9 SCC 377: 1997 (3) Serv LJ 81 SC: 1997 (2) Supreme 165

(e) No concentration of wealth

Article 39 (c) says that the state shall direct its policy towards securing the prevention of concentration of wealth to the common detriment.

(f) Equal pay for equal work

Article 35 (d) says that the state shall direct its policy towards securing equal pay for equal work for both men and women.

(g) Welfare of children

Art 39 (e) says that the state shall direct its policy towards securing the protection of the strength and health of workers and avoiding circumstances which force citizens to enter avocation unsuited to their age and strength.

(h) Bonded Labour

Art 39 (f) says that the state shall direct its policy towards securing the protection of childhood and youth against exploitation or moral and material abandonment.

Clause (f) was modified by the Constitution (42nd Amendment) Act, 1978, with a view to emphasize the constructive role of the State with regard to children.

In ***M. C. Mehta Vs. State of Tamil Nadu***[73] (Known as Child Labour Abolition Case), the Supreme Court held that *children below the age of 14 years cannot be employed in any hazardous industry, or mines or factory.*

In ***Randhir Singh Vs. Union of India***[74], the Supreme Court held that *equal pay for equal work though not a fundamental right is certainly a constitutional goal, and, therefore, capable of*

[73] MANU/SC/0169/1997 : AIR 1997 SC 699: 1997 AIR SCW 407: (1996) 6 SCC 756

enforcement through constitutional remedies under article 32 of the Constitution. The doctrine of equal pay for equal work is equally applicable to persons employed on a daily wages basis.

(ii) Social Security charter

Article 39-A, Art 41 to article 43-A and article 45 to article 47 is jointly called as social security charter.

(a) Equal justice and free legal aid

Article 39-A was added by 42nd Amendment of constitution. This article enjoins on the state to make provisions for providing free legal aid to the weaker section of the society and thus invest the legal process with functional relevance and promotion of social justice. The central theme of this article is that no one should be denied of justice by reason of economic or other disabilities.

This article has been inserted in the Constitution by 42nd Amendment Act, 1976. This article ordains the State to secure a legal system which promotes justice on the basis of equal opportunity. The language of article 39A is couched in mandatory terms as is clear by the use of word 'shall' twice therein.

The Supreme Court has emphasized that legal assistance to a poor or indigent accused who is arrested and put in jeopardy of his life and personal liberty is a constitutional imperative mandated not only by article 39A but also by articles 14 and 21.

---

[74] MANU/SC/0234/1982 : AIR 1982 SC 879: (1982) 1 SCC 618: 1982 SCC (Lab) 119: 1982 UJ (SC) 193: (1982) 1 SCWR 260: 1982 (1) SCJ 283.

(b) Social Service

Article 41 directs the state to ensure the people within the limit of its economic capacity and development economic, education, public assistance in cases of unemployment, old age, sickness and disablement and in other cases of undeserved want.

The State is directed by this article to ensure to the people within the limits of its economic capacity and development: (I) employment, (II) education, (III) public assistance in case of unemployment, old age, sickness and disablement and in other cases of undeserved want

In ***Sameer Vs. State***[75] the Supreme Court emphasized that it is the duty of the state under this directives (Art. 41) not only to establish educational institutions but also effectively secure right to education by admitting students to the seats available at such institutions and the states action must conform to the standard of equality and rationality underlying Art.14.

(c) Condition of work

Article 42 directs the state to make provision for securing just and human condition and for maternity relief.

In ***D.Bhuvan Mohan Patnaik Vs. State of Andhra* Pradesh**[76]. The Supreme Court has suggested that article 42 may 'benevolently' be extended to living conditions in jails. The barbarous and subtle form of punishment to which convicts and under trials are subjected to, offend against the letter and spirit of the Constiution

[75] AIR 1982 SC 66

[76] MANU/SC/0038/1974 : AIR 1974 SC 2092: 1974 SCC (Cri) 803: 1975 Cr LJ556: MANU/SC/0367/1974 : (1975) 3 SCC 185: (1975) 2 SCR 24

In ***Consumer Education and Research centre Vs. Union of India***[77], Right to health and medical care is a Fundamental Right under Art. 21 as it is essential for making the life to the workman meaningful and purposeful with dignity of person. Right to life includes right to livelihood, better standard of life, hygienic conditions in workplace and leisure. The Supreme Court went one step further and laid down guidelines to be followed by all asbestos industries either private or government by virtue of Art.42.

(d) Living wages

Article 43 says that the state shall direct its policy in securing a living wage and decent conditions of work for all workers, agricultural, industrial or otherwise as to ensure to them sufficient leisure and enjoyment of social and cultural opportunities and, in particular the State shall endeavour to promote cottage industries on an individual or co-operative basis in rural areas.

A 'living wage' is such a wage as enables the male earner to provide for himself and his family not merely the bare essential of food, clothing and shelter, but a measure of frugal comfort including education for children, protection against ill-health and requirement of essential social needs.

In ***D.S. Nakara Vs. Union of India***[78], the Constitutional Bench of the Supreme Court has held that pension is not only compensation for loyal service rendered in the past, but also by the broader significance it is a social welfare measure rendering socio-economic justice

[77] (1995) 3 SCC 42

[78] MANU/SC/0237/1982 : AIR 1983 SC 130: (1983) 1 SCC 305: 1983 SCC (Lab) 145: 1983 UJ (SC) 217: (1983) 1 SCWR 390: 1983 (1) SCJ 188

(e) Participation of workers in Management of Industries

Article 43-A directs the state to take steps by suitable legislation or in any other way to secure the participation of workers in the management of undertakings, establishments or other organisations engaged in any industry. This article has been inserted in the Constitution by 42nd Amendment Act, 1976

(f) Free and Compulsory education

Art. 45 provides that the State shall endeavour to provide early childhood care and education for all children untill they complete the age of six years.[79] This article has been substituted by the Constitution (Eighty-sixth Amendment) Act, 2002 which received assent of the President on December, 12, 2002.

In ***M.C. Mehta Vs. State of Tamil Nadu***,[80] Child labour is a big problem and remained intractable, even after about 50 years of our having become independent, despite various legislative enactments........ Prohibiting employment of a child in a number of occupations and avocations

(g) Promotion of educational and economic interests of weaker section

The State shall promote with special care the educational and economic interests of the weaker sections of the people, and, in particular of the Scheduled Castes, Scheduled Tribes, and shall protect them from social injustice and all forms of exploitation.

Article 46 provides for the promotion of educational and economic interest of scheduled castes, scheduled tribes and other weaker section so that a true egalitarian social order is established

[79] Substituted by the Constitution (86th Amendment) Act 2002

[80] AIR 1997 SC 699: 1997 AIR SCW 407: (1996) 6 SCC 756: 1997 SCC (LandS) 49: 1997 (1) Supreme 207: 1997 (1) UJ (SC) 243.

where even Harizans, tribals and other backward classes are able to get socio-economic justice and participate in the fruits of freedom and democracy on equal basis.

In ***State of Madras Vs Champakam Dorairajan***[81], The Supreme Court refused to let the fundamental right declared in article 29(2) to be whittled down by this article. In that case, although the object of the impugned 'communal order' of the Madras Government was to advance the interest of educationally backward classes of citizens, the Supreme Court held the order void for the violation of Fundamental Right under article 29(2).

In ***R. Chandevarappa Vs State of Karnataka*** [82], the Court observed that the economic empowerment to the poor dalits and tribes is an integral constitutional scheme of socio-economic democracy is a way of life of political democracy. Economic empowerment is, therefore, a basic human right and a fundamental right as part of right to life, quality and of status and dignity to the poor, weaker sections, dalits and tribes.

(h) Raising standard of living

The State shall regard the raising of the level of nutrition and the standard of living of its people and the improvement of public health as among its primary duties and, in particular, the State shall endeavour to bring about prohibition of the consumption except for medicinal purpose of intoxicating drinks and of drugs which are injurious to health

Article 47 imposes duty upon the state to raise the level of nutrition and the standard of living of its people and the improvement of public health. In particular the state should bring about

[81] MANU/SC/0007/1951 : AIR 1951 SC 226: 1951 SCJ 313: 1951 SCR 525.
[82] MANU/SC/0805/1995 : (1995) 6 SCC 309: (1995) 5 SCALE 620: JT 1995 (7) SC 93

prohibition of the consumption except for medicinal purposes of intoxicating drinks and of drugs which are injurious to health.

In ***AIIMS Students' Union Vs AIIMS***[83], the Supreme Court observed that the improvement of public health being one of the primary duties of the State, public health can be improved by having the best of doctors, specialists and super specialists.

In ***Francis Coralie Vs. Union Territory of Delhi***[84], the Supreme Court held that right to live is not restricted to mere animal existence. It means something more than just physical survival. The right to live is not continued to be the protection of any faculty or limb through which life is enjoyed or the soul communicates with the outside world. But it also includes the rights to live with human dignity and all that goes along with it, namely, the bare necessities of life such as *'adequate nutrition'*, 'clothing and shelter' and facilities for reading, writing and expressing ourselves in diverse forms, freely moving about and mixing and communicating with fellow human being and thereby gives effect to the directives given under Art.47 wherein the state was directed to raise the level of nutrition and the standard of living.

In a welfare state the primary duty of the government is to secure the welfare of the people. Providing adequate medical facilities for the people as an essential part of the obligations undertaken by the Government in a welfare State

(iii) Community Welfare Charter

Article 44,48,48-A,49,50, and Art 57 jointly known as community welfare charter.

(a) Uniform civil code

---

83 MANU/SC/0480/2001 : AIR 2001 SC 3262: 2001 AIR SCW 3143: JT 2001 (7) SC 12: MANU/SC/0480/2001 : (2002) 1 SCC 428: 2001 (4) SCJ 590: (2001) 5 SCALE 430

84 AIR 1981 SC 746

The State shall endeavour to secure for the citizens a uniform civil code throughout the territory of India. Article 44 requires the state to secure for the citizens a uniform civil code throughout the territory of India. Most modern states have uniform civil codes. We have different personal laws for different communities. Hindus are governed by their own succession, marriage, guardianship and divorce laws.So also the Christian and few other Communities. These Separate laws tend to encourage separatist tendencies. From ***Sarla Mudgal***[85] case to ***John Vallamottam*** case[86] Supreme Court also directed to make a statutory amendment to enforcement of uniform civil code but we have not yet made any worthwhile attempts to enact a uniform civil code. This provision was made to promote unity and integrity which are cherished goal enshrined in the Preamble to our Constitution. Hindu law of marriage, succession etc., have been drastically changed in the first decade of the commencement of the Constitution but there has been resistance from Muslim community in this respect and for avoiding any resentment on their part political parties in power remained reluctant to enforce a uniform civil code.

In ***Sarla Mudgal, President, Kalyani Vs. Union of India***[87], the Supreme Court observed that article 44 is based on the concept that there is not necessarily a connection between religion and personal laws

(b) Organisation of agriculture and animal Husbandry

The State shall endeavour to organise agriculture and animal husbandry on modern and scientific lines and shall, in particular, take steps for preserving and improving the breeds, and prohibiting the slaughter of cows and calves and other milch and draught cattle. Article 48

[85] Sarla Mudgal Vs. UOI, (1995) 3 SCC 635

[86] John Vallamottam Vs. Union of India. AIR 2003 SC 2902

[87] MANU/SC/0290/1995 : (1995) 3 SCC 635: 1995 Cr LJ 2926 (SC): AIR 1995 SC 1531: 1995 AIR SCW 2326: JT 1995 (4) SC 331: 1995 SCC (Cri) 569

directs the state to take steps to organise agriculture and animal husbandry on modern and scientific lines. It should take steps for preserving and improving the breeds, and prohibiting the slaughter of cows and calves and other milch and draught cattle.

In ***State of Gujarat Vs. Mirzapur Moti Kureshi Kassab Jamat***[88], upholding total ban on the slaughter of cows, calves, bulls and bullocks irrespective of their age, the Supreme Court held that a milch cattle goes through a life cycle during which it is sometimes milch and sometimes it becomes dry. This does not mean that as soon as a milch cattle ceases to produce milk, for a short period as part of its life cycle, it goes out of the purview of articles 48, and can be slaughtered. A drought cattle may lose its utility on account of injury or sickness and may be rendered useless as a drought cattle during that period. This would not mean that if a draught cattle ceases to be of utility for a short period on account of sickness or injury, it is excluded from the definition of 'drought cattle' and deprived of the benefit of article 48.

(c) Protection of environment

The State shall endeavour to protect and improve the environment and to safeguard the forests and wild life of the country. Article 48-A requires the state to take steps to protect and improve the environmental and to safeguard the forests and wild life of the country.

In ***M.C. Mehta Vs. Union of India***[89], The court has said "*articles 39(e), 47 and 48A by themselves and collectively cast a duty on the State to secure the health of the people, improve*

[88] MANU/SC/1352/2005 : AIR 2006 SC 212: 2005 AIR SCW 5723: (2005) 8 SCC 534: 2005 (7) SCJ 701: (2005) 8 SCALE 661: 2005 (8) Supreme 697

[89] MANU/SC/0271/2003 : AIR 2003 SC 3469: 2003 Cr LJ 2045: 2003 AIR SCW 1975: JT 2003 (3) SC 505: (2003) 5 SCC 376: (2003) 3 SCALE 575: 2003 (3) Supreme 44

public health and protect and improve the environment". This article has been inserted in the Constitution by the 42nd Amendment Act, 1976.

In ***T.N. Godavarman Thirumalpad Vs. Union of India & Ors.***[90], a three-Judge Bench of this Court read Article 48-A and Article 51-A together as laying down the foundation for a jurisprudence of environmental protection and held that "*Today, the State and the citizens are under a fundamental obligation to protect and improve the environment, including forests, lakes, rivers, wild life and to have compassion for living creatures*".

In ***Rural Litigation and Entitlement Kendra & Ors. Vs. State of Uttar Pradesh & Ors.***[91], a complete ban and closing of mining operations carried on in the Mussoorie hills was held to be sustainable by deriving support from the fundamental duty as enshrined in Article 51-A(g) of the Constitution. The Court held that preservation of the environment and keeping the ecological balance unaffected is a task which not only Governments but also every citizen must undertake. It is a social obligation of the State as well as of the individuals.

In ***Subhas Kumar Vs. State of Bihar***[92], and in the series of cases filed by the public spirited lawyer M.C. Mehta (which will be dealt later) it was held that the Right to live includes right to get pollution free environment, water and air and thereby Art.48A was given the status of Fundamental Right.

(d) Protection of monuments

[90] (2002) 10 SCC 606
[91] 1986 (Supp) SCC 517
[92] AIR1991SC 420

It shall be the obligation of the State to protect every monument or place or object of artistic or historic interest declared by or under law made by Parliament to be of national importance, from spoilation, disfigurement, destruction, removal, disposal or export, as the case may be.

Article 49 requires the state to protect every monuments or place or object of artistic or historic, interest, to be of national importance from spoliation, disfigurement, destruction, removal, disposal or export.

In ***M.C. Mehta Vs. Union of India***[93], having regard to article 49 and clause (g) of article 51A of Constitution of India the Supreme Court in a public interest litigation, prevented the "Taj Heritage Corridor Project", one of the main purposes of which was to divert river Yamuna and to reclaim 75 acres of land between Agra Fort and the Taj Mahal from using the reclaimed land for constructing food plazas, shops and amusement activities

(e) Separation of judiciary from executive

Article 50 requires the state to take step to separate the judiciary from the executive in the public services of the state.

In ***Baldev Raj Guliani Vs. Punjab and Haryana High Court***[94], the Supreme Court has interpreted this provision to further enhance the prestige, dignity and independence of the subordinate judiciary

(f) Promotion of International Peace and Security

The State shall endeavour to-

(a)promote international peace and security;

---

[93] AIR 2007 SC 1087: 2007 AIR SCW 1025: 2007 (1) Crimes 375: MANU/SC/5296/2006 : (2007) 1 SCC 110: (2006) 12 SCALE 391: 2007 (1) SCC (Cri) 264: 2007 (1) Supreme 219

[94] MANU/SC/0537/1976 : AIR 1976 SC 2490: (1976) 4 SCC 201: (1977) 1 SCR 425

(b)maintain just and honourable relations between nations;

(c)foster respect for international law and treaty obligations in the dealings of organised peoples with one another; and

(d)encourage settlement of international disputes by arbitration

Art 51 provides that the state should strive to promote international peace and security, maintain just and honourable relations between nations, foster respect for international law and treaty obligations in the dealings of organised peoples with one another and encourage settlement of international disputer by arbitration.

In ***People's Union for Civil Liberties Vs. Union of India***[95], International Law today is not confined to regulating the relation between the States. Today matters of social concerns such as health, education and economics apart from human rights falls within the ambit of the international regulations.

In ***Addl. Distt. Magistrate, Jabalpur Vs. Shivakant Shukla***[96], Khanna, J. observed *that if there be a conflict between the municipal law on the one side and the international law or the provisions of any treaty obligations on the other, the court would give effect to municipal law.*

(g) Organisation of village Panchayats

The State shall take steps to organise village panchyats and endow them with such powers and authority as may be necessary to enable them to function as units of self-government.

[95] MANU/SC/0274/1997 : AIR 1997 SC 1203: 1997 AIR SCW 1234: 1997 (1) Cr CJ 374: 1997 (1) Crimes 190: JT 1997 (2) SC 311: (1997) 3 SCC 433: 1997 (1) SCJ 480: (1997) 1 SCR 923: (1997) 1 SCALE 706: 1997 SCC (Cri) 434: 1997 (2) Supreme 429

[96] MANU/SC/0062/1976 : AIR 1976 SC 1207: (1976) 2 SCC 521: 1976 Cr LJ 945: 1976 UJ (SC) 610:MANU/SC/0179/1976 : (1976) 3 SCC 454: (1976) 3 SCR 929: 1976 Supp SCR 172.

The Constitution 73rd Amendment Act, 1992 introducing the panchayats in Part IX (articles 243-243-O) is a major step in the direction of implementing this directive principle.

Art. 40 emphasises on the decentralised democracy through full blooded panchyats. It provides for organisation of panchayats. It placed responsibility for home rule on the rural poor.

The idea underlying this constitutional provision is to introduce democracy at the grassroots. This provision does not prescribe as to what powers should be given to the panchayats or what their structure should be and so the panchayat laws may vary from one State to another. The village panchayats are envisaged by the article as the basic democratic institutions of a pyramid of the democratically organised and functioning self-governing units .

Chapter IV

Fundamental Rights, Directive Principles and Fundamental Duties in Indian Constitution

---

Synopsis

1. *Fundamental Rights*
2. *Directive Principles of State Policy*
3. *Fundamental Duties*
4. *Relationship between the Fundamental Rights, Directive Principles and Fundamental Duties*
5. *Report of the National Committee to Review the Working of Indian Constitution on Fundamental Rights, Directive Principles and Fundamental Duties (JS Verma Committee Report)*
6. *Report of the National Commission to review the Working of the Consitution (Venkatchaliah Committee Report)*

The Fundamental Rights, Directive Principles of State Policy and Fundamental Duties of the Constitution of India that prescribe the fundamental obligations of the State to its citizens and the duties of the citizens to the State. These sections comprise a constitutional bill of rights for government policy making and the behavior and conduct of citizens. These sections are considered vital elements of the constitution, which was developed between 1947 and 1949 by the Constituent Assembly of India.

The Fundamental Rights are defined as the basic the Constitution, apply irrespective of race, place of birth, religion, caste, creed or sex. They are enforceable by the courts, subject to specific restrictions.

The Directive Principles of State Policy are guidelines for the framing of laws by the government. These provisions, set out in Part IV of the Constitution, are not enforceable by the courts, but the principles on which they are based are fundamental guidelines for governance that the State is expected to apply in framing and passing laws.

The Fundamental Duties are defined as the moral obligations of all citizens to help promote a spirit of patriotism and to uphold the unity of India. These duties, set out in Part IV-A of the Constitution (under a constitutional amendment) concern individuals and the nation. Like the Directive Principles, they are not legally enforceable.

Fundamental Rights

The Fundamental Rights, embodied in Part III of the Constitution, guarantee civil rights to all Indians, and prevent the State from encroaching on individual liberty while simultaneously placing upon it an obligation to protect the citizens' rights from encroachment by society. Seven fundamental rights were originally provided by the Constitution - right to equality, right to freedom, right against exploitation, right to freedom of religion, cultural and educational rights, right to property and right to constitutional remedies. However, the right to property was removed from Part III of the Constitution by the 44th Amendment in 1978. The purpose of the Fundamental Rights is to preserve individual liberty and democratic principles based on equality of all members of society. They act as limitations on the powers of the legislature and executive, under Article 13, and in case of any violation of these rights the Supreme Court of India and the High Courts of the states have the power to declare such legislative or executive action as unconstitutional and void. These rights are largely enforceable against the State, which as per the wide definition provided in Article 12, includes not only the legislative and executive wings of the federal and state governments, but also local administrative authorities and other agencies and institutions which discharge public functions or are of a governmental character. However, there are certain rights - such as those in Articles 15, 17, 18, 23, 24 - that are also available against private individuals. Further, certain Fundamental Rights - including those under Articles 14, 20, 21, 25 - apply to persons of any nationality upon Indian soil, while others - such as those under Articles 15, 16, 19, 30 - are applicable only to citizens of India.

The Fundamental Rights are not absolute and are subject to reasonable restrictions as necessary for the protection of public interest. In the *Kesavananda Bharati v. State of Kerala* case in 1973, the Supreme Court, overruling a previous decision of 1967, held that the Fundamental Rights could be amended, subject to judicial review in case such an amendment violated the basic structure of the Constitution. The Fundamental Rights can be enhanced, removed or otherwise altered through a constitutional amendment, passed by a two thirds majority of each House of Parliament. The imposition of a state of emergency may lead to a temporary suspension any of the Fundamental Rights, excluding Articles 20 and 21, by order of the President. The President may, by order, suspend the right to constitutional remedies as well, thereby barring citizens from approaching the Supreme Court for the enforcement of any of the Fundamental Rights, except Articles 20 and 21, during the period of the emergency. Parliament may also restrict the application of the Fundamental Rights to members of the Indian Armed Forces and the police, in order to ensure proper discharge of their duties and the maintenance of discipline, by a law made under Article 33.

Here an attempt has been made by the author to elaborate the detailed provisions of Fundamental Rights.

PART III

FUNDAMENTAL RIGHTS

General

12. Definition.—In this Part, unless the context otherwise requires, "the State includes the Government and Parliament of India and the Government and the Legislature of each of the States and all local or other authorities within the territory of India or under the control of the Government of India.

13. Laws inconsistent with or in derogation of the Fundamental Rights.

(1) All laws in force in the territory of India immediately before the commencement of this Constitution, in so far as they are inconsistent with the provisions of this Part, shall, to the extent of such inconsistency, be void.

(2) The State shall not make any law which takes away or abridges the rights conferred by this Part and any law made in contravention of this clause shall, to the extent of the contravention, be void.

(3) In this article, unless the context otherwise requires,—

(a) "law" includes any Ordinance, order, bye-law, rule, regulation, notification, custom or usage having in the territory of India the force of law;

(b) "laws in force" includes laws passed or made by a Legislature or other competent authority in the territory of India before the commencement of this Constitution and not previously repealed, notwithstanding that any such law or any part thereof may not be then in operation either at all or in particular areas.

(4) Nothing in this article shall apply to any amendment of this Constitution made under article 368[97].

Right to Equality

14. Equality before law.—The State shall not deny to any person equality before the law or the equal protection of the laws within the territory of India.

15. Prohibition of discrimination on grounds of religion, race, caste, sex or place of birth.—

(1) The State shall not discriminate against any citizen on grounds only of religion, race, caste, sex, place of birth or any of them.

(2) No citizen shall, on grounds only of religion, race, caste, sex, place of birth or any of them, be subject to any disability, liability, restriction or condition with regard to—

(a) access to shops, public restaurants, hotels and places of public entertainment; or

(b) the use of wells, tanks, bathing ghats, roads and places of public resort maintained wholly or partly out of State funds or dedicated to the use of the general public.

(3) Nothing in this article shall prevent the State from making any special provision for women and children.

(4) Nothing in this article or in clause (2) of article 29 shall prevent the State from making any special provision for the advancement of any socially and educationally backward classes of citizens or for the Scheduled Castes and the Scheduled Tribes.[98]

(5) Nothing in this article or in sub-clause (g) of clause (1) of article 19 shall prevent the State from making any special provision, by law, for the advancement of any socially and educationally backward classes of citizens or for the Scheduled Castes or the Scheduled Tribes in

---

[97] 1Ins. by the Constitution (Twenty-fourth Amendment) Act, 1971, s. 2.

[98] Added by the Constitution (First Amendment) Act, 1951, s. 2.

so far as such special provisions relate to their admission to educational institutions including private educational institutions, whether aided or unaided by the State, other than the minority educational institutions referred to in clause (1) of article 30.[99]

16. Equality of opportunity in matters of public employment.—

(1) There shall be equality of opportunity for all citizens in matters relating to employment or appointment to any office under the State.

(2) No citizen shall, on grounds only of religion, race, caste, sex, descent, place of birth, residence or any of them, be ineligible for, or discriminated against in respect of, any employment or office under the State.

(3) Nothing in this article shall prevent Parliament from making any law prescribing, in regard to a class or classes of employment or appointment to an office under the Government of, or any local or other authority within, a State or Union territory, any requirement as to residence within that State or Union territory prior to such employment or appointment.

(4) Nothing in this article shall prevent the State from making any provision for the reservation of appointments or posts in favour of any backward class of citizens which, in the opinion of the State, is not adequately represented in the services under the State.

(4A) Nothing in this article shall prevent the State from making any provision for reservation in matters of promotion, with consequential seniority, to any class or classes of posts in the services under the State in favour of the Scheduled Castes and the Scheduled Tribes which, in the opinion of the State, are not adequately represented in the services under the State. [100]

(4B) Nothing in this article shall prevent the State from considering any unfilled vacancies of a year which are reserved for being filled up in that year in accordance with any provision for

[99] Ins. by the Constitution (Ninety-third Amendment) Act, 2005, s. 2 (w.e.f. 20-1-2006).
[100] Ins. by the Constitution (Seventy-seventh Amendment) Act, 1995, s. 2.

reservation made under clause (4) or clause (4A) as a separate class of vacancies to be filled up in any succeeding year or years and such class of vacancies shall not be considered together with the vacancies of the year in which they are being filled up for determining the ceiling of fifty per cent. reservation on total number of vacancies of that year. [101]

(5) Nothing in this article shall affect the operation of any law which provides that the incumbent of an office in connection with the affairs of any religious or denominational institution or any member of the governing body thereof shall be a person professing a particular religion or belonging to a particular denomination.

17. Abolition of Untouchability.—

"Untouchability' is abolished and its practice in any form is forbidden. The enforcement of any disability arising out of 'Untouchability' shall be an offence punishable in accordance with law.

18. Abolition of titles.—

(1) No title, not being a military or academic distinction, shall be conferred by the State.

(2) No citizen of India shall accept any title from any foreign State.

(3) No person who is not a citizen of India shall, while he holds any office of profit or trust under the State, accept without the consent of the President any title from any foreign State.

(4) No person holding any office of profit or trust under the State shall, without the consent of the President, accept any present, emolument, or office of any kind from or under any foreign State.

Right to Freedom

19. Protection of certain rights regarding freedom of speech, etc.—

(1) All citizens shall have the right—

[101] Ins. by the Constitution (Eighty-first Amendment) Act, 2000, s. 2 (w.e.f. 9-6-2000).

(a) to freedom of speech and expression;

(b) to assemble peaceably and without arms;

(c) to form associations or unions;

(d) to move freely throughout the territory of India;

(e) to reside and settle in any part of the territory of India; and * * * * *

(g) to practise any profession, or to carry on any occupation, trade or business.

(2) Nothing in sub-clause (a) of clause (1) shall affect the operation of any existing law, or prevent the State from making any law, in so far as such law imposes reasonable restrictions on the exercise of the right conferred by the said sub-clause in the interests of the sovereignty and integrity of India, the security of the State, friendly relations with foreign States, public order, decency or morality, or in relation to contempt of court, defamation or incitement to an offence.[102]

(3) Nothing in sub-clause (b) of the said clause shall affect the operation of any existing law in so far as it imposes, or prevent the State from making any law imposing, in the interests of the sovereignty and integrity of India or public order, reasonable restrictions on the exercise of the right conferred by the said sub-clause.

(4) Nothing in sub-clause (c) of the said clause shall affect the operation of any existing law in so far as it imposes, or prevent the State from making any law imposing, in the interests of the sovereignty and integrity of India or public order or morality, reasonable restrictions on the exercise of the right conferred by the said sub-clause.

(5) Nothing in sub-clauses (d) and (e) of the said clause shall affect the operation of any existing law in so far as it imposes, or prevent the State from making any law imposing, reasonable

[102] 3Subs. by the Constitution (First Amendment) Act, 1951, s. 3, for cl. (2) (with retrospective effect).

restrictions on the exercise of any of the rights conferred by the said sub-clauses either in the interests of the general public or for the protection of the interests of any Scheduled Tribe.

(6) Nothing in sub-clause (g) of the said clause shall affect the operation of any existing law in so far as it imposes, or prevent the State from making any law imposing, in the interests of the general public, reasonable restrictions on the exercise of the right conferred by the said sub-clause, and, in particular, nothing in the said sub-clause shall affect the operation of any existing law in so far as it relates to, or prevent the State from making any law relating to,—

(i) the professional or technical qualifications necessary for practising any profession or carrying on any occupation, trade or business, or

(ii) the carrying on by the State, or by a corporation owned or controlled by the State, of any trade, business, industry or service, whether to the exclusion, complete or partial, of citizens or otherwise.

20. Protection in respect of conviction for offences.—

(1) No person shall be convicted of any offence except for violation of a law in force at the time of the commission of the Act charged as an offence, nor be subjected to a penalty greater than that which might have been inflicted under the law in force at the time of the commission of the offence.

(2) No person shall be prosecuted and punished for the same offence more than once.

(3) No person accused of any offence shall be compelled to be a witness against himself.

21. Protection of life and personal liberty.—

No person shall be deprived of his life or personal liberty except according to procedure established by law.

21A. The State shall provide free and compulsory education to all children of the age of six to fourteen years in such manner as the State may, by law, determine.[103]

22. Protection against arrest and detention in certain cases. —

(1) No person who is arrested shall be detained in custody without being informed, as soon as may be, of the grounds for such arrest nor shall he be denied the right to consult, and to be defended by, a legal practitioner of his choice.

(2) Every person who is arrested and detained in custody shall be produced before the nearest magistrate within a period of twenty-four hours of such arrest excluding the time necessary for the journey from the place of arrest to the court of the magistrate and no such person shall be detained in custody beyond the said period without the authority of a magistrate.

(3) Nothing in clauses (1) and (2) shall apply—

(a) to any person who for the time being is an enemy alien; or

(b) to any person who is arrested or detained under any law providing for preventive detention.

(4) No law providing for preventive detention shall authorise the detention of a person for a longer period than three months unless—

(a) an Advisory Board consisting of persons who are, or have been, or are qualified to be appointed as, Judges of a High Court has reported before the expiration of the said period of three months that there is in its opinion sufficient cause for such detention: Provided that nothing in this sub-clause shall authorise the detention of any person beyond the maximum period prescribed by any law made

by Parliament under sub-clause (b) of clause (7); or

(b) such person is detained in accordance with the provisions of any law made by Parliament under sub-clauses (a) and (b) of clause (7).

---

[103] Ins by the Constitution (Eighty-sixth Amendment) Act, 2002, s. 2

(5) When any person is detained in pursuance of an order made under any law providing for preventive detention, the authority making the order shall, as soon as may be, communicate to such person the grounds on which the order has been made and shall afford him the earliest opportunity of making a representation against the order.

(6) Nothing in clause (5) shall require the authority making any such order as is referred to in that clause to disclose facts which such authority considers to be against the public interest to disclose.

(7) Parliament may by law prescribe—

(a) the circumstances under which, and the class or classes of cases in which, a person may be detained for a period longer than three months under any law providing for preventive detention without obtaining the opinion of an Advisory Board in accordance with the provisions of sub-clause (a) of clause (4);

(b) the maximum period for which any person may in any class or classes of cases be detained under any law providing for preventive detention; and

(c) the procedure to be followed by an Advisory Board in an inquiry under sub-clause (a) of clause (4).

Right against Exploitation

23. Prohibition of traffic in human beings and forced labour.—

(1) Traffic in human beings and begar and other similar forms of forced labour are prohibited and any contravention of this provision shall be an offence punishable in accordance with law.

(2) Nothing in this article shall prevent the State from imposing compulsory service for public purposes, and in imposing such service the State shall not make any discrimination on grounds only of religion, race, caste or class or any of them.

24. Prohibition of employment of children in factories, etc. —

No child below the age of fourteen years shall be employed to work in any factory or mine or engaged in any other hazardous employment.

Right to Freedom of Religion

25. Freedom of conscience and free profession, practice and propagation of religion.—

(1) Subject to public order, morality and health and to the other provisions of this Part, all persons are equally entitled to freedom of conscience and the right freely to profess, practise and propagate religion.

(2) Nothing in this article shall affect the operation of any existing law or prevent the State from making any law—

(a) regulating or restricting any economic, financial, political or other secular activity which may be associated with religious practice;

(b) providing for social welfare and reform or the throwing open of Hindu religious institutions of a public character to all classes and sections of Hindus.

Explanation I.—The wearing and carrying of kirpans shall be deemed to be included in the profession of the Sikh religion.

Explanation II.—In sub-clause (b) of clause (2), the reference to Hindus shall be construed as including a reference to persons professing the Sikh, Jaina or Buddhist religion, and the reference to Hindu religious institutions shall be construed accordingly.

26. Freedom to manage religious affairs.—

Subject to public order, morality and health, every religious denomination or any section thereof shall have the right—

(a) to establish and maintain institutions for religious and charitable purposes;

(b) to manage its own affairs in matters of religion;

(c) to own and acquire movable and immovable property; and

(d) to administer such property in accordance with law.

27. Freedom as to payment of taxes for promotion of any particular religion.—

No person shall be compelled to pay any taxes, the proceeds of which are specifically appropriated in payment of expenses for the promotion or maintenance of any particular religion or religious denomination.

28. Freedom as to attendance at religious instruction or religious worship in certain educational institutions.—

(1) No religious instruction shall be provided in any educational institution wholly maintained out of

State funds.

(2) Nothing in clause (1) shall apply to an educational institution which is administered by the State but has been established under any endowment or trust which requires that religious instruction shall be imparted in such institution.

(3) No person attending any educational institution recognised by the State or receiving aid out of State funds shall be required to take part in any religious instruction that may be imparted in such institution or to attend any religious worship that may be conducted in such institution or

in any premises attached thereto unless such person or, if such person is a minor, his guardian has given his consent thereto.

Cultural and Educational Rights

29. Protection of interests of minorities.—

(1) Any section of the citizens residing in the territory of India or any part thereof having a distinct language, script or culture of its own shall have the right to conserve the same.

(2) No citizen shall be denied admission into any educational institution maintained by the State or receiving aid out of State funds on grounds only of religion, race, caste, language or any of them.

30. Right of minorities to establish and administer educational institutions. —

(1) All minorities, whether based on religion or language, shall have the right to establish and administer educational institutions of their choice.

(1A) In making any law providing for the compulsory acquisition of any property of an educational institution established and administered by a minority, referred to in clause (1), the State shall ensure that the amount fixed by or determined under such law for the acquisition of such property is such as would not restrict or abrogate the right guaranteed under that clause.[104]

(2) The State shall not, in granting aid to educational institutions, discriminate against any educational institution on the ground that it is under the management of a minority, whether based on religion or language.

31. [Compulsory acquisition of property.] Rep.by the Constitution (Forty-fourth Amendment) Act, 1978, s. 6 (w.e.f. 20-6-1979).

---

[104] Ins. by the Constitution (Forty-fourth Amendment) Act, 1978, s. 4 (w.e.f. 20-6-1979).

Saving of Certain Laws[105]

31A. Saving of laws providing for acquisition of estates, etc.—

(1) Notwithstanding anything contained in article 13, no law providing for—

(a) the acquisition by the State of any estate or of any rights therein or the extinguishment or modification of any such rights, or

(b) the taking over of the management of any property by the State for a limited period either in the public interest or in order to secure the proper management of the property, or

(c) the amalgamation of two or more corporations either in the public interest or in order to secure the proper management of any of the corporations, or

(d) the extinguishment or modification of any rights of managing agents, secretaries and treasurers, managing directors, directors or managers of corporations, or of any voting rights of shareholders thereof, or

(e) the extinguishment or modification of any rights accruing by virtue of any agreement, lease or licence for the purpose of searching for, or winning, any mineral or mineral oil, or the premature termination or cancellation of any such agreement, lease or licence, shall be deemed to be void on the ground that it is inconsistent with, or takes away or abridges any of the rights conferred by article 14 or article

Provided that where such law is a law made by the Legislature of a State, the provisions of this article shall not apply thereto unless such law, having been reserved for the consideration of the President, has received his assent:

Provided further that where any law makes any provision for the acquisition by the State of any estate and where any land comprised therein is held by a person under his personal cultivation, it shall not be lawful for the State to acquire any portion of such land as is within the ceiling limit

[105] Ins. by the Constitution (Forty-second Amendment) Act, 1976, s. 3 (w.e.f. 3-1-1977).

applicable to him under any law for the time being in force or any building or structure standing thereon or appurtenant thereto, unless the law relating to the acquisition of such land, building or structure, provides for payment of compensation at a rate which shall not be less than the market value thereof.

(2) In this article,—

(a) the expression'estate' shall, in relation to any local area, have the same meaning as that expression or its local equivalent has in the existing law relating to land tenures in force in that area and shall also include—

(i) any jagir, inam or muafi or other similar grant and in the States of Tamil Nadu and Kerala, any janmam right;

(ii) any land held under ryotwari settlement;

(iii) any land held or let for purposes of agriculture or for purposes ancillary thereto, including waste land, forest land, land for pasture or sites of buildings and other structures occupied by cultivators of land, agricultural labourers and village artisans;

(b) the expression "rights", in relation to an estate, shall include any rights vesting in a proprietor, sub-proprietor, under-proprietor, tenure-holder, raiyat, under-raiyat or other intermediary and any rights or privileges in respect of land revenue.

31B. Validation of certain Acts and Regulations.—

Without prejudice to the generality of the provisions contained in article 31A, none of the Acts and Regulations specified in the Ninth Schedule nor any of the provisions thereof shall be deemed to be void, or ever to have become void, on the ground that such Act, Regulation or provision is inconsistent with, or takes away or abridges any of the rights conferred by, any provisions of this Part, and notwithstanding any judgment, decree or order of any court or

Tribunal to the contrary, each of the said Acts and Regulations shall, subject to the power of any competent Legislature to repeal or amend it, continue in force.[106]

31C. Saving of laws giving effect to certain directive principles.—

Notwithstanding anything contained in article 13, no law giving effect to the policy of the State towards securing[all or any of the principles laid down in Part IV] shall be deemed to be void on the ground that it is inconsistent with, or takes away or abridges any of the rights conferred by article 14 or article 19; and no law containing a declaration that it is for giving effect to such policy shall be called in question in any court on the ground that it does not give effect to such policy: Provided that where such law is made by the Legislature of a State, the provisions of this article shall not apply thereto unless such law, having been reserved for the consideration of the President, has received his assent.

31D. [Saving of laws in respect of anti-national activities.] Rep. by the Constitution (Forty-third Amendment) Act, 1977, s.2 (w.e.f.13-4-1978).[107]

Right to Constitutional Remedies

32. Remedies for enforcement of rights conferred by this Part.—

(1) The right to move the Supreme Court by appropriate proceedings for the enforcement of the rights conferred by this Part is guaranteed.

(2) The Supreme Court shall have power to issue directions or orders or writs, including writs in the nature of habeas corpus, mandamus, prohibition, quo warranto and certiorari, whichever may be appropriate, for the enforcement of any of the rights conferred by this Part.

[106] Ins. by the Constitution (First Amendment) Act, 1951, s. 5
[107] Ins. by the Constitution (Forty-second Amendment) Act, 1976, s. 5 (w.e.f. 3-1-1977)

(3) Without prejudice to the powers conferred on the Supreme Court by clauses (1) and (2), Parliament may by law empower any other court to exercise within the local limits of its jurisdiction all or any of the powers exercisable by the Supreme Court under clause (2).

(4) The right guaranteed by this article shall not be suspended except as otherwise provided for by this Constitution.

32A. [Constitutional validity of State laws not to be considered in proceedings under article 32.] Rep. by the Constitution (Forty-third Amendment) Act, 1977, s. 3 (w.e.f. 13-4-1978).[108]

33. Power of Parliament to modify the rights conferred by this Part in their application to Forces, etc.—Parliament may, by law, determine to what extent any of the rights conferred by this Part shall, in their application to,—

(a) the members of the Armed Forces; or

(b) the members of the Forces charged with the maintenance of public order; or

(c) persons employed in any bureau or other organisation established by the State for purposes of intelligence or counter intelligence; or

(d) persons employed in, or in connection with, the telecommunication systems set up for the purposes of any Force, bureau or organisation referred to in clauses (a) to (c), be restricted or abrogated so as to ensure the proper discharge of their duties and the maintenance of discipline among them.[109]

34. Restriction on rights conferred by this Part while martial law is in force in any area.—Notwithstanding anything in the foregoing provisions of this Part, Parliament may by law indemnify any person in the service of the Union or of a State or any other person in respect of any act done by him in connection with the maintenance or restoration of order in area within the

[108] Ins. by s. 6, ibid. (w.e.f. 1-2-1977).

[109] 1Subs. by the Constitution (Fiftieth Amendment) Act, 1984, s. 2, for art. 33

territory of India where martial law was in force or validate any sentence passed, punishment inflicted, forfeiture ordered or act done under martial law in such area.

35. Legislation to give effect to the provisions of this Part.—

Notwithstanding anything in this Constitution,—

(a) Parliament shall have, and the Legislature of a State shall not have, power to make laws—

(i) with respect to any of the matters which under clause (3) of article 16, clause (3) of article 32, article 33 and article 34 may be provided for by law made by Parliament; and

(ii) for prescribing punishment for those acts which are declared to be offences under this Part;

and Parliament shall, as soon as may be after the commencement of this Constitution, make laws for prescribing punishment for the acts referred to in sub-clause (ii);

(b) any law in force immediately before the commencement of this Constitution in the territory of India with respect to any of the matters referred to in sub-clause (i) of clause (a) or providing for punishment for any act referred to in sub-clause (ii) of that clause shall, subject to the terms thereof and to any adaptations and modifications that may be made therein under article 372, continue in force until altered or repealed or amended by Parliament.

Explanation.— In this article, the expression "law in force" has the same meaning as in article 372.

Directive Principles

The Directive Principles of State Policy, embodied in Part IV of the Constitution, are directions given to the State to guide the establishment of an economic and social democracy, as proposed by the Preamble. They set forth the humanitarian and socialist instructions that were the aim of social revolution envisaged in India by the Constituent Assembly. The State is expected to keep these principles in mind while framing laws and policies, even though they are non-justiciable in nature. The Directive Principles may be classified under the following categories: ideals that the State ought to strive towards achieving; directions for the exercise of legislative and executive power; and rights of the citizens which the State must aim towards securing. Despite being non-justiciable, the Directive Principles act as a check on the State; theorised as a yardstick in the hands of the electorate and the opposition to measure the performance of a government at the time of an election. Article 37, while stating that the Directive Principles are not enforceable in any court of law, declares them to be "fundamental to the governance of the country" and imposes an obligation on the State to apply them in matters of legislation. Thus, they serve to emphasise the welfare state model of the Constitution and emphasise the positive duty of the State to promote the welfare of the people by affirming social, economic and political justice, as well as to fight income inequality and ensure individual dignity, as mandated by Article 38, in order to ensure equitable distribution of land resources. Article 39 lays down certain principles of policy to be followed by the State, including providing an adequate means of livelihood for all citizens, equal pay for equal work for men and women, proper working conditions, reduction of the concentration of wealth and means of production from the hands of a few, and distribution of community resources to "sub serve the common good". These clauses highlight the Constitutional objectives of building an egalitarian social order and establishing a welfare state, by bringing about a social revolution assisted by the State, and have been used to support the nationalisation of mineral resources as well as public utilities. Further, several legislations pertaining to agrarian reform and land tenure have been enacted by the federal and state governments, in order to ensure equitable distribution of land resources. Articles 41-43 mandate the State to endeavour to secure to all citizens the right to work, a living wage, social security, maternity relief, and a decent standard of living. These provisions aim at establishing a socialist state as envisaged in the Preamble. Article 43 also places upon the State the responsibility of promoting cottage industries, and the federal government has, in furtherance of this, established several Boards for the promotion of khadi, handlooms etc., in coordination with the state governments. Article 39A requires the State to provide free legal aid to ensure that opportunities for securing justice are available to all citizens irrespective of economic or other disabilities. Article 43A mandates the State to work towards securing the participation of workers in the management of industries. The State, under Article 46, is also mandated to promote the interests of and work for the economic uplift of the scheduled castes and scheduled tribes and protect them from discrimination and exploitation. Several enactments, including two Constitutional amendments, have been passed to give effect to this provision. Article 44 encourages the State to secure a uniform civil code for all citizens, by eliminating discrepancies between various personal laws currently in force in the country. However, this has remained a "dead letter" despite numerous reminders from the Supreme Court to implement the provision.[89] Article 45 originally mandated the State to provide free and compulsory education to children between the ages of six and fourteen years, but after the 86th Amendment in 2002, this has been converted into a Fundamental Right and replaced by an obligation upon the State to secure childhood care to all children below the age of six. Article 47 commits the State to raise the standard of living and improve public health, and prohibit the consumption of intoxicating drinks and drugs injurious to health. As a consequence, partial or total prohibition has been introduced in several states, but financial constraints have prevented its full also mandated by Article 48 to organise agriculture and improving breeds and prohibiting slaughter of cattle environment and safeguard the forests and wildlife of the country, while Article 49 places an obligation upon the State to ensure the preservation of monuments and objects of national importance State to ensure the separation of judiciary from executive in public services, in order to independence, and federal legislation has been enacted to achieve this objective. Article 51, must also strive for the promotion of international peace and security, and Parliament has been empowered under Article 253 to make laws giving effect to international treaties.

Here an attempt has been made by the author to elaborate the detailed provisions of Directive Principles.

PART IV

DIRECTIVE PRINCIPLES OF STATE POLICY

36. Definition.—

In this Part, unless the context otherwise requires, 'the State' has the same meaning as in Part III.

37. Application of the principles contained in this Part.—

The provisions contained in this Part shall not be enforceable by any court, but the principles therein laid down are nevertheless fundamental in the governance of the country and it shall be the duty of the State to apply these principles in making laws.

38. State to secure a social order for the promotion of welfare of the people.—(1) The State shall strive to promote the welfare of the people by securing and protecting as effectively as it may a social order in which justice, social, economic and political, shall inform all the institutions of the national life.

(2) The State shall, in particular, strive to minimise the inequalities in income, and endeavour to eliminate inequalities in status, facilities and opportunities, not only amongst individuals but also amongst groups of people residing in different areas or engaged in different vocations.

39. Certain principles of policy to be followed by the State.—

The State shall, in particular, direct its policy towards securing—

(a) that the citizens, men and women equally, have the right to an adequate means of livelihood;

(b) that the ownership and control of the material resources of the community are so distributed as best to subserve the common good;

(c) that the operation of the economic system does not result in the concentration of wealth and means of production to the common detriment;

(d) that there is equal pay for equal work for both men and women;

(e) that the health and strength of workers, men and women, and the tender age of children are not abused and that citizens are not forced by economic necessity to enter avocations unsuited to their age or strength;

(f) that children are given opportunities and facilities to develop in a healthy manner and in conditions of freedom and dignity and that childhood and youth are protected against exploitation and against moral and material abandonment.

39A. Equal justice and free legal aid.—

The State shall secure that the operation of the legal system promotes justice, on a basis of equal opportunity, and shall, in particular, provide free legal aid, by suitable legislation or schemes or in any other way, to ensure that opportunities for securing justice are not denied to any citizen by reason of economic or other disabilities.[110]

40. Organisation of village panchayats.—

The State shall take steps to organise village panchayats and endow them with such powers and authority as may be necessary to enable them to function as units of self-government.

41. Right to work, to education and to public assistance in certain cases.—

[110] Ins. by the Constitution (Forty-second Amendment) Act, 1976 s. 8,

The State shall, within the limits of its economic capacity and development, make effective provision for securing the right to work, to education and to public assistance in cases of unemployment, old age, sickness and disablement, and in other cases of undeserved want.

42. Provision for just and humane conditions of work and maternity relief.—

The State shall make provision for securing just and humane conditions of work and for maternity relief.

43. Living wage, etc., for workers.—

The State shall endeavour to secure, by suitable legislation or economic organisation or in any other way, to all workers, agricultural, industrial or otherwise, work, a living wage, conditions of work ensuring a decent standard of life and full enjoyment of leisure and social and cultural opportunities and, in particular, the State shall endeavour to promote cottage industries on an individual or co-operative basis in rural areas.

43A. Participation of workers in management of industries.—

The State shall take steps, by suitable legislation or in any other way, to secure the participation of workers in the management of undertakings, establishments or other organisations engaged in any industry.[111]

44. Uniform civil code for the citizens.—

The State shall endeavour to secure for the citizens a uniform civil code throughout the territory of India.

45. Provision for early childhood care and education to children below the age of six years.

–The State shall endeavour to provide early childhood care and education for all children until they complete the age of six years.[112]

[111] Ins. by the Constitution (Forty-second Amendment) Act, 1976, s. 9 (w.e.f. 3-1-1977).

[112] Art. 45 shall stand substituted by the Constitution (Eighty-sixth Amendment) Act, 2002, s. 3

46. Promotion of educational and economic interests of Scheduled Castes, Scheduled Tribes and other weaker sections.—The State shall promote with special care the educational and economic interests of the weaker sections of the people, and, in particular, of the Scheduled Castes and the Scheduled Tribes, and shall protect them from social injustice and all forms of exploitation.

47. Duty of the State to raise the level of nutrition and the standard of living and to improve public health.—

The State shall regard the raising of the level of nutrition and the standard of living of its people and the improvement of public health as among its primary duties and, in particular, the State shall endeavour to bring about prohibition of the consumption except for medicinal purposes of intoxicating drinks and of drugs which are injurious to health.

48. Organisation of agriculture and animal husbandry.—

The State shall endeavour to organise agriculture and animal husbandry on modern and scientific lines and shall, in particular, take steps for preserving and improving the breeds, and prohibiting the slaughter, of cows and calves and other milch and draught cattle.

48A. Protection and improvement of environment and safeguarding of forests and wild life.—

The State shall endeavour to protect and improve the environment and to safeguard the forests and wild life of the country.

49. Protection of monuments and places and objects of national importance.—It shall be the obligation of the State to protect every monument or place or object of artistic or historic interest, declared by or under law made by Parliament to be of national importance, from spoliation, disfigurement, destruction, removal, disposal or export, as the case may be.

50. Separation of judiciary from executive.—

The State shall take steps to separate the judiciary from the executive in the public services of the State.

51. Promotion of international peace and security.—

The State shall endeavour to—

(a) promote international peace and security;

(b) maintain just and honorable relations between nations;

(c) foster respect for international law and treaty obligations in the dealings of organized peoples with one another; and

(d) encourage settlement of international disputes by arbitration.

Fundamental Duties

The Fundamental Duties of citizens were added to the Constitution by the 42nd Amendment in 1976, upon the recommendations of the Swaran Singh Committee that was constituted by the government earlier that year. Originally ten in number, the Fundamental Duties were increased to eleven by the 86th in 2002, which added a duty on every parent or guardian to ensure that their child or ward was provided opportunities for education between the ages of six and fourteen years. The other Fundamental Duties obligate all citizens to respect the national symbols of India, including the Constitution, to cherish its heritage preserve its composite culture and assist in its defense. They also obligate all Indians to promote the spirit of common brotherhood, protect the environment and public property, develop scientific temper, abjure violence, and strive towards excellence in all spheres of life. Citizens are morally obligated by the Constitution to perform these duties. However, like the Directive Principles, these are non-justifiable, without any legal sanction in case of their violation or non-compliance. There is reference to such duties in international instruments such as the Universal Declaration of Human Rights and International Covenant on Civil and Political Rights, and Article 51A brings the Indian Constitution into conformity with these treaties. Here an attempt has been made by the author to elaborate the detailed provisions of Fundamental Duties.

PART IVA[113]

FUNDAMENTAL DUTIES

51A. Fundamental duties.—

It shall be the duty of every citizen of India—

(a) to abide by the Constitution and respect its ideals and institutions, the National Flag and the National Anthem;

(b) to cherish and follow the noble ideals which inspired our national struggle for freedom;

(c) to uphold and protect the sovereignty, unity and integrity of India;

(d) to defend the country and render national service when called upon to do so;

(e) to promote harmony and the spirit of common brotherhood amongst all the people of India transcending religious, linguistic and regional or sectional diversities; to renounce practices derogatory to the dignity of women;

(f) to value and preserve the rich heritage of our composite culture;

(g) to protect and improve the natural environment including forests, lakes, rivers and wild life, and to have compassion for living creatures;

(h) to develop the scientific temper, humanism and the spirit of inquiry and reform;

(i) to safeguard public property and to abjure violence;

---

[113] Ins. by the Constitution (Forty-second Amendment) Act, 1976, s. 11 (w.e.f. 3-1-1977).

(j) to strive towards excellence in all spheres of individual and collective activity so that the nation constantly rises to higher levels of endeavour and achievement,

(k) who is a parent or guardian to provide opportunities for education to his child or, as the case may be, ward between the age of six and fourteen years.[114]

Relationship between the Fundamental Rights, Directive Principles and Fundamental Duties

The Directive Principles have been used to uphold the Constitutional validity of legislations in case of a conflict with the Fundamental Rights. Article 31C, added by the 25th Amendment in 1971, provided that any law made to give effect to the Directive Principles in Article 39(b)–(c) would not be invalid on the grounds that they derogated from the Fundamental Rights conferred by Articles 14, 19 and 31. The application of this article was sought to be extended to all the Directive Principles by the 42nd Amendment in 1976, but the Supreme Court struck down the extension as void on the ground that it violated the basic structure of the Constitution. The Fundamental Rights and Directive Principles have also been used together in forming the basis of legislation for social welfare. The Supreme Court, after the judgment in the *Kesavananda Bharati case*, has adopted the view of the Fundamental Rights and Directive Principles being complementary to each other, each supplementing the other's role in aiming at the same goal of establishing a welfare state by means of social revolution.Similarly, the Supreme Court has used the Fundamental Duties to uphold the Constitutional validity of statutes which seeks to promote the objects laid out in the Fundamental Duties. These Duties have also been held to be obligatory for all citizens, subject to the State enforcing the same by means of a valid law. The Supreme

[114] Ins. by the Constitution (Eighty-sixth Amendment) Act, 2002,

Court has also issued directions to the State in this regard, with a view towards making the provisions effective and enabling a citizens to properly perform their duties.[115]

Report of the National Committee to review the Working of Indian Constitution on Fundamental Rights, Directive Principles and Fundamental Duties[116]

Chapter 3

Fundamental Rights, Directive Principles And Fundamental Duties

CONTENTS

[115] Wikipedia

[116] http://lawmin.nic.in/ncrwc/finalreport/v1ch3.htm

Definition of 'the State'

Heads of Discrimination

Reservation for Minorities

Freedom of Press and Freedom of Information

Rights against Torture and Inhuman, Degrading and Cruel Treatment and Punishment

Right to Compensation for being Illegally Deprived of one's Right to Life or Liberty

Right to Travel Abroad and Return to one's Country

Right to Privacy

Right to Work

Preventive Detention

Right to Justice and Legal Aid

Right to Property

Article 31B and Ninth Schedule

Suspension of articles 17, 23, 24,25 and 32 during Emergency

Capital Punishment

Right to Education

Rights of Children

Right to Safe Drinking Water, Clean Environment, etc.

Right to Freedom of Religion

Special Provision Relating to Language Spoken by a Section of Population of a State

D. **Directive Principles**

Principles of Governance

Justiciability and Enforceability

Right to Social Security and to Work

Right to Health

Right to Food and Freedom from Hunger, Clothing and Housing or Shelter

Right to Education

New Challenges to Education Policy

Control of Population

Right to Culture

Promotion of Inter-Religious harmony and inter-faith values

Mechanism for Realization of Directive Principles

Credibility of Socio-Economic Data

E. **Fundamental Duties**

The Background

Usefulness of Duties

Spirit of Harmony and Dignity of Women

Composite Culture

CHAPTER 3

Fundamental Rights, Directive Principles And Fundamental Duties

A. Fundamentals of the Constitution

1 The Constitution which lays down the basic structure of a nation's polity is built on the foundations of certain fundamental values. The vision of our founding fathers and the aims and objectives which they wanted to achieve through the Constitution are contained in the Preamble, the Fundamental Rights and the Directive Principles. These three may be described as the soul of the Constitution and the testament of the founding fathers to the succeeding generations together with the later Part on Fundamental Duties.

B. Vision of Socio-Economic Change

The Preamble

2.1 The vision of socio-economic change through the Constitution is reflected in its lofty Preamble. The Preamble expresses the ideals and aspirations of a renascent India. At independence, emerging out of a long period of foreign domination and oppression under a feudal system, the people were grimly struggling to be reborn into a life of dignity and hope. The past was heavy on their shoulders, and the future uncertain. There was social and economic exploitation around. There were a whole host of social ills such as illiteracy, superstition, sati, child-marriage, agrarian exploitation, child-labour, bonded labour, gender-inequality, bedeviling the society and polity.

2.2 The framers of the Constitution sought to unite the vast country with its great diversity of languages and creeds within a common bond of constitutional justice based on the great ideals of liberty, equality, fraternity and justice. Framers showed an uncompromising respect for human dignity, an unquestioning commitment to equality and non-discrimination, and an abiding concern for the poor and the weak. They made a bold attempt to base the constitutional foundations on the firm faith that all classes of people, followers of all faiths, and particularly the traditionally under-privileged should all join to work for harmony, progress, prosperity and nation building.

2.3 The Preamble through its noble words promised Justice, social, economic and political; Liberty of thought, expression, belief, freedom of faith and worship; Equality of status and of opportunity and to promote Fraternity, assuring the dignity of the individual and the unity and integrity of the Nation. Speaking of the imperatives of social democracy, Dr. Ambedkar said:

"it was, indeed, a way of life, which recognizes liberty, equality and fraternity as the principles of life and which cannot be divorced from each other: Liberty cannot be divorced from equality; equality cannot be divorced from liberty. Nor can liberty and equality be divorced from fraternity. Without equality, liberty would produce the supremacy of the few over the many.

Equality without liberty would kill individual initiative. Without fraternity, liberty and equality could not become a natural course of things."

The Socio-economic Agenda

3.1 The scheme of the Constitution for the realisation of the socio-economic agenda comprises of both the justiciable Fundamental Rights as well as the non-justiciable Directive Principles. The judicial contribution to the synthesis and the integration of the Fundamental Rights and the Directive Principles in the process of "constitutionalising" social and economic rights has been crucial to the realisation of the Directive Principles not only as a means to effectuate Fundamental Rights but also as a source of laws for a welfare state.

3.2 The Constitution makes it mandatory to protect and promote freedoms, and to assure every citizen a decent standard of living. It makes a strong commitment to promoting the well-being of all citizens without any discrimination on the grounds of caste, creed, community or gender.

C. Fundamental Rights

Background and Approach

4.1 Constitutional guarantees for the human rights of our people were one of the persistent demands of our leaders throughout the freedom struggle. By the year 1949, when the

Constituent Assembly had completed the drafting of the Fundamental Rights Chapter, it had before it the 'Universal Declaration of Human Rights, 1948.

4.2 The International Covenant on Civil and Political Rights,1966 (ICCPR) broadly referred to the inherent right to life and liberty and the right against arbitrary deprivation of those rights and its various aspects (Articles 6 to 14); privacy, family, etc. (Article 17); freedom of conscience and religion (Article 18); freedom of expression and information (Article 19); Right of peaceful assembly (Article 21); freedom of association (Article 22); rights of minorities (Article 27); etc. The International Covenant on Economic, Social and Cultural Rights, 1966 (ICESCR) broadly referred to the "right to work" and its various aspects (Articles 6 and 7); right to form trade unions for promotion of economic or social interests and the right to strike (Article 8); right to social security and social insurance (Article 9); family, marriage, children and mothers' rights (Article 10); adequate standard of living, right to food, clothing and housing, freedom from hunger (Article 11); physical and mental health (Article 12); education (Article 13); compulsory primary education (Article 14) and culture (Article 15). The treaty obligations under the covenant enjoined the State Parties to ensure these rights without discrimination and "to take steps" to promote them "to the maximum of its available resources", with a view to achieving "progressively" the full realisation of these rights. The Directive Principles of State Policy in Part IV of the Constitution are indeed the precursor to economic, social and cultural rights specified in the ICESCR.

4.3 During the last three decades, a vast number of human rights have found place in new constitutions and bills of rights of more than eighty countries and of supra-national entities.

Countries which enacted these new constitutions have had the benefit of all the developments in the human rights jurisprudence which have taken place since 1950. Also, our Supreme Court has by judicial interpretation expanded the scope of the fundamental rights, particularly in relation to article 21, and this has included more civil and political rights which were not explicit in Part III.

4.4 A new development is that of the principle of 'basic structure' of the Constitution enunciated by the Supreme Court in 1973 in *Kesavananda Bharati vs. State of Kerala* .As to what are these basic features, the debate still continues. The Supreme Court has also held that the scope of certain fundamental rights could be adjudged by reading into them or reading them not only in the light of the Directive Principles of State Policy but also international covenants or conventions which were in harmony with the Fundamental Rights.

4.5 The Commission feels that after fifty years, time is ripe to review and enlarge suitably the contents of some of the Fundamental Rights, particularly those Fundamental Rights which have been judicially deduced.

Definition of 'the State'

5 Fundamental rights guaranteed by the Constitution are, in the absence of specific constitutional provisions, mainly enforceable against 'the State' . The definition of 'the State' in article 12 being an 'inclusive' one, courts have ruled that where there is pervasive or predominant governmental control or significant involvement in its activity, such bodies, entities and organizations fall within the definition of 'the State' .

It is recommended that in article 12 of the Constitution, the following Explanation should be added:-

'Explanation - In this article, the expression "other authorities" shall include any person in relation to such of its functions which are of a public nature.'

Heads of discrimination

6 In articles 15 and 16, prohibition against discrimination should be extended to "ethnic or social origin; political or other opinion; property or birth" .

Reservation for minorities

7.1 There was a plea on behalf of some minority communities for an express provision for reservation in favour of minorities both in articles 15 (4) and 16 (4). The Commission, upon due consideration of the representations, felt that no special provision was necessary inasmuch as, under the existing provision of articles 14, 15 and 16, it is open to the State to make reservation if it is of the opinion that such reservation is necessary and justified.

7.2 The Commission noted that the ultimate aim of affirmative action of reservation should be to raise the levels of capabilities of people of the disadvantaged sections and to bring them at par with the other sections of society.

Freedom of Press and Freedom of Information

8.1 Article 19(1)(a) refers to 'freedom of speech and expression'. It is proposed that the article must expressly include the freedom of the press and other media, the freedom to hold opinion and to seek, receive and impart information and ideas. It is also proposed to amend article 19(2) by adding a further restriction on disclosure of information received in confidence except if required in public interest.

The Commission recommends that article 19(1) (a) and (2) be amended to read as follows:

"Art. 19(1): All citizens shall have the right -

(a) *to freedom of speech and expression which shall include the freedom of the press and other media, the freedom to hold opinions and to seek, receive and impart information and ideas;"*.

19(2): "*Nothing in sub-clause (a) of clause (1) shall affect the operation of any existing law, or prevent the State from making any law, in so far as such law imposes reasonable restrictions on the exercise of the right conferred by the said sub-clause in the interests of the sovereignty and integrity of India, the security of the State, friendly relations with foreign States, public order, decency or morality, or in relation to contempt of court, defamation or incitement to an offence, or preventing the disclo-sure of information received in confidence except when required in public interest.*".

8.2 A mere legislation by the Parliament by amending the Contempt of Courts Act, 1971 alone may not suffice because the power of the Supreme Court and the High Courts to punish for contempt is recognized in the Constitution. Therefore, the Commission recommends that an appropriate proviso to article 19(2) of the Constitution may be added as under:-

"Provided that, in matters of contempt, it shall be open to the Court to permit a defence of justification by truth on satisfaction as to the bona fides of the plea and it being in public interest. ".

Rights against torture and inhuman, degrading and cruel treatment and punishment

9. Torture and inhuman, degrading and cruel treatment and punishment grossly violate human dignity. The Supreme Court has implied a right against torture, etc. by way of interpretation of article 21 which deals with the right to life and liberty. The Universal Declaration of Human Rights 1948 and the ICCPR prohibit such acts in article 5 and article 7 respectively.

It is, therefore, recommended that the existing article 21 may be re-numbered as clause (1) thereof, and a new clause (2) should be inserted thereafter on the following lines: -

"(2) No one shall be subjected to torture or to cruel, inhuman or degrading treatment or punishment."

Right to compensation for being illegally deprived of one's right to life or liberty

10 Article 9(5) of the ICCPR states, "any one who has been victim of unlawful arrest or detention shall have an enforceable right to compensation." In D.K. Basu vs. State of West Bengal

[1], the Supreme Court of India held that the reservation made by India to this clause while acceding to the Convention does not come in the way of the Court's awarding compensation in the cases of illegal arrest or detention. The High Courts in India have also been awarding compensation.

It is, therefore, recommended as under:-

After clause (2) in article 21 as proposed in para 3.9, a new clause (3) should be added on the following lines :-

"(3) *Every person who has been illegally deprived of his right to life or liberty shall have an enforceable right to compensation.*"

Right to travel abroad and return to one's country

11 The Supreme Court has spelt out in articles 14 and 21 the right to travel abroad and return to one's country. Again, this right finds a place in article 13(2) of the Universal Declaration of Human Rights, 1948 as well as in articles 12(2),(3) and (4) of the ICCPR.

It is, therefore, recommended that after article 21, a new article, say article 21A, should be inserted on the following lines:-

"21A. (1) Every person shall have the right to leave the territory of India and every citizen shall have the right to return to India.

(2) Nothing in clause (1) shall prevent the State from making any law imposing reasonable restrictions in the interests of the sovereignty and integrity of India, friendly relations of India with foreign States and interests of the general public."

Right to Privacy

12 The Supreme Court has included 'Right to Privacy' in the Right to 'Life' under article 21.

It is, therefore, proposed that a new article, namely, article 21-B, should be inserted on the following lines:

"21-B. (1) Every person has a right to respect for his private and family life, his home and his correspondence.

(2) Nothing in clause (1) shall prevent the State from making any law imposing reasonable restrictions on the exercise of the right conferred by clause (1), in the interests of security of the

State, public safety or for the prevention of disorder or crime, or for the protection of health or morals, or for the protection of the rights and freedoms of others.

Right to Work

13.1 It is in the rural sector that widespread poverty, underemployment, malnutrition, lack of access to healthcare and oppressive social customs that bear down heavily on women and children create a social landscape of appalling misery. It is here that a major action plan has to be launched to create additional jobs, to enhance incomes of those at the bottom rung of the social ladder and to create the physical and social infrastructure of a vibrant economy.

13.2 The Commission, therefore, recommends that a new article, say article 21-C, may be added to make it obligatory on the State to bring suitable legislation for ensuring the right to rural wage employment for a minimum of eighty days in a year.

Preventive Detention

14.1 Article 22 (3)(b) permits 'preventive detention' and the rule in clause (2) of article 22 which requires production before the nearest magistrate within 24 hours does not also apply in such cases. No doubt, several preventive detention laws have been upheld by the courts. But, being detention without trial, there is a view that such a detention is a negation of the rule of law and the principles of fair trial. The arrest is supposed to be made on the basis of information that the person is likely to commit some serious offences. There are complaints that this law is misused quite frequently.

14.2 While the Commission does not propose to recommend deletion of clauses dealing with preventive detention under article 22, it recommends the following changes :-

(i) The first and second provisos and Explanation to article 22(4) as contained in section 3 of the Constitution (44th Amendment) Act, 1978 should be substituted by the following provisos and the said section 3 of the 1978 Act as amended by the proposed legislation should be brought into force within a period of not exceeding three months :-

"Provided that an Advisory Board shall consist of a Chairman and not less than two other members, and the Chairman and the other members of the Board shall be serving judges of any High Court :

Provided further that nothing in this clause shall authorize the detention of any person beyond a maximum period of six months as may be prescribed by any law made by Parliament under sub-clause(a) of clause (7)" .

(ii) In clause (7) of article 22 of the Constitution, in sub-clause (b), for the words "the maximum period" , the words "the maximum period not exceeding six months" shall be substituted.

Right to justice and legal aid

15.1 The Commission recommends that after article 30, the following article should be added as article 30A:

"**30A: Access to Courts and Tribunals and speedy justice**

(1) Everyone has a right to have any dispute that can be resolved by the application of law decided in a fair public hearing before an independent court or, where appropriate, another independent and impartial tribunal or forum.

(2) The right to access to courts shall be deemed to include the right to reasonably speedy and effective justice in all matters before the courts, tribunals or other fora and the State shall take all reasonable steps to achieve the said object."

15.2 Legal aid is essential for effective implementation of the various rights included in Part III to help the needy and the indigent. The Commission recommends that article 39A in Part IV be shifted to Part III as a new article 30B to read as under:-

"**39B. Equal justice and free legal aid**: *The State shall secure that the operation of the legal system promotes justice, on a basis of equal opportunity, and shall, in particular, provide free legal aid, by suitable legislation or schemes or in any other way, to ensure that opportunities for securing justice are not denied to any citizen by reason of economic or other disabilities."*

Right to property

16.1 After the 44th Amendment of the Constitution, right to property has ceased to be a fundamental right. Under article 300A, it has become a constitutional right. One other important aspect is with regard to deprivation or acquisition of agricultural and homestead land belonging to weaker sections. Before such deprivation takes place, the persons so deprived must be provided lands of quality as nearly as may be equal to the lands such persons were previously occupying or otherwise adequately rehabilitated.

16.2 The Commission recommends that article 300-A should be recast as follows:-

"**300-A** *(1) Deprivation or acquisition of property shall be by authority of law and only for a public purpose.*

(2) There shall be no arbitrary deprivation or acquisition of property:

Provided that no deprivation or acquisition of agricultural, forest and non-urban homestead land belonging to or customarily used by the Scheduled Castes and the Scheduled Tribes shall take place except by authority of law which provides for suitable rehabilitation scheme before taking possession of such land."

Article 31B and Ninth Schedule

17 A number of enactments unrelated to the rationale underlying articles 31B have come to be included in the Ninth Schedule with a view to keep them secure from attack on the ground that such enactment or a provision thereof is inconsistent with any provision of Part III of the Constitution. In the Consultation Paper on 'Enlargement of Fundamental Rights, it was proposed that article 31B be suitably amended to provide that the laws to be included in the Ninth Schedule must, in pith and substance, relate to agrarian reforms or land reforms or laws to give effect to the directive principles in article 39(b) and 39(c). After further discussion, the Commission recommends that in article 31-B, the following proviso should be added at the end, namely :-

"*Provided that the protection afforded by this article to Acts and Regulations which may be hereafter specified in the Ninth Schedule or any of the provisions thereof, shall not apply unless such Acts or Regulations relate* -

(a) in pith and substance to agrarian reforms or land reforms;

(b) to reasonable quantum of reservation under articles 15 and 16;

(c) to provisions for giving effect to the policy of the State towards securing all or any of the principles specified in clause (b) or clause (c) of article 39."

Suspension of articles 17, 23, 24, 25 and 32 during emergency

18.1 Article 359 deals with "Suspension of the enforcement of the rights conferred by Part III during emergencies". Clause (1) permits suspension of the right to move court but excludes article 20 (retrospectivity of law relating to offences, double jeopardy and self-incrimination) and article 21 (Life and liberty not to be deprived except according to procedure established by law which after Maneka Gandhi's case means fair, reasonable and just procedure).

18.2 The Commission recommends that clauses (1) and (1A) of article 359 should be amended by substituting for "(except articles 20 and 21)", the following-

"(except articles 17,20,21,23,24,25 and 32)"

Capital Punishment

19 Section 121 of the Indian Penal Code permits death sentence or life imprisonment to be imposed for the offences of waging war against the Government of India, or attempts to wage such a war or abetment of such a war. The Commission, after due deliberations, has not thought it appropriate to recommend, at this stage, any change in the existing law relating to imposition of death penalty.

Right to Education

20.1 At the time when the Commission released its Consultation Paper on the subject, Constitution (93rd Amendment) Bill was under consideration. But the proposed Amendment covers the Right to Free and Compulsory Education only between the years 6 and 14 years. The

Commission is of the view that the Right to Free and Compulsory Education should also be extended to the children upto the age of fourteen years and that the right to education beyond the age of 14 years may depend upon the economic capacity and the stage of development of the State.

20.2 The Commission feels that the constitutional commitment for free and compulsory education for all children until the age of fourteen should under no circumstances be diluted and the State should fulfill this solemn obligation to the nation. The responsibility for the universalisation of elementary education should be entrusted to Panchayats and local self government institutions. It is recommended that the relevant provisions in the Constitution (93rd Amendment) Bill, 2001 making the right to education of children from six years till the completion of fourteen years as a Fundamental Right should be amended and enlarged to read as under:-

"*30-C Every child shall have the right to free education until he completes the age of fourteen years; and in the case of girls and members of the Scheduled Castes and the Scheduled Tribes, until they complete the age of eighteen years.*" .

Rights of Children

21.1 Article 39(e) in the Directive Principles in Part IV refers to the duty of the State to direct its policy to see that children of tender age are not abused. Article 39 (f) refers to a similar duty on the State to give opportunities and facilities to children to develop in a healthy manner and with dignity and in conditions which are free and where childhood and youth are protected against exploitation and moral and material abandonment.

21.2 The Commission recommends that the following article should be added -

"Art. 24A. Every child shall have the right to care and assistance in basic needs and protection from all forms of neglect, harm and exploitation."

Right to safe drinking water, clean environment, etc.

22.1 Gandhiji had once said that freedom for him would mean the availability of safe drinking water to every person in every village of India. This has still not become a reality.

22.2 Right to healthy environment and its protection and the right to development are group-rights and are loosely described as 'third generation rights'. The right to sustainable development has been declared by the UN General Assembly as an inalienable human right. The Declaration recognizes that 'human being is the central subject of the development process and that the development policy shall make the human being the main participant and beneficiary of development. "Development" is defined as a 'comprehensive economic, social, cultural and political process, which aims at the constant improvement of the well being of the entire population in development and in the fair distribution of benefits there from. The Rio Conference of 1992 declared human beings as centres of concern for sustainable development. Human beings are, it is said, entitled to a healthy and protective life in harmony with nature

(Principle 1). "In order to achieve 'sustainable development' environmental protection shall constitute an integral part of the development process and cannot be considered in isolation of it". The 1997 Earth Summit meeting of 100 nations in New York affirmed these principles.

22.3 The Commission recommends that after the proposed article 30-C, the following article may be added as article 30-D :-

"*Art. 30-D. Right to safe drinking water, prevention of pollution, conservation of ecology and sustainable development.* -

Every person shall have the right -

(a) to safe drinking water;

(b) to an environment that is not harmful to one's health or well-being; and

(c) to have the environment protected, for the benefit of present and future generations so as to -

(i) prevent pollution and ecological degradation;

(ii) promote conservation; and

(iii) secure ecologically sustainable development and use of natural resources while promoting justifiable economic and social development.".

Right to Freedom of Religion

23.1 A number of institutions of Sikhs and Buddhists suggested certain changes in article 25(2). Explanation II to article 25 provides that reference to Hindus in sub-clause (b) of clause (2) should be construed as including a reference to Sikhs etc.

23.2 The Commission, without going into the larger issue on which the contention is based, is of the opinion that the purpose of the representations would be served if Explanation II to article 25 is omitted and sub-clause (b) of clause (2) of that article is reworded as follows:-

"(b) providing for social welfare and reform or the throwing open of Hindu, Sikh, Jaina or Buddhist religious institutions of a public character to all classes and sections of these religions. "

Special provision relating to language spoken by a section of population of a State

24 In order to make the rights available to minorities under articles 29 and 30 meaningful, the Commission feels that the provisions contained under article 347 need some modification. Before the President directs that use of any language spoken by a section of the population of a State be recognized in a State for such purposes as he may specify, he has to ensure that a substantial proportion of the population of that State so desires. The explanation "substantial proportion of the population" had been a subject matter of controversy and different constructions have been placed up on it. It shall be desirable that some optimum level of population with a view to take necessary action under this constitutional provision is prescribed.

In article 347 of the Constitution, for the words "a substantial proportion of the population", the words "not less than ten per cent of the population" should be substituted.

D. Directive Principles

Principles of Governance

25.1 It is only during the last two or three decades that there has been a perceptible shift in intellectual discourse in the academia towards problems and principles of good governance as contradistinguished from issues of government and politics. Our founding fathers, however, were far-sighted people. They realised even in the late 1940s the difference and in article 37 specifically spoke of certain "principles" being "fundamental" in the "governance of the country". Also, the State was enjoined "to apply these principles in making laws."

25.2 The founding fathers were conscious of the fact that mere political democracy, i.e., getting the right to vote once in five years or so was meaningless unless it was accompanied by social and economic democracy. Political equality was not possible unless men were made equal on the social and economic plane as well. Right to vote for a hungry and illiterate man without clothing and shelter meant little. Dr. Ambedkar had said:

"*We do not want merely to lay down a mechanism to enable people to come and capture power. The Constitution also wishes to lay down an ideal before those who would be forming the government. That ideal is of economic democracy.*"

25.3 The Supreme Court has, in a number of judgements, referred to the importance of the Directive Principles. It has called these principles the "conscience" of the Constitution and also as the core of the Constitution. These principles are the "goals" to be achieved by Part III of the Constitution. They are intended to ensure "distributive justice" for removal of inequalities and disabilities and to achieve a fair division of wealth amongst the members of the society. The Supreme Court held that the courts can look at the Directive Principles for the purpose of interpretation of the fundamental rights. The courts will adopt that interpretation which makes the fundamental rights meaningful and efficacious. The courts have to make every attempt to reconcile the fundamental rights with the Directive Principles remembering that the reason why the Directive Principles were left by the founding fathers as non-enforceable was to give the Government sufficient latitude to implement them.

25.4 The Directive Principles are indeed the precursor to the Economic, Social and Cultural Rights specified in the International Covenant on Economic, Social and Cultural Rights, 1966 (ICESCR). They reflect the consensus on the intrinsic necessity of these means and envisage State action which would facilitate the transfer and distribution of power -- leading to transmission of power to the citizens and this is loosely called "empowerment" of the people. Democracy will become real when in practice there is sharing of power and responsibility by all sections of the people and it becomes illusory when it is about pursuit of power by the dominant sections alone. The Directive Principles cannot be confined to mere rhetoric or to ad hoc policies of electoral appeasement or handouts.

25.5 The comparable provisions of the Directive Principles of State Policy enshrined in the Constitution of India and the ICESCR are given below :-

Art. of Indian Constitution	Articles of ICESCR
Article 39	Articles 3, 6 (1) and 7
Article 41	Article 6 and 7
Article 42	Articles 7 and 10.2
Article 43	Articles 11 (1), 11(2) and 15
Article 45	Articles 13 (1), (2)(a), (3) and (4) and 14
Article 47	Articles 12(1), (2), (a) to (d)
Article 51	Articles 1.3 and 2 (1)

25.6 The concept of a division among human rights is no longer accepted in contemporary human rights discourse. Further, recent constitutional changes in the East European states have set at naught some of the reasons for the divide. Again, the description of the Civil and Political rights as ‘negative’ rights which prohibit the State from interfering with rights of the individuals and the description of the Economic, Social and Cultural rights as ‘positive’ rights which require affirmative action by the State is not accepted by jurists any longer. The theory that the former rights are justiciable and the latter rights are not justiciable has not also been accepted by scholars. The existence of any basis for such division is described as a 'myth' and inaccurate generalization

[1].

25.7 The Vienna World Conference on Human Rights, 1993 reaffirmed that the Civil, Political and the Economic, Social and Cultural Rights are 'universal, interdependent and indivisible.' The European Social Charter 1961 (revised charter 1996) and Protocols; the American Convention on Human Rights, 1969 (effective from 1978); the African Charter of Human Rights and Peoples' Rights, 1981 (effective from 1986) and finally the Human Rights Act, 1998 (UK) (which incorporates several provisions of the European Convention) and the South African Convention, 1996 deal with Civil, Political and Economic, Social and Cultural Rights covering the whole gamut of rights.

25.8 The Father of the Nation, Mahatma Gandhi stated in the Second Round Table Conference in London, long before the UN Declaration of Human Rights, 1948 that his aim was "to establish a political society in India in which there would be no distinction between high class of people and low class of people, that women should enjoy the same rights as men; and dignity, justice, social, economic and political, would be ensured to the teeming millions of India."

25.9 In the Annual Report of the National Human Rights Commission 1997-98, this is what is stated about our country:

"It is said that one third of the world's poor are Indians, who lacked clean drinking water, basic sanitation and minimum standards of health care, food and nutrition….Persistence of such a situation constitutes a failure of governance which had urgently to be remedied for it is on the pillars of good governance that promotion of human rights in the final analysis rests."

Justiciability and Enforceability

26.1 The judiciary is not suited, according to several writers to enforce some of the ICESCR rights. Where the resources of the nation are involved and a question of priority arises, the remedy cannot be judicial. However, the concept here is not "justiciability" at the instance of individuals in courts of law, but the concept is one of "enforceability" which means that the State must "recognize", and "take steps", by adopting "legislative" or other measures for the "full realisation" and "to the maximum of the State's available resources, both " individually and through international assistance and co-operation". These are the words actually used by the ICESCR and have been the subject matter of voluminous literature. These rights are described as "entitlements" of the people and give rise to "obligations" on the part of the State parties. The enforcement must first be of the "minimum core obligations" as stated in Para 10 of the General Comment No.3 of 1990 of the U.N. Committee on Economic, Social and Cultural Rights.

26.2 It is felt that an appropriate mechanism must be devised to oblige the State to take action step by step and progressively for the realisation of these rights to the maximum within the resources of the State.

26.3 The Commission recommends that the heading of Part IV of the Constitution should be amended to read as "DIRECTIVE PRINCIPLES OF STATE POLICY AND ACTION".

Right to Social Security and to Work

27.1 Article 41 directs the State to make effective provision for securing the right to work, to education and to public assistance in cases of unemployment, old age, sickness and disablement, and in other cases of undeserved want. This is social security in its widest sense. It is a measure of the distance the country still has to travel to build a good society. The present situation, as revealed by successive UNDP reports, is one of hardship and deprivation for very large sections of our people. Poverty eradication continues to be a major challenge for social and economic policy. The 'trickle-down' theory did not work but neither did the direct anti-poverty programmes.

27.2 Safety nets like the Public Distribution System (PDS), the Integrated Rural Development Programmes, and the targeted programmes for women and children have also not had the measure of success that was hoped for. Even the step up in growth rates following the introduction of the new economic strategy of liberalization has not succeeded in generating substantial increases in employment that alone would reduce poverty and increase the sense of security among the people. It is clear that a many-sided approach has to be developed to increase growth rates, to structure labour intensive projects spread through the length and breadth of the country and to help the vulnerable sections of the people to take advantage of government programmes intended for their welfare.

27.3 The Commission, therefore, recommends the initiation of a strategic Plan of Action to create a large number of employment opportunities in five years to realize and exploit the enormous potential in creating such employment opportunities. The components of this plan may include:

(1) Improvement of productivity in agriculture that will activate a chain of activities towards increased income and employment opportunities.

(2) Integrated horticulture that will include production of fruits, vegetables and flowers, cut-flowers for export and medicinal plants as well as establishment of bio-processing industries aimed primarily at value-addition of agricultural products.

(3) Intensification of animal husbandry programs and production of quality dairy products.

(4) Integrated Program of Intensive Aquaculture including use of common property resources like village ponds and lakes.

(5) Afforestation and Wasteland Development to bring an additional 12 million hectares under forest plantation and contribute to rural asset building activity.

(6) Soil and Water Conservation to support afforestation and Natural Resource Conservation towards eco-friendly agriculture.

(7) Water Conservation and Tank Rehabilitation.

(8) Production and use of organic manures through vermiculture and other improved techniques and production of organic health foods from them.

27.4 The State should provide opportunity to every person to gain his living by work which he freely chooses or accepts - which shall include the technical and vocational guidance and training programmes, polices and techniques to achieve steady economic, social and cultural development and full and productive employment under conditions safeguarding fundamental political and economic freedom to the individual. The right to work does not mean that everybody is to be employed by the State. It only means that the State has to develop "employment opportunities" both in the public and private sector.

27.5 The resource requirement for the implementation of this plan can be met by integrating the plethora of government programmes and changing their focus towards employment generation and income enhancing activities. Institutionally, this plan of action can succeed only if programmes are people-oriented and developed in a participatory mode. A change in mindset where people are regarded as "partners in development" rather than "beneficiaries" is necessary.

27.6 The foregoing considerations suggest a complete change in emphasis insofar as growth strategy is concerned. What is important is how work, productive work, will enhance incomes for the individual and the community. It is essential to make a beginning toward making the right to work the integral component of growth and development strategy. The Commission has carefully examined the relevant economic data on the subject and has come to the conclusion that a realistic approach to the right to work is not only desirable, it is entirely feasible.

Right to Health

28.1 The right to health has been treated by the Supreme Court as part of the right to 'life' in article 21.But, the right to health is not a right to be 'healthy'. It means a right both to certain 'freedoms' and 'entitlements'. The freedoms include the right to control ones' health and body, including sexual and reproductive freedom and the right to be free from interference, such as by non-consensual medical treatment and experimentation. Entitlements include a right to a system of health protection with equality of opportunity to enjoy the highest attainable level of health - a right to the enjoyment and availability of facilities, good services and conditions such as physical accessibility, economic accessibility and information accessibility. It must be qualitative and should include the right to healthy working conditions and preventive medicine.

28.2 The State has to "respect, protect and fulfill" its obligations in these areas for children, adults and those in old age

As of today, free medical treatment in government hospitals is totally inadequate. Nor is it available always in close neighbourhood. It is not possible to deal extensively with the pathetic conditions of medical care provided by government hospitals in our country. It is a fact of life that the poorer and weaker sections of society are unable to afford the extraordinary expense involved in the medical care provided by private hospitals. There is, therefore, an urgent need to see that, progressively, the State allocates adequate funds in this behalf.

Right to Food and Freedom from Hunger, Clothing and Housing or Shelter

29.1 The State must recognize the right of everyone to an adequate standard of living for himself and his family, including adequate food, clothing and housing and to the continuous improvement of living conditions; the State shall also have to recognize the right of everyone to be free from hunger. It shall then have to initiate programmes to improve methods of production, conservation and distribution of food by making full use of technical and scientific knowledge, by disseminating knowledge of the principles of nutrition and by developing or reforming agrarian system in such a way as to achieve the most efficient development and utilization of natural resources; and to take into account, the problem of both food-importing and food-exporting countries and to ensure an equitable distribution of world food supplies in relation to need.

29.2 It is well-known that while the godowns of the Food Corporation of India are overflowing and even rotting with excess food grains, there are reports of starvation deaths across the country. Further, quite a good percentage of food grains are lost due to inadequate conservation and also during distribution. This must be avoided by introducing proper systems.

29.3 The State must ensure right to housing or shelter. The Government of India formulated the National Housing Policy 1988, 1994, and the National Housing and Habitat Policy, 1998. There are various schemes for weaker sections, slum developments, etc.. As already stated, this right has been recognized by the Supreme Court of India as part of the right to life under article 21[4].

29.4 The Commission is convinced that the realization of the right to food, clothing and housing requires the State to prepare long range and short range plans for proper allocation of necessary funds.

Right to Education

30.1 Article 45 under the Directive Principles had envisaged free and compulsory education within ten years for all children till the age of 14. The national goal of universalisation of elementary education has still not been reached. Education for all remains an objective with the target date being pushed forward after every review. Increase in literacy rates to 72 per cent by 2007 and to 80 per cent by 2012, and universal access to primary education by 2007, have been set as goals in the approach paper to the Tenth Plan.

30.2 It should also be laid down in article 45 that the State shall make provision for education beyond the age of fourteen years within the limits of its economic capacity and stage of development.

New Challenges to Education Policy

31.1 We live in an age of rapid social, economic and technological change. Educational policy and programmes have to reflect the changed requirements in content and techniques of delivery. There has been a paradigm shift from a teaching to a learning process. Information and communication technology have to be harnessed to the goal of achieving education for all. The need for autonomy, continuous review, flexibility and clarity have to be built into policy. The educational system should impart moral and ethical values essential for good citizenship.

31.2 Autonomy for the education budget should be ensured. Some sanctity should be attached to the core provisions, such as teachers' salaries. There is a strong case for constitutional protection for the service conditions of teachers. Moreover, there is need to insulate educational institutions from needless litigation.

31.3 The Commission recommends that an independent National Education Commission should be set up every five years to report to Parliament on the progress of the constitutional directive regarding compulsory education and on other aspects relevant to the knowledge society of the new century. The model of the Finance Commission may be usefully looked into.

Control of Population

32 The Commission noted with concern that proper planning and monitoring of the socio-economic development of the country is considerably hampered and neutralized by the exponential growth of population.

The Commission, therefore, recommends that the following article should be added as a directive principle of state policy after article 47 of the Constitution:

"Art. 47A. Control of Population:- The State shall endeavour to secure control of population by means of education and implementation of small family norms."

Right to Culture

33.1 Article 49 of the Directive Principles requires the State to protect monuments and places and objects of national importance. For the purpose of protecting culture in all its facets and in developing it, the State has to set apart necessary resources.

33.2 More than five decades of experience with the working of our Constitution and the laws has borne out that democracy in a meaningful sense, depends on a pluralistic ethos permeating the polity. Our national life must be accommodative of the myriad variegations that make up the unique mosaic of India's society. The framework of our many and elaborate structures of government must exemplify the architecture of an inclusive society and one of the means is to promote civil society initiatives for inter-religions and social harmony.

33.3 All considered, as advised by experience and by present and emerging needs, it is felt that a mechanism may be brought into being which can advance the cause of inter-faith harmony and solidarity. This can be done under the auspices of the National Human Rights Commission.

Promotion of Inter-Religious harmony and inter-faith values

34.1 Past experience indicates that in sensitive areas and localities of the country where inter-religious conflicts have sprung up out of trivial incidents resulting in conflagration, extensive damage to life and property. The setting up of "Mohalla Committees" with the participation of prominent members of different communities to take note of early warning symptoms and alerting the administration in preventing them have produced enduring beneficial results. In particular, the endeavours made in Bhiwandi, in the State of Maharashtra, after the tragic riots there, have emphasised the value of such measures.

34.2 The Commission, therefore, recommends the setting up of an inter-faith mechanism to promote such civil society initiatives. In the Commission' s view, this can be done under the auspices of the National Human Rights Commission set up under section 3 of the Protection of Human Rights Act, 1993 which, inter alia, provides for the participation of "the Chairpersons of the National Commission for Minorities, the National Commission for Scheduled Castes and Scheduled Tribes and the National Commission for Women" who shall be deemed to be the Members of the Commission for the discharge of functions specified in clauses (b) to (j) of the section 12 of the said Act. The Chairpersons of the National Commission for Backward Classes and National Commission for Safai Karamcharis should be co-opted to this body. This body could, in addition to its other statutory functions, also function as mechanism for promotion of inter-religious harmony. With an appropriate statutory enablement by way of enlargement of section 12 of the said Act, the purpose could be achievedwithout additional expenditure for setting up a separate mechanism. Section 12 of the said Act could be amended by the addition of clause (k), which shall read as under:

"(k) promoting through civil society initiatives, inter-faith and inter-religious harmony and social solidarity" .

By this simple statutory enablement, with consequential amendment in Section 3(3), the Chairpersons of all the aforesaid Commissions who meet and interact would, in collaboration with the National Foundation for Communal Harmony (established under the Ministry of Home Affairs, Government of India), would be able to oversee the installation and working of "

Mohalla Committees" and other civil society initiatives in sensitive areas which particularly require promotion of inter-faith harmony.

Mechanism for realisation of Directive Principles

35.1 The State should devise appropriate mechanisms for realisation of Directive Principles. The Commission does not propose to recommend a complaints procedure inasmuch as it is more concerned with a procedure which will ensure proper allocation of resources for the realization of the right to work, health, food, clothing, housing, education and culture. Domestic bodies in various countries have different composition, membership and powers.

35.2 In the view of the Commission, there must be a body of high status which first reviews the state of the level of implementation of the Directive Principles and Economic, Social and Cultural Rights and in particular (i) the right to work, (ii) the right to health, (iii) the right to food, clothing and shelter, (iv) Right to Education upto and beyond the 14th year, and (v) the Right to Culture. The said body must estimate the extent of resources required in each State under each of these heads and make recommendations for allocation of adequate resources, from time to time. For ensuring that the Directive Principles of State Policy are realized more effectively, the following procedure is suggested:-

(i) The Planning Commission shall ensure that there is special mention/emphasis in all the plans and schemes formulated by it, on the effectuation/realization of the Directive Principles of State Policy.

(ii) Every Ministry/Department of the Government of India shall make a special annual report indicating the extent of effectuation/realization of the Directive Principles of State Policy, the shortfall in the targets, the reasons for the shortfall, if any, and the remedial measures taken to ensure their full realization, during the year under report.

(iii) The report under item (ii) shall be considered and discussed by the Department Related Parliamentary Standing Committee, which shall submit its report on the working of the Department indicating the achievements/failures of the Ministry/Department along with its recommendations thereto.

(iv) Both the above Reports i.e. (ii) and (iii) above shall be discussed by the Planning Commission in an interactive seminar with the representatives of various NGOs, Civil Society Groups, etc. in which the representatives of the Ministry/Department and the Departmental Related Parliamentary Standing Committee would also participate. The report of this interaction shall be submitted to the Parliament within a time bound manner.

(v) The Parliament shall discuss the report at (iv) above within a period of three months and pass a resolution about the action required to be taken by the Ministry/Department.

35.3 A similar mechanism as mentioned above may be adopted for the States.

Credibility of Socio-economic Data

36 The Report of the National Statistical Commission (2001) stresses the importance of availability of adequate, credible and timely socio-economic data generated by the statistical system, both for policy formulation and for monitoring progress of the sectors of economy and

pace of socio-economic change. The Commission endorses the recommendations of the National Statistical Commission and stresses the importance of their implementation.

E. Fundamental Duties

The Background

37.1 Ten Fundamental Duties of the citizen are incorporated in article 51A, Part IVA of the Constitution. Inserted by the Constitution (Forty-second Amendment) Act, 1976 it was part of a large number of changes brought about during the Emergency. But after the end of the Emergency, when the new Parliament reviewed the whole position and in most cases restored the pre-emergency position, article 51A was one that emerged unscathed because it was considered by all parties to be an unexceptionable charter of principles which citizens could usefully absorb and practice.

37.2 Constitutions of some countries of the world contain provisions for Fundamental Duties. The inclusion of Fundamental Duties in our Constitution also brings it in line with Article 29(1) of the Universal Declaration of Human Rights which says: "Everyone has the duties to the community in which alone the free and full development of the personality is possible." Exercise of fundamental rights entails duties to the community which ensures the free and full development of human personality.

37.3 In the last quarter-century since the Amendment, several judgments of High Courts and the Supreme Court have quoted these Fundamental Duties, where applicable, to lend further support to their decisions.

37.4 A consultation paper on the subject of "Effectuation of Fundamental Duties" prepared for the Commission by the Citizenship Development Society was circulated for eliciting public opinion. Responses received were carefully examined by the Commission along with the report of the Justice Verma Committee on Fundamental Duties.

37.5 The Government of India appointed the committee "to operationalise the suggestions to teach Fundamental Duties to the citizens of India" in the year 1998 under the chairmanship of Justice J.S. Verma. The Committee submitted its report in October 1999. The Commission feels that it is, therefore, not necessary for it to cover the same ground again. It finds itself in full agreement with the report of the Verma Committee. The salient recommendations of the Committee are at Annexure 1
to the Consultation Paper on "Effectuation of Fundamental Duties of Citizens".

Usefulness of Duties

38.1 Fundamental Duties of citizens serve a useful purpose. In particular, no democratic polity can ever succeed where the citizens are not willing to be active participants in the process of governance by assuming responsibilities and discharging citizenship duties and coming forward to give their best to the country. Some of the fundamental duties enshrined in article 51A have been incorporated in separate laws. For instance, the first duty includes respect for the National Flag and the National Anthem. Disrespect is punishable by law. To value and preserve the rich heritage of the mosaic that is India should help to weld our people into one nation but much more than article 51A will be needed to treat all human beings equally, to respect each religion and to confine it to the private sphere and not make it a bone of contention between different communities of this land. In sum, the Commission believes that article 51A has travelled a great distance since it was introduced in the Forty-second Amendment and further consideration should be given to ways and means to popularise the knowledge and content of the Fundamental Duties and effectuate them.

38.2 The most important task before us is to reconcile the claims of the individual citizen and those of the civic society. To achieve this, it is important to orient the individual citizen to be conscious of his social and citizenship responsibilities and so shape the society that we all become solicitous and considerate of the inalienable rights of our fellow citizens. Therefore, awareness of our citizenship duties is as important as awareness of our rights. Every right implies a corresponding duty but every duty does not imply a corresponding right. Man does not live for himself alone. He lives for the good of others as well as of himself. It is this knowledge of what is right and wrong that makes a man responsible to himself and to the society and this knowledge is inculcated by imbibing and clearly understanding one' s citizenship duties. The fundamental duties are the foundations of human dignity and national character. If every citizen performs his duties irrespective of considerations of caste, creed, colour and language, most of the malaise of the present day polity could be contained, if not eradicated, and the society as a whole uplifted. Rich or poor, in power or out of power, obedience to citizenship duty, at all costs and risks, is the essence of civilized life.

Spirit of Harmony and Dignity of Women

39.1 Some further thought needs to be given to clauses (e) and (f) of article 51A. Article 51A(e) desires the promotion of harmony and the spirit of common brotherhood among all the people of India transcending religious, linguistic and regional or sectional diversities and renunciation of practices derogatory to the dignity of women. It is couched in broad terms but it should be clear that attacks on minority communities or minority opinions are frowned upon. Respect for both are essential and the wording lends support to a broad humanism to cover such differences as may exist or better still, co-exist. Two thoughts can be distilled. The first is that the objective will not be reached unless there is a determined effort to restrict religious practices to the home on the justified premise that one's religion is a personal matter and is not conducive to mass assertiveness. The other is the status of women.

39.2 Lip service is being paid to the doctrine of gender equality. The fact remains that generally women are still regarded as inferior both at home and workplace although the Commission has noticed an improvement, however dissatisfied it may be with the degree of the improvement.

39.3 It is necessary to separate religious precepts from civil law. Civil law as the name implies is a matter for society not for religious leaders and it would seem to us to be axiomatic that in matters of civil rights, laws of property and inheritance and marriage and divorce, although practices may differ, legal rights that accrue must be the same. For example, a marriage may be solemnised according to religious or social custom but the rights of a woman in the case of divorce must be the same no matter what her religion is. As the Supreme Court held in the Shahbanoo case, an abandoned wife is an abandoned wife and it does not matter whether she professes one religion or another. She is entitled to alimony. Progress in these directions will be slow but it is necessary that progress is seen to be made. The key lies in education.

39.4 Clause (e) of article 51A also seems to cover the need to regard all human beings equally. In this connection, it is necessary to consider the question of the uplift¬ment of the Scheduled Castes and other disadvantaged sections of our society. The scourge must be eradicated. The Constitution gave us ten years to do the job; the provision has been extended to fifty years and we are in our sixth ten-year period but we are no nearer the goal. The discrimination is two-fold. It is economic-condemning whole sections of our society numbering millions to menial jobs as part of the evil of treating them as sub-human. We have provided for reservation of jobs to these people, we have even given them separate constituencies to represent them. It has created a vested interest in backwardness. The other adverse result is that it has had no effect on their status in society, which continues to be determined by birth and not human worth and human personality. It is this social stigma which still plagues our people and the struggle to restore to them basic human dignity has made no significant progress. While the Commission appreciates the context in which affirmative action became necessary, it feels that reservation of jobs and seats in the legislatures will not help this aspect of the matter.

39.5 It is quite clear to the Commission that the disease of considering human beings as high or low based on the accident of birth is a disease rooted in the mind and it is in the mind that the defences of a society based on human dignity and equality must be constructed. Logically this leads directly to the conclusion that the key lies in education. The time to begin training our young people to respect the National flag and sing the National anthem, to respect women, to hold all religions equal and deserving of as much respect as one's own, to accept that all human beings are born equal and are entitled to equal treatment are among principles best taught by examples when the child is too young to understand but not too young to obey. The focus must, therefore, shift to education which has suffered from serious neglect. Schools restrict admissions on unacceptable criteria, teachers themselves are untrained and often politicised, as is the curriculum. Despite these hardships, many of our young people have done well.

Composite culture

40.1 Clause (f) of article 51A requires us to value and preserve the rich heritage of our composite culture. It follows that we may not break each other's places of worship, set fire to religious texts, or beat up one another's priests or obstruct those who exercise their Fundamental Right under article 25 to profess, practice and propagate religion. Composite culture means culture drawn from many strands. Here again education in its broadest and best sense can provide the corrective to the aberrations that have occurred.

40.2 Education is not confined only to the time spent in schools and colleges. Education begins at birth in the subconscious and continues till death. Anyone who says that he has nothing more to learn is already brain-dead. It follows that the influences that play on a child at home are of great importance. Parents should understand that education begins at home, the examples they set, the environment of enlightenment and tolerance that is necessary to produce good citizens cannot be sub-contracted to formal schooling important though this is. Schemes should, therefore, be framed that include parents in social activities that have as their objective the country's age-old traditions, its welcome to the persecuted of every faith, its virtues of tolerance of and respect for all religions and a certain pride in belonging to this land and in being considered as Indian. The highest office in our democracy is the office of citizen; this is not only a platitude, it must translate into reality. The distinction is not illusory. This country has given far too much indulgence to an attitude of mind that acts on the question 'what is there in it for me? Education and the process of inculcating unselfishness and a sense of obligation to one's fellowmen should inspire the question - where does my duty lie? The transformation has the potential to make our nation strong, invincible and able to command the respect of the world.

40.3 (i) The Commission recommends that the first and foremost step required by the Union and State Governments is to sensitise the people and to create a general awareness of the provisions of fundamental duties amongst the citizens on the lines recommended by the Justice Verma Committee
18 on the subject. Consideration should be given to the ways and means by which Fundamental Duties could be popularized and made effective; (ii) right to freedom of religion and other freedoms must be jealously guarded and rights of minorities and fellow citizens respected; (iii) reform of the whole process of education is an immediate but immense need, as is the need to free it from governmental or political control; it is only through education that will power to

adhere to our Fundamental Duties as citizens can be inculcated; and (iv) duty to vote at elections, actively participate in the democratic process of governance and to pay taxes should be included in article 51A. The Commission fully endorses the other recommendations of the Justice Verma Committee on operationalisation of Fundamental Duties of Citizens and strongly suggests their early implementation.

40.4 The Commission also recommends that the following should be incorporated as fundamental duties in article 51A of the Constitution -

(i) *To foster a spirit of family values and responsible parenthood in the matter of education, physical and moral well-being of children.*

(ii) Duty of industrial organizations to provide education to children of their employees.

Report of the National Commission to review the Working of the Consitution[117]

[117] http://lawmin.nic.in/ncrwc/finalreport/v1ch3.htm

The Commission submitted its report in two volumes to the Government on 31st March, 2002 by Justice M.N. Venkatachaliah.

Chapter 3: Fundamental Rights, Directive Principles And Fundamental Duties

Fundamental Rights

(1) In article 12 of the Constitution, the following Explanation should be added:-

'*Explanation - In this article, the expression "other authorities" shall include any person in relation to such of its functions which are of a public nature.*' [Para 3.5]

(2) In articles 15 and 16, prohibition against discrimination should be extended to "ethnic or social origin; political or other opinion; property or birth". [Para 3.6]

(3) Article 19(1)(a) and (2) should be amended to read as follows:

"Art. 19(1): All citizens shall have the right -

(a) to freedom of speech and expression which shall include the freedom of the press and other media, the freedom to hold opinions and to seek, receive and impart information and ideas."

19(2): "Nothing in sub-clause (a) of clause (1) shall affect the operation of any existing law, or prevent the State from making any law, in so far as such law imposes reasonable restrictions on the exercise of the right conferred by the said sub-clause in the interests of the sovereignty and integrity of India, the security of the State, friendly relations with foreign States, public order, decency or morality, or in relation to contempt of court, defamation or incitement to an offence, or preventing the disclo-sure of information received in confidence except when required in public interest." [Para 3.8.1]

(4) A Proviso to article 19(2) of the Constitution should be added as under:-

"Provided that, in matters of contempt, it shall be open to the Court to permit a defence of justification by truth on satisfaction as to the bona fides of the plea and it being in public interest." [Paras 3.8.2 and 7.42]

(5) The existing article 21 may be re-numbered as clause (1) thereof, and a new clause (2) should be inserted thereafter on the following lines: -

"(2) No one shall be subjected to torture or to cruel, inhuman or degrading treatment or punishment." [Para 3.9]

(6) After clause (2) in article 21 as proposed in para 3.9, a new clause, namely, clause (3) should be added on the following lines:-

"(3) Every person who has been illegally deprived of his right to life or liberty shall have an enforceable right to compensation." [Para 3.10]

(7) After article 21, a new article, say article 21-A, should be inserted on the following lines:-

"21-A. (1) Every person shall have the right to leave the territory of India and every citizen shall have the right to return to India.

(2) Nothing in clause (1) shall prevent the State from making any law imposing reasonable restrictions in the interests of the sovereignty and integrity of India, friendly relations of India with foreign States and interests of the general public." [Para 3.11]

(8) A new article, namely, article 21-B, should be inserted on the following lines:

"21-B. (1) Every person has a right to respect for his private and family life, his home and his correspondence.

(2) Nothing in clause (1) shall prevent the State from making any law imposing reasonable restrictions on the exercise of the right conferred by clause (1), in the interests of security of the State, public safety or for the prevention of disorder or crime, or for the protection of health or morals, or for the protection of the rights and freedoms of others." [Para 3.12]

(9) A new article, say article 21-C, may be added to make it obligatory on the State to bring suitable legislation for ensuring the right to rural wage employment for a minimum of eighty days in a year. [Para 3.13.2]

(10) As regards article 22, the following changes should be made:-

(i) The first and second provisos and Explanation to article 22(4) as contained in section 3 of the Constitution (44th Amendment) Act, 1978 should be substituted by the following proviso and the said section 3 of the 1978 Act as amended by the proposed legislation should be brought into force within a period of not exceeding three months:-

"Provided that an Advisory Board shall consist of a Chairman and not less than two other members, and the Chairman and the other members of the Board shall be serving judges of any High Court:

Provided further that nothing in this clause shall authorize the detention of any person beyond a maximum period of six months as may be prescribed by any law made by Parliament under sub-clause (a) of clause (7)."

(ii) In clause (7) of article 22 of the Constitution, in sub-clause (b), for the words "the maximum period", the words "the maximum period not exceeding six months" shall be substituted.[Para 3.14.2]

(11) After article 30, the following article should be added as article 30A:

"30-A: Access to Courts and Tribunals and speedy justice

(1) Everyone has a right to have any dispute that can be resolved by the application of law decided in a fair public hearing before an independent court or, where appropriate, another independent and impartial tribunal or forum.

(2) The right to access to courts shall be deemed to include the right to reasonably speedy and effective justice in all matters before the courts, tribunals or other fora and the State shall take all reasonable steps to achieve the said object." [Para 3.15.1]

(12) Article 39A in Part IV should be shifted to Part III as a new article 30-B to read as under:-

"30-B. Equal justice and free legal aid: The State shall secure that the operation of the legal system promotes justice, on a basis of equal opportunity, and shall, in particular, provide free legal aid, by suitable legislation or schemes or in any other way, to ensure that opportunities for securing justice are not denied to any citizen by reason of economic or other disabilities."

[Para 3.15.2]

(13) Article 300-A should be recast as follows:-

"300-A. (1) Deprivation or acquisition of property shall be by authority of law and only for a public purpose.

(2) There shall be no arbitrary deprivation or acquisition of property:

Provided that no deprivation or acquisition of agricultural, forest and non-urban homestead land belonging to or customarily used by the Scheduled Castes and the Scheduled Tribes shall take place except by authority of law which provides for suitable rehabilitation scheme before taking possession of such land." [Para 3.16.2]

(14) In article 31-B, the following proviso should be added at the end, namely:-

"*Provided that the protection afforded by this article to Acts and Regulations which may be hereafter specified in the Ninth Schedule or any of the provisions thereof, shall not apply unless such Acts or Regulations relate* -

(a) in pith and substance to agrarian reforms or land reforms;

(b) to reasonable quantum of reservation under articles 15 and 16;

(c) to provisions for giving effect to the policy of the State towards securing all or any of the principles specified in clause (b) or clause (c) of article 39." [Para 3.17]

(15) Clauses (1) and (1A) of article 359 should be amended by substituting for "(except articles 20 and 21)" , the following:-

"(except articles 17,20,21,23,24,25 and 32)" [Para 3.18.2]

(16) The relevant provision in the Constitution (93rd Amendment) Bill, 2001 making the right to education of children from 6 years till the completion of 14 years as a Fundamental Right should be amended and enlarged to read as under:-

"30-C. Every child shall have the right to free education until he completes the age of fourteen years; and in the case of girls and members of the Scheduled Castes and the Schedule Tribes until they complete the age of eighteen years." [Para 3.20.2]

(17) After article 24, the following article should be added:-

"*Article 24A. Every child shall have the right to care and assistance in basic needs and protection from all forms of neglect, harm and exploitation.*" [Para 3.21.2]

(18) After the proposed article 30-C, the following article may be added as article 30-D:-

"30-D. Right to safe drinking water, prevention of pollution, conservation of ecology and sustainable development. -

Every person shall have the right -

(a) to safe drinking water;

(b) to an environment that is not harmful to one's health or well-being; and

(c) to have the environment protected, for the benefit of present and future generations so as to

(i) prevent pollution and ecological degradation;

(ii) promote conservation; and

(iii) secure ecologically sustainable development and use of natural resources while promoting justifiable economic and social development." [Para 3.22.3]

(19) Explanation II to article 25 should be omitted and sub-clause (b) of clause (2) of that article should be reworded to read as follows:-

"(b) providing for social welfare and reform or the throwing open of Hindu, Sikh, Jaina or Buddhist religious institutions of a public character to all classes and sections of these religions." [Para 3.23.2]

(20) It shall be desirable that some optimum level of population with a view to take necessary action under this constitutional provision is prescribed. In article 347 of the Constitution, for the words "a substantial proportion of the population", the words "not less than ten per cent of the population" should be substituted. [Para 3.24]

Directive Principles

(21) The Commission recommends that the heading of Part IV of the Constitution should be amended to read as "*Directive Principles of State Policy And Action*" . [Para 3.26.3]

(22) A strategic Plan of Action should be initiated to create a large number of employment opportunities in five years to realize and exploit the enormous potential in creating such employment opportunities. The components of this plan may include:

(1) Improvement of productivity in agriculture that will activate a chain of activities towards increased income and employment opportunities.

(2) Integrated horticulture that will include production of fruits, vegetables and flowers, cut-flowers for export and medicinal plants as well as establishment of bio-processing industries aimed primarily at value-addition of agricultural products.

(3) Intensification of animal husbandry programs and production of quality dairy products.

(4) Integrated Program of Intensive Aquaculture including use of common property resources like village ponds and lakes.

(5) Afforestation and Wasteland Development to bring an additional 12 million hectares under forest plantation and contribute to rural asset building activity.

(6) Soil and Water Conservation to support afforestation and Natural Resource Conservation towards eco-friendly agriculture.

(7) Water Conservation and Tank Rehabilitation.

(8) Production and use of organic manures through vermiculture and other improved techniques and production of organic health foods from them. [Para 3.27.3]

(23) The Commission recommends that an independent National Education Commission should be set up every five years to report to Parliament on the progress of the constitutional directive regarding compulsory education and on other aspects relevant to the knowledge society

of the new century. The model of the Finance Commission may be usefully looked into.[Para 3.31.3]

(24) After article 47, the following article should be added, namely:-

47A. "Control of population.- The State shall endeavour to secure control of population by means of education and implementation of small family norms." .[Para 3.32]

(25) An inter-faith mechanism to promote such civil society initiatives should be set up. This may be done under the auspices of the National Human Rights Commission set up under section 3 of the Protection of Human Rights Act, 1993 which, inter alia, provides for the participation of "the Chairpersons of the National Commission for Minorities, the National Commission for Scheduled Castes and Scheduled Tribes and the National Commission for Women" who shall be deemed to be the Members of the Commission for the discharge of functions specified in clauses (b) to (j) of the section 12 of the said Act. This body could, in addition to its other statutory functions, also function in collaboration with the National Foundation for Communal Harmony as a mechanism for promotion of inter-religious harmony for inter alia overseeing the installation and working of "Mohalla Committees" and other civil society, initiatives in sensitive areas. With an appropriate statutory enablement by way of enlargement of section 12 of the said Act, the purpose could be achieved without additional expenditure for setting up a separate mechanism. Section 12 of the said Act with consequential amendments to section 3(3) could be amended by the addition of clause (k), which shall read as under:

"(k) promoting through civil society initiatives, inter-faith and inter-religious harmony and social solidarity." [Para 3.34.2]

(26) There must be a body of high status which first reviews the state of the level of implementation of the Directive Principles and Economic, Social and Cultural Rights and in

particular (i) the right to work, (ii) the right to health, (iii) the right to food, clothing and shelter, (iv) Right to Education up to and beyond the 14th year, and (v) the Right to Culture. The said body must estimate the extent of resources required in each State under each of these heads and make recommendations for allocation of adequate resources, from time to time. For ensuring that the Directive Principles of State Policy are realized more effectively, the following procedure should be followed:-:-

(i) The Planning Commission should ensure that there is special mention/emphasis in all the plans and schemes formulated by it, on the effectuation/realization of the Directive Principles of State Policy.

(ii) Every Ministry/Department of the Government of India should make a special annual report indicating the extent of effectuation/realization of the Directive Principles of State Policy, the shortfall in the targets, the reasons for the shortfall, if any, and the remedial measures taken to ensure their full realization, during the year under report.

(iii) The report under item (ii) should be considered and discussed by the Department Related Parliamentary Standing Committee, which shall submit its report on the working of the Department indicating the achievements/failures of the Ministry/Department along with its recommendations thereto.

(iv) Both the Reports mentioned at items (ii) and (iii) above should be discussed by the Planning Commission in an interactive seminar with the representatives of various NGOs, Civil Society Groups, etc. in which the representatives of the Ministry/Department and the Departmental Related Parliamentary Standing Committee would also participate. The report of this interaction shall be submitted to the Parliament within a time bound manner.

(v) The Parliament should discuss the report at item (iv) above within a period of three months and pass a resolution about the action required to be taken by the Ministry/Department concerned. A similar mechanism as mentioned above may be adopted by the States. [Paras 3.35.2 and 3.35.3]

(27) The Report of the National Statistical Commission (2001) stresses the importance of availability of adequate, credible and timely socio-economic data generated by the statistical system, both for policy formulation and for monitoring progress of the sectors of economy and pace of socio-economic change. The Commission endorses the recommendations of the National Statistical Commission and stresses the importance of their implementation.

Fundamental Duties

(28) For effectuating Fundamental Duties, the following steps should be taken:-

(i) The first and foremost step required by the Union and State Governments is to sensitise the people and to create a general awareness of the provisions of fundamental duties amongst the citizens on the lines recommended by the Justice Verma Committee on the subject. Consideration should be given to the ways and means by which Fundamental Duties could be popularized and made effective;

(ii) Right to freedom of religion and other freedoms must be jealously guarded and rights of minorities and fellow citizens respected;

(iii) Reform of the whole process of education is an immediate but immense need, as is the need to free it from governmental or political control; it is only through education that will power to adhere to our Fundamental Duties as citizens can be inculcated;

(iv) Duty to vote at elections, actively participate in the democratic process of governance and to pay taxes should be included in article 51A; and

(v) The other recommendations of the Justice Verma Committee on operationalisation of Fundamental Duties of Citizens should be implemented at the earliest. [Para 3.40.3]

(29) The following should also be incorporated as fundamental duties in article 51A of the Constitution –

(i) To foster a spirit of family values and responsible parenthood in the matter of education, physical and moral well-being of children.

(ii) Duty of industrial organizations to provide education to children of their employees.

[Para 3. 40.4]

Chapter V

Comparative Study of Fundamental Rights and Directive Principles in Indian Constitution and other Constitutions

---

Synopsis

(1) Fundamental Rights under Indian Constitution and other Constitutions

(A Right to Equality in Indian Constitution and other Constitutions

i. *Equality before law in Indian Constitution and other Constitutions*

ii. *Prohibition of discrimination on grounds of religion, race, caste, sex or place of birth in Indian Constitution and other Constitutions*

iii. *Equality of Opportunity in matters of public employment in Indian Constitution and other Constitutions*

iv. *Abolition of Untouchability in Indian Constitution and other Constitutions*

v. *Abolition of title in Indian Constitution and other Constitutions*

(B) Right to Freedom in Indian Constitution and Other Constitutions

i. *Freedom of Speech and Expression and its limitations in Indian Constitution and other Constitutions*

ii. *Freedom of Assembly and its limitations in Indian Constitution and other Constitutions*

iii. *Freedom of Association and Union and its limitations in Indian Constitution and other Constitutions*

iv. *Freedom of movement and residence and its limitation in Indian Constitution and other Constitutions*

v. *Right to Property in Constitutions*

(C) Right against Exploitation in Indian Constitution and other Constitutions

i. *Prohibition of traffic in human beings and forced labour in Indian Constitution and other Constitutions*

ii*. Prohibition of employment of Children in factories, etc in Indian Constitution and other Constitutions*

(D) Right to Freedom of Religion in Indian Constitution and other Constitutions

i*. Freedom of conscience and free profession Practice and Propagation of religion in Indian Constitution and other Constitutions*

ii. *Freedom to manage religious affairs in Indian Constitution and other Constitutions*

iii. *Freedom not to pay Taxes for religious Promotion in Indian Constitution and other Constitutions*

iv*. Freedom not to attend religious instructions in Indian Constitution and other Constitutions*

(E) Cultural and Educational Rights in Indian Constitution and other Constitutions

i. Protection of interest of Minorities in Indian Constitution and other Constitutions

ii. Right to Minorities to Establish and Administer Educational Institutions in Indian Constitution and other Constitutions

(F) Saving of Certain laws in Indian Constitution and other Constitutions

i. Saving to laws providing for acquisition of estates, etc. (Article 31-A)

ii. Validation of certain Acts and Regulations (Article 31-B)

iii. Saving of laws giving effect to certain Directive Principles(Article 31-C)

(G) Right to Constitutional Remedies in Indian Constitution and other Constitutions

i. India: Article 32

ii. India: Article 33

iii. India: Article 34

iv. India: Article 35

(2) Directive Principles under Indian Constitution and other Constitutions

(A) Social and Economic charter in Indian Constitution and other Constitutions

i. Social order based on Justice in Indian Constitution and other Constitutions

ii. Economic Justice in Indian Constitution and other Constitutions

(B) Social Security charter in Indian Constitution and other Constitutions

i. Equal Justice and Free Legal Aid in Indian Constitution and other Constitutions

ii. Social Services in Indian Constitution and other Constitutions

iii. Condition of work in Indian Constitution and other Constitutions

iv. Living wages in Indian Constitution and other Constitutions

v. Participation of Workers in Management of Industries in Indian Constitution and other Constitutions

vi. Free and Compulsory Education in Indian Constitution and other Constitutions

vii. Promotion of Educational and Economic Interests of weaker section in Indian Constitution and other Constitutions

viii. Raising standard of living in Indian Constitution and other Constitution

(C) Community Welfare Charter in Indian Constitution and other Constitutions

i. Organisation of Village Panchayats in Indian Constitution and other Constitutions

ii. Uniform Civil Code in Indian Constitution and other Constitutions

iii. Organisation of Agriculture and Animal husbandry in Indian Constitution and other Constitutions

iv. Protection of Environment in Indian Constitution and other Constitutions v. Protection of Monuments in Indian Constitution and other Constitutions

vi. Separation of Judiciary From executive in Indian Constitution and other Constitutions

vii. Promotion of International Peace in Indian Constitution and other Constitutions

---

(1) Fundamental Rights under Indian Constitution and other Constitutions

Generally all democratic countries have a written or un-written Constitution with a special guarantee to people about Fundamental Rights. Even non-democratic countries guarantee fundamental rights to people just to show society at large that they have regard and respect for the fundamental rights of human beings. Today's position is that roughly all modern constitutions of countries who are members of UNO have a provision of fundamental rights either directly or indirectly. Here I am placing an article wise study of Fundamental Right of the Indian Constitution along with a study of corresponding Fundamental Rights under foreign Constitution as follows:

A. Right to Equality in Indian Constitution and other Constitutions

(i) Equality before law in Indian Constitution and other Constitutions

(a) India: ***Article 14*** provides that the state shall not deny to any person equality before the law or the equal protection of the laws within the territory of India.

(b) USA: ***section 1*** of the 14th Amendment. "No state shall deny to any person within its jurisdiction the equal protection of the laws.

(c) Eire: ***Section 40 (1):*** "All citizens shall, as human persons be held equal before law."

(d) Burma: ***Section 13***: "All citizens irrespective of birth, religion, sex or race are equal before law; that is to say, there shall not be any arbitrary discrimination between one citizen or class of citizens and another."

(e) Argentina: ***Article 16*** prohibits the prerogative of blood or of birth, personal privileges and titles of nobility. All inhabitants are equal before the law and if they satisfy the requirements of fitness they are all equally admissible for employment. Taxation is equal as also public burdens.

(f) Chile: ***Article 10*** -All inhabitants of the republic are assured equality before the law and also practice of all beliefs, liberty and conscience and the free exercise of all religious that may not be contrary to morality, good usage or to public order. No privileged class is recognised nor any from of slavery. Any alien who does slave traffic cannot live in chile nor be naturalized in the republic.

(g) Nicaragua: ***Article 106*** treats all Nicaraguans as equal before the law except in regard to women on account of the differences inherent in their nature or where the good of the family is concerned. Article 107 denies all privileges by reason of birth, nobility, race or social status.

(h) Uruguay: ***Article 8*** guarantees that all persons are equal before the law, no other difference being recognized among them other than that of talent or virtue.

(ii) Prohibition of discrimination on grounds of religion, race, caste, sex, or place of birth in Indian Constitution and other Constitutions

(a) India : ***Article 15*** provides that Prohibition of discrimination on grounds of religion, race, caste, sex or place of birth:

1. The state shall not discriminate against any citizen on grounds only of religion, race, caste, sex, place of birth or any of them.

2. No citizen shall, on grounds only of religion, race, caste, sex, place of birth or any of them, be subject to any disability, liability restriction or condition with regard to:

a. access to shops, public restaurants, hotels and places of public entertainment, or

b. the use of wells, tanks, bathing ghats, roads, and places of public resort maintained wholly or partly out of state Funds or dedicated to the use of the general public.

3. Nothing in this Article shall prevent the state from making any special provision for women and children.

4. Nothing in this article or in clause (2) of article 29 shall prevent the state from making any special provision for the advancement of any socially and educationally backward classes of citizens or for the Scheduled Tribes.

(b) USA: The 15th Amendment (1870), ***Section 1***, runs: "The right of the citizens of the united States to vote shall not be denied or abridged by the United States or by any state on account of race, colour or previous condition."

"The right of citizens of the United State to vote shall not be denied or abridged by the United States or by any state on account of sex."

(c) Australia: ***Section 117*** of the Constitution Act postulates: "A subject of the queen, a resident in any state shall not be subject in any other state to any disability or discrimination which may not be applicable to him if he were a subject of the queen resident in such other state."

(d) Switzerland: ***Article 60*** of the Constitution states: "Every canton is bound to accord to the citizens of the other confederated states the same treatment as to its own citizens in regard to legislation and judicial proceedings."

Equality is further assured by ***Article 4***, which says that "In Switzerland there are no subjects; nor any privileges of rank, birth, person or family."

(e) **Japan:** ***Article 14*** which states that "...There shall be no discrimination in political economic, or social relations because of race, creed, sex, social status or family origin."

(iii) Equality of opportunity in matters of public employment in Indian Constitution and other Constitutions.

(a) India : ***Article 16*** provides

(1) there shall be equality of opportunity for all citizens in matters relating to employment or appointment to any office under the state.

2. No citizen shall, on grounds only of religion, race, caste, sex, descent, place of birth, residence or any of them, be ineligible for or discriminated against in respect of any employment or office under the state.

3. Nothing in this Article shall prevent parliament from making any law prescribing, in regard to a class or classes of employment or appointment to an office under the government of , or any local or other authority within, a state or union territory any requirement as to residence within that State or Union territory prior to such employment or appointment.

4. Nothing in this Article shall prevent the state from making any provisions for the reservation of appointments or posts in favour of any backward class of citizens, which, in the opinion of the state, is not adequately represented in the services under the state.

4-A: Nothing in this article shall prevent the state from making any provision for reservation in matters of promotion ot any class or classes of posts in the services under the state in favour of the Scheduled Castes and the Scheduled Tribes which, in the opinion of the States, are not adequately represented in the services under the State.

4-B: Nothing in this article shall prevent the state from considering any unfilled vacancies of a year which are reserved for being filled up in that year in accordance with any provision for reservation made under clause (4) or clause (4-A) as a separate class of vacancies to be filled up in any succeeding year or years and such class of vacancies shall not be considered together with the vacancies of the year in which they are being filled up for determining the ceiling of fifty percent reservation on total number of vacancies of that year[118].

5. Nothing in this article shall affect the operation of any law which provides that the incumbent of an office in connection with the affairs of any religious or denominational institution or any member of the governing body thereof shall be a person professing a particular religion or belonging to a particular denomination.

(b) United State of America: Article VI, ***Section 3***, of the U.S Constitution provides that "...No religious test shall be required as a qualification to any office or public trust under the United States.

(c) Australia: ***Section 116*** of the Australian Constitution provides that "...No religious test shall be required as a qualification for any office or public trust under the commonwealth."

(d) Burma: ***Section 14*** of the Burmese Constitution provides that "...There shall be equality of opportunity for all citizens in matters of public employment and in the exercise of carrying on any occupation, trade, business or profession."

(e) Government of India Act, 1935: ***Section 275*** says, "A person shall not be disqualified by sex, for being appointed to any occupation or be ineligible for office under the crown in India."

(iv) Abolition of Untouchability in Indian Constitution and other Constitutions

[118] Clause 4-B of Article 16 is inserted by the Constitution(Eighty First Amendment) Act, 2000

(a) India : ***Article 17*** provides that "Untouchability" is abolished and its practice in any form is forbidden. The enforcement of any disability arising out of Untouchability shall be an offence punishable in accordance with law.

(b) There is no parallel to this in any other constitution unless one draws the analogy of the Negroes of South Africa.

(v) Abolition of Titles in Indian Constitution and other Constitutions

(a) India : ***Article 18*** provides that

1. No titles, not being a Military or Academic distinction shall be conferred by the state.
2. No citizen of India shall accept any titles from any foreign state.
3. No person who is not a citizen of India shall, while he holds any office of profits or trust under the state, accept, without the consent of the president, any title from any foreign state.
4. No person holding any office of profit or trust under the state shall, without the consent of the president, accept any present, emolument, or office of any kind from or under any foreign state.

(b) United state of America: ***Article 1,*** Section 9-No title of nobility shall be granted by the United States. And no person holding any office of profit or trust shall, without consent of the congress, accept any present emoluments, office or title of any kind whatever, from any king, prince, or foreign State.

(c) Japan: ***Article 14-*** peers and peered shall not be recognized. No privilege shall accompany any award of whichever decoration, or any other restriction nor shall any such award be valid beyond the lifetime of individuals who hold it and hereafter may receive it.

(d) Eire : ***Section 40 (2)*** Provides that "Titles of nobility shall not be conferred by the state. No title of nobility or however may be accepted by any citizen except with the prior approval of the government."

(B) Right to Freedom in Indian Constitution and other Constitutions

(i) Freedom of Speech and expressions and its limitations in Indian Constitution and other Constitutions.

(a) India : ***Article 19 (1)(a)*** and ***19(2)*** provides that all citizens shall have the right to freedom of speech and expression.

(b) United Nations: ***Article 17*** of the United Nations Declarations of Human Rights postulates that "Every one has the right to freedom of opinion and expression, this right includes the freedom to hold opinion without interference and to seek, receive and import information and ideas, through any media and regardless of frontiers."

(c) USA: The first amendment to the Constitution (1791) states that "The congress shall make on laws abridging the freedom of speech or of the press."

(d) Germany: ***Article 188*** of the Weimar Constitution 1919 postulated that "Every German has the right within the limits of general laws to express his opinion freely by word of mouth, writing, printed matter or picture, or in any conditions of his work or appointment and no one is permitted to injure him on account of his making use of such rights."

"No censorship shall be enforced, but restrictive regulations may be introduced by law in reference to cinematographic entertainments. Legal measures are also admissible for the purpose of combating bad and obscene literature as well as for the protection of youth in public exhibitions and performances."

(e) Eire: ***Section 40 (6) (1)*** States: "The state guarantees liberty for the exercise of the following rights subject to public order and morality"

The right of the citizens to express freely their convictions and opinions…"

The education of public opinion being however, a matter of such grave "import to the common good, the state shall endeavour that organs of public opinions such as the radio, the press, the cinema, while preserving their rightful liberty of expression, including criticism of governmental policy, shall not be used to undermine public order or morality or the authority of the state. The publication or utterance of blasphemous seditious or indecent matter is an offence which shall be punishable in accordance with law."

(f) France: The preamble to the constitution of the Fourth France Republic (1789) declares: "No one should be disturbed on account of his opinions, even religious, provided their manifestation does not derange the public order established by law."

"The free communication of ideas and opinion is one of the most precious of the rights of men. Every citizen, then, can freely speak, write and print, subject to responsibility for the abuse of this freedom in cases determined by law."

(g) Burma: ***Article 17 (j)*** Provides that there shall be liberty for the exercise of the following rights, subject to law, public order and morality that the right of the citizens to express freely their convictions and opinions.

(h) Japan: ***Article XXI*** Declares "Freedom of assemblies association, speech and press and all other forms of expression are guaranteed. No censorship shall be maintained nor shall the secrecy of any means of communication be violated.

(i) Federation of Nigeria: ***Section 25(1)*** guarantees freedom of expression including freedom to hold opinions and to receive and impart ideas and information without interference.

(2) Nothing in this section shall invalidate any law that is reasonably justiciable in a democratic society:

a. In the interests of defence, public safety public order, public morality or public health.
b. For the purpose of protecting the rights, reputation and freedom of other persons, preventing the disclosure of information received in confidence, maintaining the authority and independence of the courts or regulating telephone, wireless broadcasting, television, or the exhibition of cinematographic films or;
c. Imposing restrictions upon persons holding office under the state, members of the armed forces of the Federation or members of a police Force."

(j) There are some common rights which is guaranteed by other Constitutions :

a. Privacy of Correspondence:

Article 10 of Federal Republic of Germany, article 110 of Nicargua, article 24 of CostaRica, Article 33 of Rumania and Article 23 of Czechoslovakia provides privacy of correspondence.

b. Right of petitioning to public authorities

Art. 17 of Germany, Article 27 of Luxemburg, Article 21 of Korea, Article 31 of Costa Rica, Article 35 of Rumania and Article 23 of Czechoslovakia provides rights of Petitioning to public authorities.

c. Sanctuary offered for victims of political persecution:

Article 31 and Article 35 of Rumania deals with these Right.

d. Right to Work

Article 19 of Rumania, Article 17 of Korea, Article 10 of Luxemburg and Article 26 of Czechoslovakia provides Right to work.

E. Right to Leisure

Article 22 of Rumania, Article 12 of Czechoslovakia and Article 16 of Germany provides Right to Leisure.

f. Right to Education

Article 22 of Rumania and Article 12 of Czechoslovakia provides Right to Education.

(ii) Freedom of Assembly and Restrictions in Indian Constitution and other Constitution.

(a) India : Article 19 (1)(b) and Clause (3) Provides the Freedom of Assembly and its restrictions.

(b)USA: The first Amendment states that "The Congress shall make on law…abridging…the right of people peaceably to assemble." The 14th Amendment guarantees to protect the above right. "No states shall make or enforce any law which shall abridge the privileges or immunities of the citizen of the United States, nor shall any state deprive any person of life, liberty, or property without due process of law nor deny to any person within its jurisdiction the equal protection of laws.

(c) Eire: ***Section 40 (6) (1)*** of the Constitution postulates that the State guarantees liberty for the exercise of the right of the citizen to assemble peaceably and without arms.

Provision may be made by law to prevent or control meetings which are determined in accordance with law to be calculated to cause breach of the peace or to be in danger or nuisance to the vicinity of either house of the parliament.

(d) Burma: ***Section 17 (11)*** of its Constitution states that "There shall be liberty in the exercise of the right to assemble, subject to law, public order and morality.

(e) Japan: ***Article XXI*** postulates that the rights of assembly…are guaranteed.

(f) Germany: ***Article 8*** lays down that in case of open-air meetings the right to assemble may be limited by legislation.

(g) Czechoslovakia: ***Article 24*** states that the right of assembly cannot be exercised so as to endanger the popular democratic, system of public peace and order.

(h) Rumania: ***Article 21*** states that freedom of press, of speech, of assembly and freedom to hold meetings, processions and demonstrations are guaranteed.

iii. Freedom of association and unions and its limitation in Indian Constitution and other Constitutions.

(a) India: ***Article 19 (1)(C)*** and ***19(4)*** deals with freedom of association and unions and its limitations.

(b) USA: No specific guarantee in the Constitution but law prohibiting them is one of judicial growth.

(c) Eire: ***Article 46 (6)*** extends the guarantee subject to public order and morality. "The right of citizens to form associations and unions is guaranteed. Laws however, may be enacted for the regulation and control in public interest of the exercise of the right but it shall not contain political religious or class distinction.

(d) Burma: ***Article 17 (3)-*** Provides that subject to law, public order and morality, the right of the citizens to form associations and unions. Any association or organisation whose object or activity is intended or likely to undermine the Constitution is forbidden.

(e) Germany: ***Article 9***- Provides that all Germans have the right to form unions, societies, and associations, not contrary to the notions of international understanding and forbidden by Law.

(f) Costa Rica: ***Article 25*** postulates that no one may be forced to join any association.

(g) Rumania: ***Article 32*** prohibits the associations of a fascist or anti-democratic nature. Otherwise the right of associations and organisations is guaranteed to citizens.

(h) Luxemburg: ***Article 26*** states that the founding of religious corporations may be authorized by law.

(i) Korea: ***Article 18*** entitles workers to share in profits.

(j) Czechoslovakia: ***Article 24*** postulates the right of assembly and association are guaranteed in so far as they do not endanger the popular democratic system or public peace and order. The exercise of such rights may be governed by law. Article 25 states that for the protection of their rights, employees may associate in the United Trade Union and are entitled to defend their interest through it. The United Trade Unions are assured of extensive participations in the control of the National Economy. The interest of the persons employed in individual work and offices are represented by the United Trade Union Organization.

(k) Hungary: ***Article 56*** states the guarantee of the right of associations for the purposes of developing the social, economic, and cultural activities of the workers.

(l) Pakistan: ***Article*** *7* provides that "Every person shall have the right to form association or unions subject to any reasonable restriction imposed by law in the interest of morality or public order."

iv. Freedom of Movement and residence and its limitation in Indian Constitution and other Constitution

(a) India : ***Article 19 (1) (c)*** and ***19 (4)*** provides freedom of movement and residence and its limitation.

(b) USA: There is no specific guarantee in US Constitution. It is covered by **Section 1**, of 14th Amendment of the Constitution.

(c) Czechoslovakia*:* ***Section*** *7* enunciates:

1. Every citizen may reside or sojourn in any place within the Czechoslovak Republic. The right may only be limited in the public interest in virtue of the law.
2. The right to emigrate abroad only may be limited in the virtue of the law.

(d) Germany: ***Article 11*** States:

1. All Germans enjoy freedom of movement throughout the federal territory.
2. This rights shall only be restricted by legislation, where lack of adequate means of existence would involve a special burden on the community or where it is necessary for the protection of youth against neglect, for combating the risk of epidemic or for the prevention of punishable acts.

Article III of the German Reich is provided that "All Germans enjoy the right of exchange of domicile within the whole Reich. Every one has the right to stay in any part of the realm that the chooses, to settle there, acquire landed property and pursue any means of livelihood."

(e) Switzerland: ***Article 45*** provides that "Every Swiss citizen has the right to settle in any part of Switzerland, subject to the production of a certificate of origin or similar document. The right of settlement may by way of exception be refused to or withdrawn from persons who have been deprived of their civic rights as the result of a penal conviction. The right of Settlement may also be withdrawn from persons who have been repeatedly sentenced for grave misdemeanors and from persons who become a permanent burden upon public charity, and whose commune or canton of origin refuses to provide adequate assistance for them after having been officially requested to provide it. In cantons in which domiciliary relief is provided, permission for settlement may be made conditional, in case of citizens of the canton , upon the person being capable of work and not having a permanent charge upon public charity in their former domicile in the canton of origin. The canton in which a Swiss citizen settles may not require from him any security or impose any special charge upon him in respect of each settlement. Similarly, communes may not impose on Swiss citizens domiciled within their area any charges other than those imposed upon their own citizens."

(f) Dazing: ***Article 75*** provides that "All nationals shall enjoy freedom of movement within the free city and shall have the right to stay and to settle at any place they may choose, to acquire real property and to earn their living in any way. The right shall not be curtailed without legal sanctions."

(g) Japan: ***Article XXII*** states that "Every person shall have freedom to choose and change his residence and to choose his occupation to the extent that it dose not interfere with the public welfare."

(h) Yugoslavia: It is provided that "No citizen may be expelled from one part of the country or another nor obliged to reside in a specified place save in such cases as may be expressly determined by law, No person may in any circumstances be expelled from his domicile without sentence by a court."

(i) Burma: ***Article 17 (IV)*** provides that "Subject to law, public order and morality, the right of every citizen to reside and settle in any part of the Union is guaranteed."

(j) Rumania: ***Article 28*****:** "guaranteed the individual liberty of the citizen."

(k) Nicaragua***: Article 55*** guarantees "The right to move in any country. There is both the right to emigrate and immigrate."

(l) Korea: ***Article 10*** states that "All citizens shall be free from limit residence, restrictions on domicile or restrictions on change of domicile."

v. Right to Property Indian Constitutions and other Constitutions

(a) India: *"****Article 19 (1) (f)****.* Provided the right to property. This article is deleted From the list of Fundamental rights[119]. Now it is a simple legal right under Article 300-A.

(b) USA: The ***14th Amendment*** states, "...Nor shall any state deprive any person of life liberty or property without due process of law." The ***5th Amendment*** states that "No person shall be...deprived of life, liberty or property without due proceed of law, nor shall private property be taken for public use without just compensations."

(c) Burma: ***Article 17 (iv)*** guarantees to every citizen the right to acquire property subject to law, public order and morality."

(d) The Government of India Act (1935) ***Section 298*** of the Act postulated:

1. "No subject of his majesty domiciled in India shall on grounds only of religion, place of birth, descent, colour or any of them...be prohibited on any such grounds from acquiring, holding or disposing of property or carrying on any occupation, trade, business or profession in India."

---

[119] Omitted by the Constitution (44th Amendment) Act, 1978

2. “Nothing in this section shall affect the operation of an law which prohibits, either absolutely or subject to exceptions, the sale or mortgage of agricultural land situated in any particular area and owned by a person belonging to some class of persons engaged in or connected with agriculture in that area, to any person not belonging to that class.”

(e) Virginia: ***Article 1*** postulates that "all men are by nature equally free and independent and have certain inherent rights of which, when they enter into a state of society, they cannot by any compact, deprive or divest their posterity, namely the enjoyment of life and liberty with the means of acquiring and possessing property and obtaining happiness and safety.”

(f) France: ***Article XVII*** states that “The right to property being inviolable and sacred no one ought to be deprived of it, except in cases of evident public necessity, legally ascertained and on condition of a previous just indemnity.”

(g) Rumania: ***Article** 7* postulates that “The common property of the people constitutes the material basis of the economic progress and national independence of the Rumanian People’s Republic. It is the duty of all citizens to protect and develop the common property of the people.

***Article 8**:* provides that Private property and the right to inherent property are recognized and guaranteed by law. Private property acquired by work and thrift enjoys special protection.

(h) Czechoslovakia: ***Section 8*** *says that* subject to the general provisions of law, every citizen may acquire fixed and other property in any place in the Czechoslovakia Republic and carry on a gainful occupation there.

Section 9

1. Private ownership may only be restricted by law.

2. Expropriation may only take place in virtue of the law and on payment of compensation, unless it is laid down by law that compensation shall not be payable.
3. No person shall misuse the right of property to the detriment of the community.

(i) Hungary: ***Section 8*** provides :

1. The Constitution recognizes and protects all property acquired by work.
2. Private property and private enterprise must not be harmful to the public interest.
3. The Constitution guarantees the right of inheritance.

(j) Germany: ***Section 22.***

1. Property is guaranteed by the constitution. The scope and limitations of ownership are determined by the laws and social obligations towards the community.
2. The right of inheritance as regulated by civil law is guaranteed. The share of the State in the inheritance is prescribed by law.

Section 23: provides that "Property restrictions and expropriations can only be imposed for the good of the community and in virtue of a law.

They shall be accompanied by suitable compensation unless the law otherwise determines."

(k) Costa Rica: ***Article 44*** states that Property shall be inviolable; no one shall be deprived of the property save in the public interest lawfully proved and with prior compensation in conformity with the law. In case of war or internal disorder, it is not necessary that compensation should precede, provided the payment must be made within two years after end of the emergency. The Legislative Assembly may, for reasons of public necessity, by a vote of two third of its members, impose limitations on property in the social interest.

VI. The freedom of profession, trade, or business and its limitation in Indian Constitution and other Constitutions

(a) India : ***Article 19(1)(g)*** and ***19(6)*** provides the freedom of profession, trade or business and limitation thereon.

(b) Burma: ***Article 17 (iv)*** holds that "Subject to law, public order and morality, the right to follow any occupation, trade, business or profession"

(c) Switzerland: ***Article 31*** guarantees "freedom of trade and industry throughout the confederation," but reserves the following to the state, viz., salt and gunpowder monopolies, federal duties, import duties of wine and other alcoholic beverages.

(d) Germany: ***Article 12*** States that "All the Germens have the right of free choice of occupation, place of employment and place of training. The pursuit of an occupation may be regulated by legislation. No one shall be forced to do a particular job except in virtue of an established general obligation to perform a public service laying equally upon all."

(e) Nicaragua: ***Article 82*** of the Constitution extends a guarantee to citizens the right to freely adopt any profession industry or trade not contrary to morality, public health or security.

(f) Rumania: ***Article 19*** postulates that "All citizens have the right to work. The state gradually secures the full exercise of this right by the planned organization and development of the national economy."

(g)Czechoslovakia: ***Article 26*** declares that:

1. All citizens have the right to work.
2. His work is secured in particular by organization of work directed by the state in accordance with a planned economy.

Article 27 states:

1. All working members of the population possess the right to just remuneration for the work done.
2. This right is secured by the state wages policy, which is administered with the United Trade Union Organization and directed towards the constant raising of standards of living of the working population.
3. Remuneration shall be governed by the quality and quantity of the work and by the benefit which it brings to the community.
4. In equal conditions, men and women are entitled to equal remuneration for equal work.

(h) Hungary : ***Article 9*** States:

1. In the Hungarian People's Republic, labour is the foundation of the social order.
2. Every able-bodied citizen has the right and the duty to work to the best of his ability, and is bound in honour to do so.
3. By their labour, by participation in work competitions, by strengthening labour discipline and improving working methods, the workers serve the cause of building up socialism.
4. The Hungarian people's Republic strives to apply in practice the socialist principle: "From each according to his ability, to each according to his work."

(i) Costa Rica ***: Article 56*** postulates that "Work is the right of the individual and an obligation towards society. The state must ensure that all have an honest and useful occupation which is properly paid and must prevent such occupation from giving rise to conditions which in any way impair the liberty or dignity of the individual or reduce labour to the level of a mere commodity. The state guarantees the right to a free choice of employment."

(j) USA: There is no specific provision in the Constitution of the United States guaranteeing the right of freedom of profession or freedom of trade, occupation, etc. The 14th amendment assuring the citizens that state shall deprive any person of life, liberty or property without due process of any contains the guarantee to the individual freedom to practice any profession or trade he chooses.

VII . Protection in respect of conviction for offence in Indian Constitution and other Constitutions.

(a) India : ***Article 20*** provides:

1. No person shall be convicted of any offence except for a violation of a law in force at the time of the commission of the act charged as an offence, nor be subject to a penalty greater than that which might have been inflicted under the law in force at the time of the commission of the offence.
2. No person shall be prosecuted and punished for the same offence more than once.
3. No person accused of any offence shall be compelled to be a witness against himself.

(b) USA: ***Article 9 (3)*** postulates that: "No ex post facto law shall be passed. No person shall be...subject for the same offence to be twice put in jeopardy of life or limb...No person shall be compelled in any criminal case to be a witness against himself."

(c) Eire: ***Article 15 (5)*** Says: "The Oireachtas shall not declare acts to be infringements of the law which ere not so at the date of their commission."

(d) Burma: ***Article 24*** States that : "No person shall be convicted of crime except for violation of a law in force at the time of commission of the act charged as an offence nor shall he be subject to a penalty greater than that applicable at the time of the commission of the offence.'

(e) Japan: ***Article 39*** Says that :

1. "No person shall be held criminally liable for an act which was lawful at the time is was committed."

2. "No person shall be held criminally liable for an act…of which he has acquitted nor shall be in any way be placed in double jeopardy."

3. "No person shall be compelled to testify against himself."

(f) Czechoslovakia: ***Article 35*** Says that "Penalties may only be provided or imposed in virtue of the law."

(g) Costa Rica: ***Article 34*** reads that "No law shall be given retrospective effect to the prejudice of any person or of his vested property rights or of any judicial situation."

Article 36 provides that "In Criminal matters, no one shall be compelled to be a witness against himself, or against his spouse, parents, children or collateral relatives of blood or marriage up to the third degree."

Article 42 provides that "One and the same judge shall be not act as such at different stages of proceedings foe the decision of one and the same point. No one shall be tried more than once for the same offence."

(h) Government of India Act, 1935 Provides

1. No provision existed provision existed prohibiting ex post facto laws.

2. No provision existed regarding autrefois convict or autrefois acquit. but Section 403 of the Criminal procedure code, embodied the principle of autrefois convict or autrefois acquit.

(i) United Nations: ***Article 11(2)*** postulates that "No one shall be held guilty of any penal offence on account of any act or omission which did to constitute a penal offence, under national or international law at the time when it was committed. Nor shall a heavier penalty be imposed than one that was applicable at the time the penal offence was committed."

VIII. Protection of life and liberty in Indian Constitution and other Constitutions.

(a) India : ***Article 21*** provides that "No person shall be deprived of his life or personal liberty except according to procedure established by law."

(b) USA: The ***5th and 4th Amendment*** of the Constitution of USA says that "No personal shall be … deprived of his life, liberty or property without due process of law"

(c) Japan: ***Article XXXI*** says that "No citizen shall be deprived of his personal liberty nor shall any other criminal penalty be imposed, except according to procedure established by law."

(d) Eire: ***Article 40 (4)*** provides that "No citizen shall be deprived of his personal liberty save in accordance with law."

(e) Burma: ***Article 16*** states that "No citizen shall be deprived of his personal liberty, nor his dwelling entered nor his property confiscated save in accordance with law."

(f) Rumania: ***Article 28*** provides that "The individual liberty of the citizens is guaranteed. No person shall be arrested and detained for more than 48 hour without a warrant from the department of prosecutions from the examining authorities appointed by law or an authorization from the courts in conformity with the provisions of the law."

Article 29 states that "The home is inviolable. No person shall enter a citizen's home or residence without his consent save in his presence and in virtue of a written order from the competent authority or if the citizen is caught in the act of committing an offence."

Article 30 states that "No person shall be condemned and suffer any penalty save in virtue of a judicial decision pronounced in conformity with the law."

(g) Czechoslovakia : ***Article 2*** says that " Personal Freedom is guaranteed. It may be limited or withdrawn only in virtue of the law.

Article 3 states:

1. No person shall be tried except in the cases laid down by the law and then only by court or authority competent under the manner prescribed by law.
2. Unless caught in the act of committing an offence no person shall be arrested except on the written order of a judge, reason therefore The order shall be delivered at the time of arrest or if this is not possible within 18 hours there after.
3. No person shall be taken into custody by a public official except in the case prescribed by law; he must then be either released within 48 hours or brought before a court or authority which is competent to proceed with the case from the view of its nature."

(h) The federal Republic of Germany (old): ***Section 2*** provides:

1. Every one has the right to develop his personality freely in so far as does not violate the rights of others or offend against the Constitutional order or moral law.
2. Every one has the right of personal security of life and limb. Personal liberty is inviolable. These rights can only be curtailed by virtue of a law.

(i) Hungary: ***Article 57*** states that "The Hungarian people's republic safeguards the freedom and inviolability of the home and correspondence of its citizens."

(j) Germany: ***Section 8*** states that "Personal liberty, inviolability of the home, secrecy of postal communications and the right to settle in any place desired are guaranteed. The state can only take away these freedoms in pursuance of the laws applying to all citizens."

(k) Costa Rica: ***Section 20*** of the Republic Constitution states that "Every man is free in the Republic. No one who is under the protection of its laws shall be a slave."

Section 23 states that "The home and all other private premises of persons living in the republic shall be inviolable-provided that they may be entered on written order of a competent judicial officer or to prevent offence from being committed or left unpunished or t avoid grave injury to persons or property subject to what is prescribed by law."

(l) United Nations: ***Article 3*** **and** *7* of the draft Declaration of Human Rights provides that "Every one has the right to life, liberty and security of person." "No one shall be subjected to arbitrary arrest or detention."

(m) Danzig: ***Article*** *74* states that "The liberty of the person has been declared inviolable and no limitation or deprivation of personal liberty may be imposed by public authority except by virtue of a law."

(n) Korea: The Korean Constitution states that "No citizen shall be arrested etc. unless according to law."

IX. Protection against Arrest and detention in Indian Constitution and other Constitutions.

(a) India : ***Article*** *22* provides :

1. No person who is arrested shall be detained in custody without being informed, as soon as may be, of the grounds for such arrest nor shall he be denied the right to consult and to be defended by a legal practitioner of his choice.
2. Every person who is arrested and detained in custody shall be produced before the nearest magistrate within a period of twenty four hours of such arrest excluding the time necessary for the journey from the place of arrest to the court of the magistrate and no such person shall be detained in custody beyond the said period without the authority of a magistrate
3. Nothing in clause(1) and(2) shall apply:

(a) to any person who for the time being is an enemy alien; or

(b) to any person who is arrested or detained under any law providing for preventive detention.

4. No law providing for preventive detention shall authorise the detention of a person for a longer period than three months unless-
    a. An Advisory Board consisting of persons who are, or have been, or are qualified to be appointed as, judges of a High Court has reported before the expiration of the said period of three months that there is in its opinion sufficient cause for such detention. Provided that nothing in this sub-clause shall authorize the detention of any person beyond the maximum period prescribed by any law made by Parliament under sub-clause (b) of clause (7); or

b. Such person is detained in accordance with the provision of any law made by Parliament under sub-clause (a) and (b) of clause (7).

5. When any person is detained in pursuance of an order made under any law providing for preventive detention, the authority making the order shall, as may be, communicate to such person the grounds on which the order has been made and shall afford him the earliest opportunity of making a representation against the order.
6. Nothing in clause (5) shall require the authority making any such order as is referred to in that clause to disclose facts which such authority considers to be against the public interest to disclose.
7. Parliament may by law prescribe-

a. The circumstances under which and the class or classes of case in which, a person may be detained for a period longer than three months under any law providing for preventive detention without obtaining he opinion of an Advisory board in accordance with the provisions of sub-clause (a) of clause (4);
b. The maximum period for which any person may in any class or classes of case be detained under any law providing for preventive detention' and
c. The procedure to be followed by an advisory board in an inquiry under sub-clause (a) of clause (4).

(b) America (USA): The *6th* Amendment provides that "In all criminal prosecutions the accused shall enjoy the right to a speedy and Public, and to be informed of the nature and cause of the accusations to be confronted with the witness against him to have compulsory process for obtaining witnesses in his favour, and to have the assistance of counsel for his defence."

(c) Japan: ***Article XXXIV*** states that "No person shall be arrested or detained without being at once informed of the charges against him or without adequate cause; and upon court in his presence and the presence of his counsel."

(C) Right against Exploitation in Indian Constitution and other Constitutions

(i) Prohibition of Traffic in Human beings and force labour in Indian Constitution and other Constitutions.

(a) India : ***Article 23*** provides that

i. Traffic in human beings and beggars and other similar forms of forced labour are prohibited and any contravention of this provision shall be an offence punishable in accordance with law.

ii. Nothing in this Article shall prevent the state from imposing compulsory service. The state from imposing compulsory service. The state shall not make any discrimination on grounds only of religion, race, caste or class or any of them.

(b) USA: 13th Amendment declares:

Section 1 Provides that "Neither slavery nor involuntary servitude except as punishment for crime where of the party shall have been duly convicted, shall exist within the United States, or any place subject to their jurisdiction.

Section 2 Provides that "The congress shall have power to enforce this Article by appropriate Legislation."

(c) Burma: ***Article 19*** states that "Traffic in human beings and Forced labour in any form, involuntary servitude except as a punishment for crime where of the party shall have been duly convicted, shall be prohibited"

Explanation: "Nothing in this section shall prevent the state from imposing compulsory service for public purpose without any discrimination on grounds of birth race religion or class."

(d) Japan: ***Article XVIII*** of the Japanese constitution of 1946 states that "no person shall be held in bondage of any kind' involuntary servitude, except as punishment for crime, is prohibited."

(e) United Nations: ***Article 4*** states that "no one shall be held in slavery or servitude' slavery and the slave trade shall be prohibited in all their forms.

(f) Federal Republic of Germany (old): ***Article 12*** enunciates:

1. "All Germans have the right of free choice of occupation, place and employment and place of training. The pursuit of occupation may be regulated by legislation.
2. No one shall be forced to do a particular job except in virtue of an establishment general obligation to perform a public service lying equally upon all.
3. Forced labour is only permissible where a sentence of imprisonment is ordered by a court."

(ii) Prohibition of Employment of Children in Factories, etc., in Indian Constitution and other Constitution

(a) India : ***Article 24*** provides that no child below the age of fourteen years shall be employed to work in any factory or mine or engaged in any other hazardous employment.

(b) Czechoslovakia: ***Article 11*** of the Constitution provides that the states guarantees to children special care and protection and in particular, takes systematic measures to increase the population of the nation.

Article 29 states:

1. Every person possesses the right to public health. All citizens possess the right to medical care and to provisions in old age and also during incapacity for work and when unable to maintain themselves.
2. Women are entitled to special care during pregnancy and maternity, and children and young persons are entitled to all facilities for full physical and mental development."

(c) Germany: ***Article 18*** of the German Democratic Republic provides that "Youth is protected against exploitation and guarded against moral, physical, and spiritual neglect. Child labour is prohibited."

(d) Costa Rica: ***Section 51*** states that the family, as a natural element and foundation of society, shall be entitled to the special protection to the state. Mothers, children, the aged and helpless invalids shall likewise be entitled to this protection.

D. Right to Freedom of Religion in Indian Constitution and other Constitution:

(i) Freedom of Conscience and Free Profession, Practice and Propagation of religion in Indian Constitution and other Constitution.

(a) India : ***Article 25*** provides that:

1. Subject to public order, morality and health and to other provision of this part, all persons are equally entitled to freedom of conscience and the right freely to profess, practice and propagate religion.
2. Nothing in this Article shall affect the operation of any existing law or prevent the state from making any law

a. regulating or restriction any economic financial, political or other secular activity, which may be associated with religious practice'

b. Providing for social welfare and reforms of the throwing open of Hindu religious institutions of a public character to all classes and section of Hindus.

Explanation: The wearing and carrying of Kirpans shall be deemed to be included in the profession of the Sikh religion. Hindus shall include Sikh, Jain or Buddhist Religions.

(b) USA: The First Amendment states that Congress shall make no law respecting an establishment of religion or prohibiting the free exercise thereof.

(c) Australia: ***Section 116*** states that "the commonwealth shall not make any law for establishment of religion or for imposing any religious observance or for prohibiting the free exercise of any religion and no religious test shall be required as a qualification for any office or public trust under the commonwealth."

(d) Japan: ***Article 20*** say that "freedom of religion is guaranteed to all… no person shall be compelled to take part in any religious act, celebration, rite or practice.

(e) Burma: ***Article 20*** declares that "all persons are equally entitled to freedom of conscience and the right freely to profess and practice religion subject to public order, morality or health and to the other provisions of this Chapter. But it shall not include any economic, financial, political or other secular activities that may be associated with religious practice. It shall not debar the state from enacting laws for the purpose of social welfare and reform.

Article 21 declares that "The state shall not impose any disabilities or make any discrimination on the ground of religious faith or belief. The abuse of religion for political purposes is forbidden and any act which is intended or likely to promote feelings of hatred, enmity or discord between racial or religious communities or sects is contrary to this constitution and may be made punishable by law."

(f) China: ***Article 36*** states that "The people shall have the freedom of religious belief."

(g) Yugoslavia: ***Article 12*** State that Liberty of religion and of conscience shall be guaranteed. All recognized religions shall be equal before law and may be practiced in public.

(h) Switzerland: ***Article 49*** Provides that liberty of conscience and creed in inviolable. No person may be compelled to became a member of any religious instruction, perform any act of religion, or incur any penalties, of any kind what so ever by reason of his religious opinions…The exercise of civil or political requirement or conditions of any kind what so ever.

"**Article 50** says that the free exercise of religion is guaranteed within limits compatible with public order and morality."

(i) Eire: ***Article 44 (2)*** states, that "Freedom of conscience and the free profession and practice of religion are subject to public order and morality guaranteed to every citizen."

1. The state guarantees not to endow any religion.
2. The state shall not impose any disabilities or make any discrimination on the ground of religious profession belief or status.

(j) France: ***Clause (1)*** of Preamble provides that "No one ought to be disturbed on account of his opinion, even religious, provided their manifestation does not derange the public order established by law."

(k) Ceylon(Sri Lanka): ***Section 29 (2)*** of the Ceylon (Constitution) order provides that "No such law shall"

a. Prohibit or restrict free exercise of any religion or

b. Make a person of any community or religion liable to disabilities or restrictions to which persons of other communities or religions are not made liable.

c. Confer on any persons of any community or religion any privilege or advantage which is not conferred on persons of other communities or religions.

(l) Rumania: ***Section 27*** says that "Freedom of conscience and religion are guaranteed by the state. The different religions may be freely organized and practiced if their ritual and practices are not contrary to the Constitution, public, safety or good morals. And religious denominations shall be regulated by law.

(m) Czechoslovakia: ***Article 15-*** guaranteed the freedom of conscience.

Article 16 provides that:

(i) Every Person has the right to profess in private and in public any religious creed or to be without religious persuasion.

(ii) All religious persuasion and persons of no religious persuasion are equal before the law.

Article 17 (1) Provides that every person is free to perform the acts connected with any religious persuasion or the absence of religious persuasion. No persons shall be constrained by direct or indirect means to take part in such acts.

(n) Germany: ***Section 4*** says that

1. Freedom of faith and conscience and freedom of religious and ideological profession are inviolable.

2. The undisturbed practice of religion is guaranteed.

3. No one shall be forced to serve in war as a combatant against his conscience.

(o) Hungary: ***Section 54*** states that "people have the liberty of conscience of all citizens and freedom of religious worship. In order to ensure liberty of conscience the Hungarian People's Republic separates the church from the state."

(p) Costa Rica: ***Section 76*** says that Roman Catholic Apostolic Religion is the religion of the state, which contributes to its maintenance without impeding the Free exercise in the republic of other forms of worship not contrary to universal morality and good behavior.

(q) United Nations: ***Article 19*** of UN Declarations of Human Right postulates that "Every one has the right to freedom of thought, conscience, and religion. This right includes freedom to change his religion or belief and freedom, either alone or in community with others and in public or private, to manifest his religion or belief in teaching practice, worship and observation."

(ii) Freedom to manage affairs in Indian Constitution and other Constitution

(a) India : ***Article 26*** provides that Subject to public order, morality and health, every religious denomination or any section thereof shall have the right to establish and maintain institutions for religious and charitable purpose; to manage its own affairs in matters of religion and to own and acquire movable and immovable property and to administer such property in accordance with law.

(b) USA: The first Amendment says that " Congress shall make no law respecting an establishment of religion.

(c) Eire : ***Article 44(2)*** states, that "Every religious denomination shall have the right to manage its own affairs, own acquire and administer movable and immovable, and maintain institutions for religious or charitable purpose and the property of any religious denomination or any educational institution shall not be diverted save for necessary works of public utility and on payment of compensation."

(d) Sri Lanka (Ceylon): ***Section 29 (2)*** provides that "No such law shall alter the constitution of any religious body except with the consent of the governing authority of that body provided that, in any case where the religious body is incorporated by law no such alteration shall be made except at the request of the governing authority of that body."

(e) Rumania: ***Section*** *27* States that the organization and functioning of the different religious denominations shall be regulated by law."

(f) Germany: ***section 41 (2)*** says that "institutions belonging to religious societies, religious acts and religious instruction shall not be misused for unconstitutional objects or in the interest of a political party."

Section 43 states that :

1. "every religious society shall order and administer its own affairs subject to the law applying to all.

2. The religious societies shall continue to be corporations in public law in so far as they were so hitherto. Other religious societies shall receive like right on application."

Section 45 **states:**

1. The forms of public support given to the religious societies in virtue of law contract of special legal title, shall be commuted by law.

2. The property and other right of the religious societies and unions in their establishment foundations and other property for purpose of public worship instruction and charity are guaranteed."

(iii) Freedom not to Pay taxes for religious Promotion in Indian Constitution and other Constitution.

(a) India : ***Article 27*** provides that "No person shall be compelled to pay any taxes, the proceeds of which are specifically appropriated in payment of expenses for the promotion of maintenance of any particular religion or religious denomination."

(b) USA: the first amendment 1791 provides that "the congress shall make no law respecting establishment of religion."

(c) Japan: ***Article 22*** stats that "No religious organization shall receive ay privileges from the states, nor exercise any political authority."

(d) Switzerland***: Article 40*** stats that "No person may be compelled to pay taxes the proceeds of which are specially appropriated in payment of the purely religious expenses of any religious community of which he is not a member."

(e) Rumania: ***Section 27*** states that “The different religions may be freely organized and practiced."

(f) Germany: ***section 4*** states:

1. freedom of faith and conscience and freedom of religions and ideological profession are inviolable .
2. the undisturbed practice of religion is guaranteed.
3. No one shall be forced to serve in wartime as a combatant against his conscience the detailed rules shall be prescribed by federal legislation.

Section 43 (4) say that " The religious societies in public law shall be entitled to levy taxes from their members on the basis of state taxation lists subject to general provisions."

Section 45 (1) states that

“the forms of public support given to the religious societies in virtue of law contract or special legal title shall be commuted by law.”

(iv) Freedom not to attend religious instruction in Indian Constitution and other Constitution.

(a) India : ***Article 28*** Provides:

1. No religious instruction shall be provided in any educational institution wholly maintained out of state funds.
2. Nothing in clause (1) shall apply to any educational institution which is administrated by the State but has been established under any endowment or trust which requires that religious instruction shall be imparted in such institutions.
3. No person attending any educational institution recognised by the state or receiving aid out of state funds shall be required to take part in any religious instruction that may be imparted in such institution or to attend any religious worship that may be conducted in such institution or in any premises attached thereto unless such person or if such person is a minor or his guardian, has given his consent thereto.

(b) Germany*: section 7 (2)* provides:

1. The person responsible for bringing up children shall have the right to decide whether the child shall attend religious instruction.
2. Religious instruction shall be part of the curriculum in all public schools other than non-denominational schools. Religious instruction shall subject to state supervision, be given in accordance with the principles of religious societies. No teacher shall be required against his will to give religious instruction.

(c) Japan: ***Article XX*** says that "legislation providing state aid for schools shall not be such as to affect prejudicially the right of any child to attend a school receiving public money without attending religious instruction in that school."

(d) Rumania: ***section 17*** states:

1. Every person is free to perform the acts connected with any religious persuasions. This right shall not, however, be exercised in a manner contrary to public order and morality. It shall not be permitted to be misused for non religious ends.
2. No person shall be constrained by direct or indirect means to take part in such acts.

(e) Germany : ***section 44*** says that The right of the church to give religious instruction in school premises is guaranteed. The religious instruction shall be given by persons chosen by the church . No one shall be forced to give or prevented from giving religious instruction . The person responsible for the child's upbringing shall decide whether it shall attend religious instruction or not.

Section 46 (1) states that "In so for as there is need for divine services and spiritual ministrations in hospitals, prisons and other public establishments the religious societies shall be allowed to perform acts of religion. No one shall be compelled to participate in such acts."

E. Cultural and Educational Rights in Indian and other Constitutions.

(i) Protection of interest of Minorities in Indian Constitution and other Constitution.

(a) India :***Article 29*** Provides

1. Any section of the citizens residing the territory of India or any part thereof having a distinct language script or culture of its own shall have the right to conserve the same.
2. No citizen shall be denied admission into any educational institution maintained by the state or receiving aid out of state funds on grounds only of religion, race, caste, language or any of them.

(b) Burma***: Article 22*** provides, that "No minority religious racial or linguistic shall be discriminated against in regard to admission into state educational institutions."

(c) Rumania: ***section 22*** states that "In the Rumania people's republic all citizens have the right to education. The state provides for the exercise of this right by organizing and developing compulsory free primary education by granting state scholarships to meritorious pupils and students and by organising and developing vocational and technical education."

Section 23 **states** that "The states encourages and supports the development of science and art and organizes research institutes, libraries publishing house, theatres, museums and musical academies."

(d) Czechoslovakia: ***section 12*** says that "All citizens have the right to education. The state takes care to ensure that every person receives education and training in accordance with his abilities and having regards to the needs of the community."

Section 13: Says that " All schools are state schools. elementary education is uniform compulsory and free."

Section 14: says that "All education and instruction shall be so arranged as to be in harmony with the results of scientific research and compatible with the democratic order."

Section 19**:**

1. freedom to engage in creative mental activity is guaranteed. Scientific research and publication of its results and likewise art and its expressions are free in so far as they do not violate the penal law.
2. cultural assets are under the protection of the state. The state ensures that they are accessible to all and supports science and art in the interests of the cultural development of the nation progress and the general welfare. In particular it takes care that creative workers are assured of favorable conditions for their work.

(e) Germany: ***section 5 (3)*** state that "Art and science, research and teaching are unrestricted. The freedom to teach does not release the teacher from his duty to be loyal to the constitution."

Section *7* says that "The whole educational system shall be under the supervision of the state and the right to establish private schools is guaranteed."

(f) Costa Rica: ***section*** *77* states that "Public education shall be organized as complete process in which the various levels are correlated from the pre school stage to the university."

Section 78 Says that "Primary education is compulsory primary preschool and secondary education is free and is provided at national expense. The state shall facilitate the higher studies of persons who lack the necessary funds."

Section 80**:** States that "Private initiative in educational matters shall receive state encouragement in the manner prescribed by law."

Section 8*7***:** states that "Freedom of teaching is a fundamental principle of university education."

Section 89**:** states that "The cultural aims of the republic include the protection of natural beauty the preservation and extension of the historic and artistic inheritance of the nation and support of private initiative for scientific and artistic progress."

(ii) Right of Minorities to establish and admission educational institutions in Indian Constitution and other Constitution

(a) India : ***Article 30*** provides :

1. All minorities, whether based on religion or language shall have the right to establish and administer educational institutions of their choice.

1-A. In making any law providing for compulsory equation of any properly of any properly of an educational institution established and administered by a minority, referred to in clause(i) the state shall ensure that the amount fixed or determined under any law for the acquisition of such property is such as would not restrict or abrogate the right guaranteed under that clause

2. The state shall not in granting aid to educational institutions discriminate against any educational institution on the ground that is under the management of a minority whether based no religion or language.

(b) Eire: ***Article 42 (3)*** of the 1937 constitution provides that "The state shall not oblige parents in violation of their conscience and lawful preference to send their children to school established by the state or to any particular type of school designated by the state."

Article 44 (4) states that "legislation providing state aid for schools shall not discriminate between schools under the management of different religious denominations."

(c) Rumania: ***section 24*** states that in the Rumanian constitution people's right of using their native language and of organizing education at all levels in the said language is guaranteed to the other nationalities living side by side with the Rumanian people.

(d) Canada: In the Canadian constitution it is stated in *section 93* that in and for each province the legislature may exclusively make in relation to education subject to and according to the following provisions.

1. Nothing in any such law shall prejudicially affect any right or privilege with respect to denominational schools which any class of persons have by law in the province or the union.

2. All the powers privileges and duties at the union by law conferred and imposed in upper Canada on the separate schools and schools trustees of the queen's roman catholic subjects shall

be and the same are hereby extended to the dissentient schools of the queen's protestant and roman catholic subjects in Quebec.

(F) Saving of certain laws in Indian Constitution and other Constitution

(i) Saving of laws providing for acquisition of estates etc.

(a) India : ***Article 31-A :***

Not withstanding anything contained in Article 13 no law providing for:

(a) the acquisition by the states of any estate or any rights therein or the extinguishments or modification of any such rights, or

(b) The taking over of the management of any property by the state for a limited period either in the public interest or in order to secure the proper management of the property, or

(c) The amalgamation of two or more corporations either in the public interest or in order to secure the proper management of any of the corporations, or

(d) The extinguishments or modification of any rights of managing agents secretaries and treasurers managing directors, directors or management of corporations or of any voting rights of shareholders thereof or

(e) The extinguishments or modification of an right accruing by virtue of any agreement leads or license for the purpose of searching for, or winning, any mineral or mineral oil, or the premature termination or cancellation of any such agreement, lease or license, shall be deemed to be void on the ground that it is inconsistent with, or takes away or abridge any of the rights conferred by Article 14, 19.

Provided that where such law is made by the Legislature of a state the provisions of this shall not apply thereto unless such law having been reserved for the consideration of the president, has received his assent.

Provided further that where any law makes any provision for the acquisition by the state of any estate and where any land comprised therein is held by a person under his personal cultivation, it shall not be lawful for the state to acquire any portion of such land as is within the ceiling limits applicable to him under any law for the time being in force or any building or structure standing thereon or appurtenant there to unless the law relating to the acquisition of such land building or structure provides for payment of compensation at rate which shall not be less than the market value thereof.

a. The expression "estate" shall in relation to any local area, have the same meaning as that expression or its local equivalent has in the existing law relating to land tenures in force in that area and shall also include:

i. Any Jagir, inam or Muafi or other similar grant and in the state of Tamilnadu and Kerala any Jenman Right;

ii. Any land held under ryotwari settlement;

iii. Any land held or let for purposes of agriculture or for purpose ancillary thereto, including waste land forest land land for pasture or sites of buildings and other structures occupied by cultivators of land agricultural labours and village artisans;

b. The expression "right", in relation to an estate, shall include any rights vesting in a proprietor, sub proprietor, under proprietor, tenure holder, raiyat, under rayat or other intermediary and any rights or privileges in respect of land revenue.

(ii) Validation of certain acts and regulations:

(a) India : ***31-B*** provides that Without prejudice to the generality of the provisions contained in article 31-a none of the Acts and Regulations specified in the Ninth schedule nor any of the Provision thereof shall be deemed to be void, or ever to have become void, on the ground that such Act, Regulation or Provision is inconsistent with, or takes away or abridges any of the rights conferred by any provisions of this part andnotwith standing any judgment, decree or order of any court or tribunal to the contrary, each of the said Acts and Regulation shall, subject to the Power any competent legislature to repeat or amend it continue in force.

(b) There is no corresponding Provision in any Foreign Constitutions.

(iii) Saving of laws giving effect to certain Directive Principles:

(a) India :***31-C*** provides that Notwithstanding anything contained in article 13, no law giving effect to the policy of the state towards securing all or any of the principles laid down in Part IV shall be deemed to be void on the ground that is inconsistent with or takes away or abridges any of the rights conferred by article 14 or19 and no law containing a declaration that it is for giving effect to such policy shall be called in question in any court on the ground that it dose not give effect to such policy.

Provided that where such law is made by the Legislature of a state, the provisions of this article shall not apply there to unless such law having been reserved for the consideration of the president has received his assent.

(b) There is no corresponding Provision in any Foreign Constitutions.

G. Right to Constitutional Remedies in Indian Constitution and other Constitution.

(i) India: Article 32 provide the

1. The right to move the Supreme Court by appropriate proceedings for the enforcement of the right conferred by this part is guaranteed.
2. The supreme court shall have power to issue directions or orders or writs including writs in the nature of Habeas corpus, Mandamus, Prohibition Quo warranto and Certiorari, whichever may be appropriate for the enforcement of any of the right conferred by this part.
3. without prejudice to the powers conferred on the supreme court by clause (1) and (2), parliament may by law empower any other court to exercise within the local limits of its jurisdiction all or any of the power exercisable by the Supreme Court under clause(2).
4. The right guaranteed under this article shall not be suspended except as otherwise provided for by this constitution.

Corresponding Foreign Provisions

(a) Burma: ***Article 15 (1)*** of the Burmese constitution is a replica of Article 32 (1) of the constitution of India.

Article 25 clause (2) states that "Without prejudice to the powers that may be vested in this behalf in other court the Supreme Court shall have power to issue direction in the nature of habeas corpus, mandamus, prohibition, quo warrant and certiorari appropriate to the rights guaranteed in this chapter."

Article 25 (3) of the Burmese constitution States that "The right to enforce these remedies shall not be suspended unless in times of war invasion rebellion, insurrection or grave emergency, the public safety may so require."

***Article 27* states that** "Except in times of invasion rebellion insurrection or grave emergency no citizen be denied redress by due process of law for any actionable wrong done to or suffered by him."

(b)USA: ***Article 1 section 9 (2)*** postulates that "The privilege of the writ of habeas corpus shall not be suspended unless when in cases of rebellion or invasion the public safety may require it ."

(c) Eire: ***Article 23 (3)*** posits that Nothing in this constitution shall be invoked to invalidate any law enacted by the oireachtas which is expressed to be for the purpose of securing the public safety and the preservation of the state in times of war or armed rebellion or to nullify any act done or purporting to be done in pursuance of such law.

"In this sub section time of war includes a time when there is taking place an armed conflict in which the state ins not a participant but in respect of which each of the house of the oireachtas shall be resolved that arising out of such armed conflict a national emergency exists affecting the vital interest of the state.[120]

"Time of war shall also include such time after termination of the said armed conflict as may elapse until each of the houses of oireachtas shall have resolved that the said national emergency occasioned by such armed conflict has ceased to exist.[121]

(d) Germany: ***Article 48*** postulates that "Where public security and order and seriously disturbed or endangered within the president of the Reich may take the measures necessary for their restoration intervening in case of need with the help of armed. Forces for this purpose he is permitted for the time being to abrogate either wholly or partially the fundamental right laid down in Article 114, 115, 117, 118, 123, 124, and 153."

---

[120] Inserted by First Amendment of the Constitution Act, 1939
Inserted by Second Amendment of the Constitution Act, 1941

"The president of the Reich must without delay, inform the Reichstag of any measures taken in accordance with paragraph 1 or 2 of this Article. Such measures shall be abrogated upon the demand of Reichstag."

"Where there is danger in delay the state government may take provisional measures of the kind indicated in paragraph 2, for its own territory. such measures shall be abrogated upon the demand of the president of the Reich or the Reichstag."

(ii) India : Article 33 Provides Parliament may, by law determine to what extent any of the rights conferred by this part shall, in their application to-

a. the members of the armed forces, or
b. the members of the force charged with the maintenance of public order; or
c. persons employed in any bureau or other organization established by the state for purpose of intelligence or counter intelligence; or
d. persons employed in or in connection with, the telecommunication system set up for the purpose of any force, bureau or organization referred to in clause (a) to (c), be restricted or abrogated so as to ensure the proper discharge of their duties and the maintenance of discipline among them.

Corresponding Foreign Provisions

(a) Burma: ***Article 28*** of the Burmese constitution is on the same lined as article 33 of India.

(b) Eire: **article 38 (4)** and (6) postulates:

1. "Military tribunals may be established for the trial of offences against military law alleged to have been committed by persons while subject to military law and also to deal with a state of war or armed rebellion.

2. “A member of the defence forced not on active service shall not be tried by any court martial or other military tribunal for an offence congnisable by the civil courts unless such offence is within the jurisdiction of any court martial or other military tribunal under any law for the enforcement of military discipline.

“The provisions of article 24 and 35 of the constitution in shall not apply to any court or tribunal set up under section (3) or section(4) of this article.”

(iii) India : Article 34 provides that

"Not withstanding anything in the foregoing provisions of this part, parliament may by law indemnify any person in the service of the union or of a state or any other person in respect of any act done by him in connection with the maintenance or restoration of order in any area within the territory of India where martial law was in force or validate any sentence passed punishment inflicted for feature ordered or other act done under martial law in such area.

No analogous provision anywhere else.

(iv) India : Article 35 Provides: Not withstanding anything is this constitution:

a) Parliament shall have and the Legislature of state not have power to make laws

1. With respect to any of the matters which under clause (3) of Article 16, clause (3) of Article 32 article 33 and Article 34 may be provided for by law made by parliament and
2. For prescribing punishment for those acts which are declared to be offence under this part,

and parliament shall, as soon as may be after the commencement of this constitution make laws for prescribing punishment for the acts referred to in sub clause (ii);

b) Any law in force immediately before the commencement of this constitution in the territory of India with respect to any of matters referred to in sub clause (i) Of clause (a) or providing for punishment for any act referred to in sub clause(ii) of that clause shall subject to the terms thereof and to any adaptations and modifications that may be made therein under Article 372 continue in force until altered or repealed or amended by parliament.

Explanation : in this article the expression "law in force" has the same meaning as in Article 372.

Corresponding Foreign Provisions

(a) Burma: ***Article 39*** provides that "The parliament shall make laws to give effect to those provision of this chapter which require such legislation and to prescribe punishment for those acts which are declared to be offences in this chapter and not already punishable."

2. Directive Principles under Indian Constitution and other Constitution

The provisions of Directive Principles found under various world constitutions corresponding to the provisions of directive principles under chapter 3 of the constitution of India. These provisions are as follows:

India Article 36 says that the State has the same meaning as in Part III.

There is no corresponding provisions anywhere

India Article 37 says that the provisions contained in the part shall not be enforceable by any court but the principle laid down are nevertheless fundamental in the governance of the country and it shall be the duty of the state to apply these principles in making laws.

Analogic provisions of Article 37:

Burma: ***Article 32*** postulates that "The principles set forth in this chapter are intended for the general guidance of the state. The application of these principles in legislation and administration shall be the care of the state but shall not be enforceable in any court of law."

Eire : ***Article 45*** *posits that* "The principles of social policy set forth in this Article are intended for the general guidance of the Oireachtas. The application of these principles in the making of laws shall be the care of the oireachtas and shall not be cognizable by any court under any of the provisions of the constitution"

A. Social and Economic character in Indian Constitution and other Constitutions

(i) Social order based in justice in Indian Constitution and other Constitutions

(a) India : Article 38 Provides

1. The state shall strive to promote the welfare of the people by securing and protecting as effectively as it may a social order in which justice social economic and political shall inform all the institution of the national life.
2. The state shall, in particular strive to minimise the inequalities in income and endeavour to eliminate inequalities in status, facilities and opportunities not only amongst individual but also amongst groups of people residing in different areas or engaged in different vocations.

(b) Eire : ***Article 45***, (1) Provides that "The state shall strive to promote the welfare of the whole people by securing and protecting as effectively as it may a social order in which justice and charity shall inform all the institutions of the national life."

(ii) Economic Justice in Indian Constitution and other Constitutions

(a) India : Article 39 Provides The state shall in particular, direct its policy towards Securing-

a. that the citizen , men and women equally have the right to an adequate means of livelihood;
b. that the ownership and control of the material resources of the community are so distributed as best to subserve to the common good;
c. that the operation of the economic system does not result in the concentration of wealth and means of production to the common detriment;
d. that there is equal pay for equal work for both men and women;
e. that the health and strength of workers, men and women and the tender age of children are not abused and that citizens are not forced by economic necessity to enter avocations unsuited to their age or strength;
f. that children are given opportunities and facilities to develop in a healthy manner and in conditions of freedom and dignity and that childhood and youth are protected against exploitation and against moral and material abandonment.

(b) Former USSR :Article 118 Provides that "Citizens of USSR have the right to work . That is the right to guaranteed employment and payment for their work in accordance with its quantity and quality. The right to work is ensured by the socialist organisation of the national economy, the steady growth of the productive forces of soviet society, the elimination of the possibility of economic crises, and the abolition of unemployment."

Article 120 provides that "Citizen of the USSR have the right to maintenance in old age and also in case of sickness or disability.

This right is ensured by the extensive development of social insurance of factory and office workers at state expense, free medical service for the working people and the provision of a wide network of health resorts for the use of the working people."

(c) Burma: ***Article (1)*** provides that "The state shall ensure that the strength and health of workers and the tender age of children shall not be abused and that they shall not be forced by economic necessity to take up occupations unsuited to their sex age and strength."

(d) Eire : ***Article 45***, (2) and (4) of the constitution Provides :

1. "The state shall, in particular direct its policy toward securing

a. that the citizen (all of whom, men and women equally have the right to an adequate means of livelihood) may through their occupations find the means of making reasonable provision for their domestic needs;

b. that the ownership and control of the material resources of the community may be so distributed amongst private individuals and the various classes as best to sub serve the common good;

c. that especially the operation of free competition shall not be allowed so to develop as to result in the concentration of the ownership or control of essential commodities in a few individuals to the common detriment."

2. The state shall favour and where necessary supplement private initiative in industry and commerce.
3. The state shall endeavour to secure that private enterprise shall be so conduced as to ensure reasonable efficiency in the production and distribution of goods and as to protect the public against unjust exploitation.

4. The state shall endeavour to secure that the strength health of workers men and women and tender age of children shall not be abused and that citizen shall not be forced by economic necessity to enter avocations unsuited to their sex age of strength."

(e) Rumania: ***section 19*** states that "All citizens have the right to work. The state gradually secures the exercise of this right by the planned organization and development of national economy."

Sections 25 provides that "Women have equal rights with men in all domains of state, economic social cultural and political life and in private law.

For equal work, women are entitled to remuneration equal to that of men."

Section 25 states that "The state safeguards public health by establishing and developing health services and by encouraging and assisting public training."

Section 26 says that The mother and children up to the age of 18 years shall enjoy special protection, prescribed by law.

(f) Czechoslovakia: ***section 1 (2)*** states that

"Men and women have equal status in the family and in the community and equal access to education and to all callings offices and dignities."

Section 26: provides:

1. All citizens possess the right to work
2. This right is secured in particular by the organization of work directed by the state in accordance with a planned economy.
3. Women are entitled in respect of pregnancy, maternity and child care to special treatment as regards their conditions of employment.

4. The law shall prescribe special conditions of employment as regards young persons, having regards to the requirements of their physical and mental development.

Section 27: provides :

1. All working members of the population possess the right to just remuneration for the work done.
2. In equal conditions men and women are entitled to equal remuneration for equal work.

Section 146: States that "The means of production are either national property of the property of the popular co operative or in the private ownership of individual produce."

Section 162: States that "By means of unified economic plan, the state directs all economic activities (in particular production, trade and transportation) so as to ensure an adequate level of national consumption, to increase the quantity, quality and flow of production and gradually raise the standard of living on the population.

(g) Costa Rica : ***Section 50*** posits that The state shall endeavour to procure the greatest will being of all the inhabitants of the country by appropriate distribution of wealth.

Section 51**:** Provides that "Mothers children the aged and helpless invalids shall likewise be entitled to this protection."

Section 56 Provides that Work is the right of the individual and an obligation towards society. The state must ensure that all have an honest and useful occupation which is properly paid, and must prevent such occupation from giving rise to conditions which in any way impair the liberty or dignity of the individual or reduce labour to the level of mere commodity.

(h) UNO: ***Article 21 (2)*** of the United Nations Declaration of Human Rights postulates that "Every one has right to equal pay for equal work."

(i) France : The preamble to constitution of 1946 postulates that "The law guarantees to women equal rights with men in all dominions."

B. Social Security character in Indian and other Constitutions

(i) Equal Justice and free Legal Aid in Indian Constitution and other Constitution

(a) India : Article 39 A provides that "the state shall secure that the operation of the legal system promotes justice, on a basis of equal opportunity, and shall in particular provide free legal aid, by suitable legislation or schemes or in any other way, to ensure that opportunities for securing justice are not denied to any citizen by reason of economic or other disabilities."

(b) No corresponding Provision anywhere.

(ii) Social services in Indian Constitution and other Constitution

(a) India : Article 41 Provides that "the state shall, within the limits of its economic capacity and development, make effective provision for securing the right to work to education and to public assistance in cases of unemployment, old age, sickness and disablement and in other cases of undeserved want."

(b) USSR (Russia): Article 42 and 43 provides that "Citizen of the USSR have the right to maintenance in old age and also in case of sickness or loss of capacity to work. This right is ensured by the expensive development of social insurance of workers and employees at state expense free medical service for the working people and the provision of a wide network of health resorts for the use of the working people."

Article 45: Provides that "Citizens of the USSR have the right to education. This right is ensured by universal compulsory elementary education including higher education, being free of charge by the system of state stipends for the overwhelming majority of students in the universities and colleges, by instruction in schools being conducted in the native language and by the organization in the factories state farms, machine and tractor stations and collective farms of free vocational technical and agronomic attaining for the working people.

(c) Burma: ***Article 33*** stipulates:

1. The state shall direct its policy towards securing to each citizen the right to work;
2. The right to maintenance in old age and sickness or loss of capacity to work;
3. The right to rest and leisure and
4. The right to education.

Article 40 further states that "The state shall ensure disabled ex servicemen a decent living and free occupational training. The children of fallen solders and children orphaned by war shall be under the special care of the state.

(d) France: "Every one has the duty to work and the right to obtain employment. Every human being who because of his age, his physical or mental condition or because of the economic situation finds himself unable to work, has the right to obtain from the community the means to lead a decent existence. The nation guarantees equal access of children and adults to education professional training and culture."

(iii) Condition of Work in Indian Constitution and other Constitution

(a) India : Article 42 Provides that the state shall make provision for just and humane conditions of work and maternity relief.

(b) Burma: ***Article 37*** states that "The state shall specially direct its policy towards protecting the interests of nursing mothers and infants by establishing maternity and infant welfare centers, children's homes and day nurseries and towards securing to mothers in employment the right to leave with pay before and after child birth.

(iv) Living of Wages in Indian Constitution and other Constitution

(a) India : Article 43 provides that the "The state shall endeavour to secure, by suitable legislation or economic organization or in any other way to all workers agricultural industrial or otherwise, work, a living wages, conditions of work ensuring a decent standard to life and full enjoyment of leisure and social and cultural opportunities and in particular the state shall endeavour to promote cottage industries on an individual or co operative."

(b) There is no corresponding provisions anywhere.

(v) Participation of Worker in Management of Industries

(a) India : Article 43-A provides that "The state shall take steps by suitable legislation or in any other way to secure the participation of worker in the management of undertaking establishments or other organizations engaged in any industry."

(b) Burma : Article 41 Provides that "The economic life of the union shall be planned with the aim of increasing the public wealth of improving the material conditions of the people and raising their cultural level of consolidating the independence of the union and strengthening the defensive capacity."

Article 42: The state shall direct its policy towards giving material assistance to economic organizations not working for private profit. Preference shall be given to cooperative and similar cooperative organisations.

(c) France: "The nation ensures to the individual and the development. It guarantees to all and notable to the child the mother and the aged worker, protection of health material security and leisure."

(d) Rumania ***Section 12*** says that "Work is the fundamental factor in the economic life of the state. It is an obligation laying upon every citizen. the state assists all working people to protect them from exploitation and raise their standard of living."

Section 20 stats that "All citizens have the right to leisure. The right to leisure is secured by regulation of the hours of work, by means of holidays with pay in accordance with the law, by the provision of rest houses, sanatoria, clubs, parks, sports grounds and institutions specially arranged for the purpose.

(e) Czechoslovakia ***: section 26*** Provides :

1. All citizen possess the right to work.
2. This right is secured in particular by the organisation of work directed by the state in accordance with a system of planned economy.
3. women are entitled in respect of pregnancy maternity and childcare to special treatment as regards their conditions of employment.
4. The law shall prescribe special conditions of employment as regards young persons having regard to the requirements of their physical and mental development.

Section 24: States:

1. All working members of the population possess the right to just remuneration for the work done.

2. The right is secured by the state wages policy, which is administered in agreement with the united union organization and directed towards the constant rising of the standard of living of the working population.
3. Remuneration shall be governed by the quality and quantity of the work and by the benefit which it brings to the community
4. In equal Conditions, men and women are entitled to equal remuneration for equal work.

***Section 29*:** States The protection of life and health at work is secured in particular by state supervision and regulations for safety precautions in work places.

(f) Germany*: Section 15* :

1. labour is protected by the state.
2. the right to work is guaranteed. The state secures every citizen of work and livelihood by direction of the economy. Where the citizen cannot be referred to suitable employment provision is made for his needs in respect of maintenance.

Section 16 *states that* Every working person has a right to rest to paid annual leave, to assistance during sickness and old age.

Section 18 :

1. The conditions of employment must be such as to safeguard the health cultural claims and family life of the working population.
2. the remuneration for work must correspond to the results and secure a decent level of existence for the workers and their dependents.

(g) Costa Rica : *Section 57* : Provides that Every worker shall be entitled to a minimum wage (fixed periodically) for the normal working day, such as to assure his well being and a decent mode of existence. Equal wages shall in every case be paid for equal work. Where conditions as regards efficiency are identical.

All matters respecting the fixing of minimum wages shall be dealt with by a technical body appointed by the law.

The ordinary hours for day work shall not exceed eight in the day and 48 in the week. The ordinary hours for night shall not exceed six in the day and 36 in the week. The remuneration for overtime shall be 50 present more than the stipulated salary or wage provided that the law.

(h) UNO : *Section 21 :* Provides that "Everyone has the right to work, to just and favorable conditions of work and pay and to protection against unemployment."

***Section 22*:**

1. everyone has the right to a standard of living including food, clothing, housing and medical care and to social services adequate for the health and well being of himself and his family and security in the event of the livelihood in circumstances beyond control .
2. Mother and child have the right to special care and assistance.

Section 24 : States that "Every one has the right to rest and leisure."

Section 23 : States that "Every one has the right to education."

Section 25 **:** States that "Every one has the right to participate in the cultural life of the community to enjoy the arts and to share in scientific advancement ."

(vi) Free and Compulsory Education in Indian Constitution and other Constitutions

(a) India : Article 45 *Provides that* "The state shall endeavour to provide early childhood Care & Education for all children until they complete the age of six year.[122]

(b) Eire : *article 42* states that the state shall provide for free primary education.

[122] Substituted by the Constitution (86th Amendment) Act 2002

(c) Burma : ***article 33*** says that In particular the state shall make provision for free and compulsory primary education.

Article 44 states that The state shall pay special attention to the young and promote their education.

(d) France : The preamble in the 1946 constitution of fourth French republic states that "The establishment of free secular public education on all levels is a duty of the state."

(e) Germany *: section 39* : States that

1. Every child must be given opportunity to develop thoroughly his physical, mental and moral powers. Attendance at the technical and secondary schools and at institutes of higher learning shall be made possible for all sections of the nation.
2. school shall be free of charge. Learning aids in compulsory schools shall be supplied without payment.

(f) Costa Rica : ***section 78:*** Says that Primary education is compulsory. Primary pre school and secondary education is free and is provided at national expense. The state shall facilitate the higher studies of persons who lack the necessary funds. The Ministry of Education shall be responsible for the awarding of scholarship and grants in aid, through a body appointed by law.

(g) Czechoslovakia: Sec 12 :

1. All citizens have the Right to Education.
2. Elementary Education is uniform. Compulsory and free.

***Section 82*:** says that "The state shall provide food and clothing for needy pupils in accordance with law.

(h) UNO : article 23 (1) Says that "Elementary and fundamental education shall be free and compulsory."

(vii) Promotion of Education and Economic interests of Scheduled Castes, Scheduled Tribes and other weaker sections in Indian Constitution and other Constitution.

(a) India : ***Article 46*** says that the state shall promote with special care the educational and economic interests of the weaker sections of the people and in particular, of the scheduled castes and the scheduled tribes and shall protect them from social injustice and all forms of exploitation.

(b) Burma: ***Article 35*** Says that: "The state shall promote with special care the educational and economic interests of the weaker and less advanced sections of the people and shall protect them from social injustice and all forms of exploitation."

(c) Eire : ***Article 45*** clause (4) (1) posits: The state pledges itself to safeguard with special care the economic interests of the weaker sections of the sport of infirm the widow orphan and the aged.

(viii) Raising Standard of Living

(a) India : Article 47 Provides that "The state shall regard the raising of the level of nutrition and the standard of living of its people and the improvement of public health as among its primary duties and in particular, the state shall endeavour to bring about prohibition of the consumption except for medicinal purposes of intoxication drinks and of drugs which are injurious to health."

(b) Burma : article 36: says that "The state regard the raising of the standard of living of its people and the improvement of public health as among its primary duties."

Article 38: says that "the state shall promote the improvement of public health by organizing and controlling health services, hospitals, dispensaries, sanatoria nursing and convalescent homes and other health institution."

Article 39 state that "The state shall take special care of the physical education of the people in general and of the youth in particular in order to increase the health and working capacity of the people and in order to strengthen the defensive capacity of the state."

C. Community Welfare charter in Indian and other Constitutions

(i) Organisation Village Panchayats

(a) India : Article 40 Provides that the "The state shall take steps to organise village panchayats and endow them with such powers and authority as may be necessary to enable them to function as units of self government.

(b) No corresponding provision anywhere.

(ii) Uniform Civil Code

(a) India : Article 44 provides that the state shall endevour to secure for the Uniform Civil Code throughout the territory of India.

(b) No corresponding provision anywhere.

(iii) Organisation of Agriculture and Animal Husbandry

(a) India: Article 48 provides that "The state shall endeavour to organize agriculture and animal husbandry on modern and scientific lines and shall in particular take steps for preserving and improving the breeds and prohibition the slaughter of cows and calves and other milch and draught cattle."

(b) No corresponding provision anywhere.

(iv) Production of Environment

(a) India : ***Article 48-A*** states that "The state shall endeavour to protect and improve the environment and to safeguard the forest and wildlife of the country."

(b) No corresponding provision anywhere.

(v) Protection of Monuments

(a) India : ***Article 49*** Provides that " It shall be the obligation of the state to protect every monument or place or object of artistic or historic interest (declared by or under law made by parliament) to be national importance from exploitation, disfigurement, destruction, removal, disposal or export as the case may be.

(b) No corresponding provision anywhere.

(vi) Separation of Judiciary from Executive

(a) India : ***Article 50*** provides that " The state shall take steps to separate the judiciary from executive in public services of the state

(b) No corresponding provision anywhere.

(vii) Promotion of International Peace and Security

(a) India : ***Article 51*** provides The state shall endevour to.

1. promote international peace and security.

2. Maintain just and honorable relations between nations:

3. Foster respect for international law and treaty obligations in the dealings of organized people with one another and

4. Encourage settlement of international dispute by arbitration

(b) French : The French republic faithful in tradition abides by the rules of international public law. It will not undertake wars of conquest and will never use it's arms against the freedom of any people. On condition of reciprocity France accepts the limitations of sovereignty necessary to the organisation and defense of peace.

(c) Eire : ***Article 29*** says: Ireland affirms its devotion to the ideal of peace and friendly cooperation amongst nations founded on International justice and morality disputes by International arbitration or judicial determination.

Ireland accepts the generally recognized principles of international law as its rule of conduct in its relation with other states.

Chapter VI

The Relationship between Directive Principles and Fundamental Rights

---

Synopsis

(1) First Phase – From Champakam Dorairajan to Fourth Amendment

(2) Second Phase – From Doctrine of Harmonious Construction to Seventeenth Amendment

(3) Third Phase – from 24th Amendment to Kesavananda Bharati Case

(4) Fourth Phase – from 42nd amendment to Minerva Mill case

(5) Fifth Phase – latest judicial trends

Fundamental Rights and Directive Principle are integral components of the same organic constitutional system and no conflict between them could have been intended by founding fathers. But the view of Supreme Court on the relationship between Fundamental Rights and Directive Principles have not been uniform throughout.

The directive principles differs from fundamental rights in this respect that while Fundamental Rights are justiciable but Directive Principles of State Policy are non-justiciable. Fundamental rights are mostly rights of the individuals against the State, whereas Directive Principles are guidelines for the State to be followed for general welfare of the society as a whole. According to article 37, Directive Principles, though they are fundamental in the governance of the country and it shall be duty of the State to apply these principles in making law, but they are non-justiciable.

There are three possible views on the relationship between Fundamental Rights and Directive Principles. The first view is that former are the superior to the latter and so the latter must give way to the former in case of repugnancy or irreconcilable conflict between the two. The second view is that Fundamental Rights and directive principle are equal in importance and hence , in case of conflict between the two an attempt must be made to harmonise them with each other. The view is that Directive Principles are superior to Fundamental Rights mainly because the constitution provide that the former are 'fundamental in the governance of the country' and it shall be the 'duty' of the state "to apply these principle in making laws" and the binding nature of law does not cease to be so merely because it can not be enforced. These different view regarding the relationship between Fundamental Rights and Directive Principles have been pronounced by the judiciary at different times .In the following chapters an attempts has been made to examine the role of judiciary in relation to the Directive Principles with the Fundamental Rights.

(1) First phase: From Champakam Dorairajan to Fourth Amendment

The first occasion of confrontation of the Supreme Court with the issue of relationship between rights and Directive Principles was presented by ***State of Madras V. Champakam Dorairajan*** [123].The fact of this case were as follows:

The government of Madras issued an order popularly known as communal government order under which the seat in the engineering and medical colleges were apportioned on a communal and religious basis. For every fourteen seat to be filled up by the selection committee, candidates were to be selected on the following basis. Non Brahmins –6,Harijan-2, Backward Hindus-2, Anglo Indians and Indian Christian-1 and Muslim –1 and Brahmins. The petitioner, a Brahmin lady contended that the Madras communal government order violated has Fundamental Rights

---

[123] AI.R. 1951 SC.226

under articles 15 (1) and 29 (2). The order was attempted to be justified by the state of Madras on the ground that it implemented the Directive Principles contained in article 46 of the constitution which imposes a duty on the state to promote the educational and economic interests of the weaker section of the people, and in particular of the scheduled caste and scheduled tribes. A full bench of the High court which heard the case did not agree these contentions of the state and held that 46 could not be interpreted in such way to as to negative the effect of the provisions contained in article 15 (1) and 29(2) or justify the enactment of any law or act of the state violating their provision. In his dissenting opinion Justice Somasundram drew the attention of the latter part of the article 37 which emphasized the fundamentals character of the directives and observed:

"*Art. 46 of the constitution is every relevant and important article to be considered in this connection..... This is the placed in the chapter relating to Directive Principles of state policy. Article 37 states that though the provision in that part are not enforceable in court, nevertheless the principles therein are fundamental in the governance of the country......... I emphasize the words fundamental in the article....... It is therefore, the duty of the state of the state respect and give effect to the principles in article 46.......The use of word 'fundamental' is significant in view of the use of the same word in part III of the constitution. The principles in this chapter are therefore, as fundamental as those in part III.*"

But the Supreme Court rejected the above contention completely and held:

" *The Directive Principle of state policy, which by article 37 are expressly made unenforceable by a court, cannot override the provisions found in part III which notwithstanding other provisions are expressly made enforceable by appropriate writs orders or directions under article 32. The chapter on Fundamental Rights is sacrosanct and not liable to be abridged by any legislature or executive act or order except to the extent provided in the appropriate article in the part IV. The Directive Principles of state policy have to conform and run as subsidiary to the chapter on the Fundamental Rights"*

In my submission, the conclusion drawn by the Supreme Court on the status of Directive Principles vis-a vis the Fundamental Rights seems to be erroneous on the following guards:

(a) The constitution contains many important mandates, which may not be enforceable by the court of law that does not mean that those provisions must run subsidiary to the chapter on Fundamental Rights.

(b) The view taken by the Supreme Court has ignored the fact that farmers of the constitution made the Directive Principles enforceable only to prevent the state from being compelled to implement them immediately as at the time of independence or at the time of commencement of the constitution, the nation was at a nascent stage and it did not have the sufficient resources to implement at once all the directive principles. But this was done not to reduce the importance of directive principles, nor to allot them inferior status in the constitution vis-a vis the Fundamental Rights.

(c) The Supreme Court while stressing on the fundamental nature orderable nature of the Directive Principles as mentioned in articles 37, ignored their fundamental nature. Article 37 of the constitution makes all the Directive Principles" fundamental in the governance of the country" Therefore the Directive Principles are not less important if not more than the Fundamental Rights.

Criticising the Judgment, Professor G.S. Sharma, pointed out that the approach of the court was purely logical and technical which reminded on the Watson-Heldane era of the Privy

Council decision with reference, to the Canadian Constitution [124]. In the words of professor P.K. Tripathi, this was perhaps that "the most damaging opinion" expressed by the court.[125] In our submission this case gave death blow to the most dynamic part of the constitution.

As a result of these judgment, the constitution(first Amendment) Act, 1951 was enacted by which clause 4 was added to the articles. This clause reads:

" Nothing in this article or in cl. (2) of article 29 shall prevent the state from making any social provision for the advancement of any socially and educationally backward classes of citizens or for the scheduled castes and the scheduled tribes."

It is quite clear from this amendment that Directive Principles are important than the Fundamental Rights. Despite this amendments the courts did not give much importance to Directive Principles and continued to hold that Directive Principles are subordinate in character. The Bombay high court in ***Jagwant Kaur Vs state of Bombay***[126], upheld the contention that *Directive Principle have to conform and run subsidiary to Fundamental Rights*. The Punjab high court in ***Omprakash Vs state of Punjab***[127], rejected the contention that as the provision of part IV could not be enforced by any court, articles 46 couldn't override article 29(2). But in ***Ajaib Singh V. state of Punjab***[128], the Punjab High Court emphasised the subordinate character of the directive principles.

The following points, therefore, emerge from the above decision, namely: -

[124] G.S Sharma, "concept leadership implicit in the Directive Principles of the state policy in the Indian constitution", 1965, Vol. 7 J.I.L.I., 173-183 at 183.

[125] P.K.Tripathi "Directive Principles of state policy; the lowers approach to them, parochial, injurious and unconstitutional", 1957 Vol. XVII. S.C.J ,2 - 8 at 7

[126] AIR 1952 Bom. 461

[127] AIR 1951 Pun. 93

[128] AIR 1952 Pun. 309

(a) The Directive Principles of state policy cannot override the provisions found in part III as the latter are made enforceable by appropriate writs or orders or directions under article 32 whereas the former are expressly made on unenforceable by any court.

(b) The chapter on Fundamental Rights is sacrosanct and not liable to be obliged by any legislature or executive Act. Or order, except to the extent provided in the appropriate articles in the part III.

(c) Directive Principles have to conform and run subsidiary to the Fundamental Rights.

(d) Any action of the state under Directive Principles is subject to the legislative and executive powers.

In ***State of Bihar Vs Kameshwar Singh***[129], the Supreme Court relying upon the Directive Principles incorporated in article 39(b) held that certain Zamindari abolition law had been passed for public purposes within the meaning of article 31(2).It was held that the state ownership or control over land was necessary preliminary step towards the implementation of Directive Principles and it could not be a public purpose. It was further held that the Directive Principles were not merely the policy but were indented to be principles fixed by the constitution for directing the state policy whatever party might come in to power.

The full bench of the Allahabad High Court in ***Buddhu Vs Municipal Board, Allahabad*** [130], held that if the prohibition of the slaughter of cows, calves, bulls and bullocks within the municipality affected the Fundamental Rights of person under articles 19(1)(g) to carry on any trade, business or occupation they choose such restriction on Fundamental Rights was justified in the view of the Directive Principles in articles 47 and 48 as a ' reasonable restriction' under articles 19 (5).

---

[129] AIR 1952 SC 252

[130] AIR 1952 Alld.753

(2) Second phase: From doctrine of harmonious construction to 17th Amendments

There was change in the attitude of the judiciary towards the Directive Principles subsequent to the Champakam Dorairajan case. In the view of the increasing recognition of the fact that although Directive Principles were non justiciable in character, the courts were to recognize their importance for the simple reason that they formed a vital part of the constitutional document. The directives were no longer to be ignored when they come into conflict with Fundamental Rights. The Supreme Court took a little uncertain and complicated view in ***Mohammad Hanif Qureshi Vs state of Bihar***[131]. In this case, the validity of UP, MP and Bihar Legislation, which banned slaughter of certain animals including cows, was challenged. It was contented that this ban prevented the petitioners from carrying on their butcher's trade and its subsidiary undertaking and therefore infringed their Fundamental Rights, inter alias, guaranteed under article 19(1) (g). Here the petitioners who were Muslim by religion were engaged in butcher's trade and its subsidiary undertaking. The state argued that the impugned acts were passed by it in discharge of its obligation contained in article 48 of the constitution. It was further argued that Directive Principles through not enforceable by any court were nevertheless fundamental in the governance of the country and the state owned a duty to give effect to them. The laws so enacted were in discharge of the fundamental obligation imposed on the state under part IV. The Directive Principles were equally fundamental and therefore, must prevail and since this enactment were made in consonance with the directive principles, they were perfectly valid. The Supreme Court rejected contention of the state *S.R.Das, C.J.* observed:

[131] AIR 1958 SC 731

" We are unable to accept this argument as sound. Article 13(2) expressly says that the state shall not make any law, which takes away or abridges the rights conferred by chapter III that enshrines Fundamental Rights. The Directive Principles cannot override this categorical restriction imposed on the legislative power of the state. A harmonious Interpretation has to be placed upon the constitution and so interpreted, it means that the state should certainly implement the Directive Principles but it must do so in such a way that its laws do not take away or abridge the Fundamental Rights for otherwise the protecting provision of chapter III will be mere rope of sand,"

S.R.Das C.J. in accordance with this view held:

(a) that a total ban on the slaughter of cows of all ages, cows, calves, and of she-buffaloes, mail and female is quite reasonable and valid and is in consonance with the Directive Principles laid down under articles 48.

(b) that a total ban on the slaughter of buffaloes or breeding of ball or working bullocks as long as these are a milch or draught cattle is also reasonable and valid, and

(c) that a total ban on the slaughter of she- buffaloes, bulls and bullocks after they cease to be capable of yielding milk or of breeding or working as draught animals cannot be supported or reasonable[132].

However the court introduced the doctrine of harmonious interpretation or construction as a new technique of interpretation in this field. In other words the Directive Principles should be implemented by the state in such a manner that they do not abridge or take away the Fundamental Rights. The Court while admitting the importance of the Directive Principles called upon the state to be cautious in their implementation and that due care are taken in the process of

[132] Shalja Chander, " justice V.R. Krishna Iyer on Fundamental Rights and directive principle", (New Delhi: Deep and Deep Publications, 1998), p.65

implementation[133]. A little, in the same year, ***In re Kerla Education Bill***[134], the Supreme Court gave a slightly more emphatic form to the doctrine of harmonious construction and thereby gave a better status to directive principle when it observed:

"*The Directive Principles have to conform to and run subsidiary to the chapter on Fundamental Rights. Nevertheless in determining the scope and ambit of the Fundamental Rights, relied on by or on behalf of any person or body the court may not entirely ignore these directive principle of state policy laid down in part IV of the constitutions should adopt the principle of harmonious construction and should attempt to give effect to both as much as possible*"

The Supreme Court observed that though the directive principles cannot overside the Fundmetnal Rights, in determining the scope and ambit of the Fundamental Right the court may not entirely ignore the Directive Principles but should adopt the principle of harmonious construction and should attempt to give effect to both as much as possible

This pronouncement of the Supreme Court admits of the fact that earlier it had ignored the Directive Principles but in future it would not do so thus these cases lay down that Directive Principle cannot override the Fundamental Rights, Seervai Justifies these decisions. He maintains that the words "fundamental" and 'duty' in article 37 in used not in the legal, but in a moral sense. The law laid down in the above cases in correct.

In ***Sajjan Singh V. state of Rajsthan***[135], Mudholkar, J., observed:

"*These Directive Principles are also fundamental in the governance of the country and the provision of part IV must be interpreted harmoniously with principles.*"

In ***Golak Nath Vs state of Punjab***[136], Subba Roa, C.J., observed :

[133] Dr.P.S. jaiswal, "Directive Principles jurisprudence and socio economic in India", (New Delhi APH publishing corporation, 1996),P. 159

[134] AIR. 1958 SC 956, 1959 SCJ 321: 1959 SCR 995

[135] AIR 1965 SC 845

"Fundamental Rights and Directive Principles of state policy enshrined in the constitution formed integrated scheme' and was elastic enough to respond to the changing needs of the society."

"In historic judgment ***Chandra Bhawan Boarding and Lodging, Bangalore v. State of Mysore*** [137], Hegde J. observed:

"We see no conflict on the whole between the provisions contained in part III & part IV. They are complementary and supplementary to each other."

(3) Third phase: from 24th amendment to Kesavananda Bharati

In the third phase of judicial activity the 25th amendment inserted article 31-c which laid down that in case of conflict between law enacted in implementing directing principle in article 39 (b) and (c) and the Fundamental Rights conferred by articles 14, 19 and 31, formers shall prevail over the latter. In ***Kesavananda Bharati Sripadagalvaru and Anr. v. State of Kerala and Anr.*** [138]**,** a thirteen-Judge Bench decision of this Court is a turning point in the history of Directive Principles jurisprudence. This decision clearly mandated the need for bearing in mind the Directive Principles of State Policy while judging the reasonableness of the restriction imposed on Fundamental Rights. In ***Kesavananda Bharati Sripadagalvaru and Anr. v. State of Kerala and Anr.*** [139], the Supreme Court by a majority held that while the first limb of article 31-c was valid, its second limb was invalid. That is, law enacted to implement article 39(b) and (c) would not be unchallengeable under article 14,19 and 31. The courts would be empowered to go in to the question whether such a law did really achieve these objectives. In Keshvanand Bharti case, the Supreme Court has said that, " Fundamental Rights and directives principles aim at the

---

[136] AIR 1967 SC 864
[137] AIR 1970 SC 2024, (1970) 2 SCR 600

[138] (1973) 4 SCC 225
[139] AIR 1973 SC 1416

same goal of bringing about social revolution and establishment of a welfare state and they can be interpreted and applied together. They are supplementary and complementary to each other. It can well be said that Directive Principles prescribed the goal to be attainted and the fundamental right lay down the means by which that goal into be achieved.

According to *Shelat and Grover.J.J.* both part III and part IV have to be balanced and harmonised. They observed:

"Both parts III and IV... have to be balanced and harmonised. Then alone the dignity of the individual can be achieved. It was to give effect to the main objective in the preamble that parts III rd and IV the were enacted. Our constitution makers did not complete any disharmony between the Fundamental Rights and the directive principles. They were meant to supplement to one another. It can well be said that the directive principle prescribed the goal to be attained and the Fundamental Rights laid down that means by which the goal was to be achieved[140].

Hegde and Mukherjea, J.J., were also of the same view regarding the relationship and status of Fundamental Rights and directives principles. They also observed:

"Parts IV the of the constitution is designed to bring about the social and economic revolution that remained to be fulfilled after independence..... to ignore parts IV is to ignore the substance provided for in the constitution, the hopes held out to the nation and the very ideals on which our constitution is built. Without faithfully implementing the Directive Principles, it is not possible to achieve the welfare state contemplated by the constitution[141].

Jag Mohan Reddy J. observed:

" There can be doubt that the object of the Fundamental Rights into ensure the ideal political democracy and present authorisation rule, while the object of the Directive Principle of state

[140] Supra Note 16 at 1582
[141] Ibid at 1641

policy is to establish a welfare state where there is a economic and social freedom without which political democracy has no meaning.[142] *"*

K.K.Mathew, J. is of the opinion that:

"Although directives are expressly made unenforceable, that does not affect its fundamental characters. ...Judicial process is also state action under article 37 and the judiciary is bound to apply the Directive Principles in the making its judgments."

According to the majority of the judges, the directive principle is not of the less significance on compared to Fundamental Rights because they are " fundamental in the governance of the country" and their aim is to provide socio- economic justice to million of Indians.

The seven-Judge Bench decision in ***Pathumma and Others v. State of Kerala and Ors.,*** (1978) 2 SCC 1, wherein the learned Judges neatly summed up the ratio of Kesavananda Bharati and other decisions which are relevant for our purpose. Pathumma holds :-

"(1) Courts interpret the constitutional provisions against the social setting of the country so as to show a complete consciousness and deep awareness of the growing requirements of society, the increasing needs of the nation, the burning problems of the day and the complex issues facing the people, which the legislature, in its wisdom, through beneficial legislation, seeks to solve. The judicial approach should be dynamic rather than static, pragmatic and not pedantic and elastic rather than rigid. This Court while acting as a sentinel on the qui vive to protect fundamental rights guaranteed to the citizens of the country must try to strike a just balance between the fundamental rights and the larger and broader interests of society so that when such a right clashes with a larger interest of the country it must yield to the latter.

---

[142] Ibid at 1715

(2) The Legislature is in the best position to understand and appreciate the needs of the people as enjoined in the Constitution. The Court will interfere in this process only when the statute is clearly violative of the right conferred on a citizen under Part III or when the Act is beyond the legislative competence of the legislature. The courts have recognised that there is always a presumption in favour of the constitutionality of the statutes and the onus to prove its invalidity lies on the party which assails it.

(3) The right conferred by Article 19(1)(f) is conditioned by the various factors mentioned in clause (5). (4) The following tests have been laid down as guidelines to indicate in what particular circumstances a restriction can be regarded as reasonable:

(a) *In judging the reasonableness of the restriction the court has to bear in mind the Directive Principles of State Policy.*

(b) *The restrictions must not be arbitrary or of an excessive nature so as to go beyond the requirements of the interests of the general public. The legislature must take intelligent care and deliberation in choosing the course which is dictated by reason and good conscience so as to strike a just balance between the freedom in the article and the social control permitted by the restrictions under the article.*

(c) No abstract or general pattern or fixed principle can be laid down so as to be of universal application. It will have to vary from case to case and having regard to the changing conditions, the values of human life, social philosophy of the Constitution, prevailing conditions and the surrounding circumstances all of which must enter into the judicial verdict.

(d) The Court is to examine the nature and extent, the purport and content of the right, the nature of the evil sought to be remedied by the statute, the ratio of harm caused to the citizen and the benefit conferred on the person or the community for whose benefit the legislation is passed.

(e) There must be a direct and proximate nexus or a reasonable connection between the restriction imposed and the object which is sought to be achieved.

(f) The needs of the prevailing social values must be satisfied by the restrictions meant to protect social welfare.

(g) The restriction has to be viewed not only from the point of view of the citizen but the problem before the legislature and the object which is sought to be achieved by the statute. In other words, the Court must see whether the social control envisaged by Article 19 (1) is being effectuated by the restrictions imposed on the fundamental right. However important the right of a citizen or an individual may be it has to yield to the larger interests of the country or the community.

(h) The Court is entitled to take into consideration matters of common report history of the times and matters of common knowledge and the circumstances existing at the time of the legislation for this purpose.

(4) Fourth phase: From 42nd amendments to Minerva mills

The directive principle of the state policy, after getting recognition in Kesavananda Bharati, got further impetus in the subsequent judgments of the Court. In ***Narendra prasad V. State of Gujarat***[143], the Supreme Court explained the role of the directive principle. The court observed:

" A particulars Fundamental Rights cannot exist in isolation in water-tight compartment, one Fundamental Rights of a may have to co-exist in harmony with the exercise of another Fundamental Rights by others and also with reasonable and valid exercise of power by the step in the Directive Principles in the interested of social welfare as a whole. The courts duty is to strike a balance between competing claims of different interests."

[143] AIR 1974 SC 2098

In **Mumbai kamgar sabha V. Abdul Bai** [144]

“The balance was, however, further shifted in favours of the Directive Principles of state policy. Recognising the importance of the social philosophy of Part IV, the Court observed:

"statutory interpretation in the creative Indian context may look for light of the ***load star*** *of Part IV of the Constitution.......... where two judicial choices are available, the construction in conformity with the social philosophy has preference."*

“In ***State of Kerla V. N.M.Thomas***[145]**,** the status relationship between the Fundamental Rights and directive principle of state policy was explained by *Fazal Ali,.J.* in the following words:

“The directive principle contained in parts IVth constitutes the stairs to climb the high edifice of a socialistic State and the Fundamental Rights are the means through which one can reach top of the edifice.”

It is submitted that from the persual of the judgments of the supreme court given after *Kesavananda Bharti,* it is evidently clear that the judicial milieu was definitely in favour of the directive principle the parliament get inspiration from this judicial milieu and thought that it was the best time when it could be introduced some constitutional charges through which the supremacy could be given to all the directive principle over the Fundamental Rights. Thus the parliament passed constitution (forty second amendment).

This amendments act amended article-31-c and established the supremacy of all the directive over the Fundamental Rights contained in articles 14, 19 or 31. The (forty second amendment) Act, 1976 three more article, that is articles 39-A, article 43-A and article 48-A, in parts IV of the constitution. The inclusion of these directive was welcome step. It is, however, interesting to note that forty second amendment though established the supremacy of all the

[144] AIR 1974 SC 1455

[145] AIR 1976 SC 490

directive principle over Fundamental Rights, yet it did not tear of the fundamental character of property right. The constitution (forty fourth) Amendments act, 1978 deleted the right to property from the Fundamental Rights. This amendments instituted a new clause (2) to article 38 in parts IV of the Constitution. The new clause also was added with a view to insure that the State removes all kinds of in equalities and provide socio-economic justice to all. The dominance of all the directive principle of the Fundamental Rights given in articles 14 or 19 continued even after these amendments. The judicial attitude regarding the status of the Directive Principles was once again changed in ***Minerva Mills ltd. V. Union of India***[146]. In this case the constitutional validity of amendments articles 31-C (as amended by the 42nd amendments) was challenged before the Supreme Court. The case was heard by the constitutional bench consisting of five *Judges (chandrachud.C.J. A.C.Gupta, N.L. Untwalia, P.S. Kailasama and P.N.Bhagwati).* The Supreme Court by **4:1** majority held that section 4 of the 42nd Constitution Amendments Act. (Which amended article 31-C) is beyond the amending power of parliament and is void. The majority opinion was a delivered by chief Justice Chandrachud and the minority opinion was the given by Justice P.N.Bhagwati.

Chandrachud, C.J., observed:

"*The Indian constitution founded on the bedrock of the balance between parts III and IV. To give absolute primacy to one over the other is to disturb the harmony of the constitution. This harmony and balance between fundamental right and Directive Principles is an essential feature of the basic structure of the constitution.*"

He further observed:

"The significance of the perception that part III and IV together constitute the core of commitment to social revolution and they, together, are conscience of the constitution.They are

146 AIR 1980 SC 1789

like two wheels of a chariat; one no less important than the other. You snap one and the other will loose its efficacy. They are like a twin formula for achieving the social revolution.[147]"

However in his forceful dissenting judgment, *Bhagwati, J.,* held Sec.4 of the Forty second Amendment as constitutional and observed that it is far from damaging the basic structure of the constitution. Justice *Bhagwati* declared the Amended article 31-C as valid. Dwelling upon the Fundamental Right and Directive principle, jurisprudence, Justice *Bhagwati* observed:

"The Fundamental Right are no doubt important and valuable in a Democracy, but there can be no real democracy without social and economic Justice to the common man and create socio-economic conditions in which there Can be social and economic justice to everyone, the theme of the directive, Principles....' The dynamic provisions of Directive Principles fertilise the static Provisions of Fundamental Rights."[148]

It is submitted that Justice Bhagawati has rightly explained the true position of the Directive Principles vis-à-vis Fundamental Rights. Article31-c was amended by the parliament with a view to provide that in case of conflict Directive Principles shall have precedence over Fundamental Rights in article 14 and 19 and the latter shall yield place to the former.

(5) Fifth phase: Latest Judicial Trend

After *Minerva Mills*, no legislative attempt was made to change the status relationship of Fundamental Rights vis-a vis directive principles. However, the Judiciary has shown its concern towards Directive Principles which is evident from the following judgment of the court. In ***Bhim***

[147] Supra Note 23 at 1806
[148] Ibid at 1847

Singh V. Union of India[149]**,** it was pointed out that *part IV of the constitution, dealing with directive principles, which seeks to build a Social justice society is basic to our constitutional order. The Directive Principles Being paramount in character and fundamental in the country's governance Have a key to play in the developmental process of the socialistic Republic that India has adopted.*"

In ***A. B. S. K. sangh (Rly) V. Union of India*** [150], Chinnappa Reddy J., observed:

"It becomes the duty of the court to apply the Directive Principles in interpretating the constitution and the laws. The directive principle should serve the courts as a code of interpretation Fundamental Rights should thus be interpreted in the light of the Directive Principles and the latter should whenever and wherever possible, be read into the former."

In ***State of Tamilnadu V. L. Abu Kavur Bai***[151], the Supreme Court held that although the Directive Principles are not enforceable yet the court should make a real attempt at harmonising and reconciling the Directive Principles and Fundamental Rights and any collision between the two should be avoided as far as possible.

In ***Central Inland Water Transport Corporation Ltd. V. Brajonath***[152], the Supreme Court explained the difference in part III and part IV in the following words:

"The difference between part iii and part IV is that while part iii prohibits the state from doing certain things, part IV enjoins upon the state to do certain things, This duty however is not enforceable in law but court cannot ignore what has been enjoyed upon the state by part IV and through the court may not be able actively to enforce the Directive Principles of State Policy by compelling the State to apply them in the governance of the country or in the making of laws the

---

[149] AIR 1981 SC 234
[150] AIR 1981 SC 298
[151] AIR 1984 SC 626
[152] AIR 1986 SC 1571

court can if the state commits a breach of its duty by acting contrary to these Directive Principles, prevent it form doing so."

In ***V. Markandeya v. State of A.P***[153] the Supreme court held that *Fundamental Rights and the Directive Principles constitute "Consciences of the Constitution". The Constitution aims at bringing about a synthesis between Fundamental Rights and Directive Principles of State Policy by giving the former a place of pride and to the latter a place of performance, together they form the core of the Constitution. They constitute its true conscience and without faithfully implementing the Directive Principles, it is not possible to achieve the Welfare State contemplated under the Constitution.*

In ***Jacob M. Pathuparambi V. Kerla Water Authority***[154], the Supreme Court once again reiterated that "*Directive Principles reflect the hopes and aspirations of the people. The principle laid down their in define the objectives and goals which the state must endeavour to achieve over a period of time. Therefore, whenever the state is required to make law it must do consistently with these principles with a view to securing social and economic freedom so essential for the establishment of an egalitarian society*".

In ***Mohini Jain V. State of Karnataka***[155], the Supreme Court once again reiterated:

"The Directive Principles which are fundamental in the governance of the country cannot be isolated from the Fundamental Rights guaranteed under part III. These principles have to read in to the Fundamental Rights. Both are supplementary to each other. The state is under constitutional mandate to create conditions in which the Fundamental Rights guaranteed to the individual under part III could be enjoyed by all."

---

[153] AIR 1989 SC 1308: (1989) 3 SCC 191
[154] (1991) 1 SSC 28
[155] (1992) 1 SSC 28

In ***Unni Krishnan V. State of Andhra Pradesh*** [156], the Supreme Court pointed out that *a right can be recognised as a Fundamental Right even though not expressly mentioned in part III and for this purpose IV can be looked in to. The Supreme Court has reiterated the same principle that the Fundamental Rights and Directive Principles of State Policy are supplementary and complementary to each other and the provisions in Part III should be interpreted having regard to the Preamble and Directive Principles of State Policy.* The court explained the inter-relationship between part III and part IV in the following words: It is thus well established by the decision of this court that provision of part III and are supplementary and complementary to each other and that Fundamental Rights are a means to achieve the goal indicated in part IV. It is also held that Fundamental Rights must be construed in the light of the Directive Principles. In ***Samantha V. State of Andhra Pradesh.***[157], it has been observed that the *Fundamental Rights and the Directive Principles of state policy are the two wheels of the chariot to achieve the establishment of the egalitarian social order through the rule of law, which is basic structure of the constitution.*

To conclude, we can say that though non-justiciable, Directive Principles prevent a picture of a socialistic (welfare) state. The directives have not received, at the hands of the court the primacy and importance, which is due to them. Today for the purpose of securing to its entire citizens justice social economic and political in a sovereign Socialistic secular democratic republic, Judges have to go far beyond the mechanical Interpretation of the provisions of the directive principles. It has been settled now that for the rule, of harmonious construction, all parts of the constitution must be read together and the court cannot ignore the directive principles.

[156] (1993) 1 SSC 645
[157] (1997) 8 SSC 191

Chapter VII

Changing Dimension of Directive Principles of the State Policy And Fundamental Duties Vis-À-Vis Fundamental Rights.

Synopsis

(A) Implementation of Directives

1. Statutory implementation of Directives

2. Judicial implementation of Directives

i. Right to Education

ii. Right to Health

iii. Right to free Legal Aid

iv. Right to Clean Environment

v. Right to Livelihood

vi. Right to Equal pay for Equal Work

vii. Right to live with Human Dignity

viii. Right to Food

(B) Enforceability of Directives

(C) Enforcement of Fundamental Duties

1. Statutory implementation of Fundamental Duties

2. Judicial implementation of Fundamental Duties

(A) Implementation of Directives

The Directive Principles of the state policy under Indian Constitution is not the hypothesis of Indian Polity. This is the stem on which the whole edifice of Constitution and Government is to stand erect.[158] The Directive Principles seek to give certain directions to the legislature and Governments in India as to how and in what manner and for what purpose, they are to exercise their power. But these principles are specifically made non-enforceable by any Court of law. Art 37 of the Constitution States: "The Provision contained in this Part shall not be enforceable by any Court, but the Principles therein laid down are nevertheless fundamental in governance of the country and it shall be the duty of the State to apply these Principles in the making laws[159]."
The first Part of Art. 37 says that "the Directive Principles are not enforceable by any Courts."From the language of first Part of Art.37 it is clear that these directives are not enforceable in any court of law.But this in not true about Directive Principles. The phrase "shall not be enforceable" has been used in article 37 only to save the state from the embarrassment of being called upon by the citizens to implement the Directive Principles immediately or at a time when their implementation would not be feasible economically, administratively or otherwise. It's second Part assets positively "the fundamental nature of the Directive Principles in the governance of the country". It is submitted that by making them fundamental in governance of the country, the Constitution makers have given them prime importance. Art 37 also says that "it shall be the duty of the State to apply the Directive Principles in making laws."

Article 37 seems to have created a position of uncertainty as to the Status of the Directive Principles vis-à-vis Fundamental Rights. But in fact there is no such uncertainty in view the

---

[158] S.I. Lasker, Directive Principles of State Policy in Indian Constitution, (New Delhi: Deep and Deep Publications, 1988) p 5.

[159] M.P. Jain, Indian Constitutional Law, 5th Edition, (Nagpur: Wadhawa & Co., 2005) p 1366

fundamental nature of Directive Principles and Constitutional duty put on the State to implement them. Art 37 specifically makes the Directive Principles as fundamental in the governance of the country and makes it mandatory for the state to apply these Principles in making laws. What is fundamental in the governance of the country can not be less important than what in fundamental to an individual. If any law is passed by the legislature which contravenes any of the Directive Principles, then that can be declared unconstitutional on the ground that it is repugnant to the supreme law of the land. It is the duty of the Courts also to apply the Directive Principles in interpreting the Constitution and laws, these principles serve as the code of interpretation for the judiciary.

From this discussion it is crystal clear that the Directive Principles of State policy have never been taken by the government in power as pious obligations, as was supposed by many of the members of the drafting committee when they were engrafted in the Constitution. The government in power always tried to implement those directives to achieve the ideals and aspiration of the people of Indian in every walk of their life.

In the era of welfare state concept, legislatures and judicature are also in favour of implementation of Directive Principles as Fundamental Rights. Today these Directive Principles are known as non-enforceable Fundamental Rights.

Now we draw our attention towards the implementation of the directives at all level i.e., social, economic and political. For the sake of convenience these implementation have been categorised in two different headings:

(1) Statutory implementation of Directives

(2) Judicial implementation of Directives

(1) Statutory implementation of Directives

Today we are living in the era of welfare State, which seeks to promote the prosperity and well being of the people. The Directive Principles strengthen and promote this concept by seeking to lay down some socio economic goals, which the various government of India have to strive to achieve. From the very beginning government always tries to implement directives at different level. At the social level Government passed Factories Act, 1948, Maternity Benefit Act 1961, Bonded labour (Abolition) Act, 1976 etc. In order to prevent the concentration of the material resources and means of production in the hands of few, a large scale reform has been introduced both in the agricultural and industrial field in pursuance of the recommendation of the planning commission. This is the implementation of directives at the economic level. For the benefit of the agricultural, industrial labours and workers Minimum Wages Act 1948, Workmen Compensation Act 1923, Employees provided fund scheme, Labour laws are made and for peaceful settlement of disputes between employee and employer, labour Tribunal has been established. To implement the provision (Article 41) of Directives regarding right to work, the National Rural Employment guarantee Act, 2005 is enforced in 200 district. In this act, it is provided that one adult member of every rural family is entitle to claim employment of 100 days. If State failed in his duty, the aggrieved person is entitled to claim employment allowances.

For the promotion of economic and educational interest of the Scheduled Caste and Scheduled Tribes, major Steps have been taken on large Scale to improve their educational and economic condition by providing them adequate facilities for free education and by granting loans to raise their economic standard.

For the improvement of public health several measures have been taken by way of education of disease like maliria, filarial, Small pox and other communicable diseases. In the view of Article 38, 39 (e), 41 and Article 47 Judiciary also held the right to health is integral facet of article 21.

The objectives laid down in article 40 have now been fulfilled by enacting the Constitution 73rd and 74th amendments acts known as the Panchayati and Nagarpalika Constitution Amendment Act, 1992.These amendments provide Constitutional Sanction to democracy at the gross root level.

Regarding preservation of forests and wild life which is deemed to be the natural wealth of the country, specific legislation have also been made. The Indian Forest Act, Indian Wild life Protection Act, 1972 and Environment Protection Act, 1986 is enacted in the view of Article 48-A.

For the Preservation and Protection of monuments and places and objects of national importance in the light of article 49, Parliament has enacted the Ancient and Historical Monuments and Archeological Sites and Remains (Declaration of National Importance) Act, 1951.

Pursuant to the direction enshrined in Article 57 of the Constitution and International Commitments, Parliament has passed the Protection of Human Rights Act 1993.

(2) Judicial implementation of Directives

In a number of decision, Supreme Court has implemented Directive Principles with great importance. In some case the SC has declared many Directive Principles as Fundamental Rights and have been enforced them. The decision taken in Kesavananda Bharti paved the way for liberal interpretations of the Fundamental Rights and gave the Directives, the status of Fundamental Rights.

Especiallly, the liberal interpretations given to Art.21 in and after the decision of ***Menaka Gandhi Vs. Union of India***[160] explores ways to implement the directive principles on par with the Fundamental Rights by giving to those directives the status of Fundamental Rights. These are:

(i) Right to Education

Article 45 requires the State to make provision within 10 years for free and compulsory education for all children until they complete the age of 14 years. Education as a necessary means of achieving socio political Justice was largely ignored until the 1992. The question whether the right to education was a Fundamental Right and enforceable as such was answered by the Supreme Court in the affirmative in ***Mohini Jain v. State of Karnataka.***[161]. In this Case, the two Judge Bench of the Supreme Court held that *the Right to Education flows directly from right to life, as the right to life and the dignity of an individual cannot be assured unless it is accompanied by the right to education, and the Fundamental Rights guaranteed under Part III of the Constitution of India, including the right to freedom of speech and expression and other rights under article 19 cannot be appreciated and fully enjoyed unless a citizen is educated and is conscious of his individualistic dignity*. The court also held that *the Directive Principles which are fundamental in the governance of the country cannot be isolated from the Fundamental*

[160] AIR 1978 SC 594, 597

[161] (1992) 3 SCC 666

Rights guaranteed under Part III. These Principles have to be read into Fundamental Rights. Both are supplementary to each other....... Without making the "Right to Education" under Article 41 of the Constitution a reality, the Fundamental Rights under Chapter III remain beyond the reach of the large majority which is illiterate."

The Zeal demonstrated in Mohini Jain which continued in the later Constitutional Bench decision in ***Unni Krishnan vs. State of A.P***[162]. where the Constitutional bench held that *the right to education upto age of 14 years is a Fundamental Rights within the meaning of article 21 of the Constitution. The Court declared "the right to education flows directly from right to life."*

The court then proceeded to examine how this right would be enforceable and to what extent. It clarified the issue thus:

The Right to Education further means that a citizen has a right to call upon the State to provide educational facilities to him within the limits of its economic capacity and development. By saying so, we are not transferring Article 41 from Part IV to Part III—we are merely relying upon Article 41 to illustrate the content of the right to education flowing from Article 21. We cannot believe that any State would say that it need not provide education to its people even within the limits of its economic capacity and development. It goes without saying that the limits of economic capacity are, ordinarily speaking, matters within the subjective satisfaction of the State. 38

The court's apprehension clearly was that recognition of such a right might open the flood gates for other claims. It clarified:

We must hasten to add that just because we have relied upon some of the directive principles to locate the parameters of the right to education implicit in Article 21, it does not follow automatically that each and every obligation referred to in Part IV gets automatically included

[162] (1993) 1 SCC 645

within the purview of Article 21. We have held the right to education to be implicit in the right to life because of its inherent fundamental importance. As a matter of fact, we have referred to Articles 41, 45 and 46 merely to determine the parameters of the said right.

In fact, the court had broken new ground in the matter of justiciability and enforceability of the DPSP. The decision in *Unnikrishnan* has been applied by the court in formulating broad parameters for compliance by the government in the matter of eradication of child labor

The declarations of the right to education as a Fundamental Rights has been further upheld and recently conformed by the eleven Judges Constitutional Bench of the Supreme Court in ***TMA Pai foundation vs. State of Karnataka***[163]. After the landmark decision, Government inserted a new article 21-A through 86th Constitutional Amendment Act, 2002. Article 21-A provides that, " the State shall provide free and compulsory education to all the children' of age of six to fourteen years in such manner as to State may; by law, determine." After this amendment education for all children of the age 6-14 years is Fundamental Rights.

(ii) Right to Health

The right to health has been treated by the Supreme Court as part of the right to life in article 21. In Indian Constitution article 38, 39(e), 41, 47 and article 48-A is related with health assistance. Article 47 declares that "the State shall regard the raising of the level of nutrition and the standard of living of its people and the improvement of Public health as among its Primary duties." The right to health also has its reference in article 38 (Social orders to Promote the welfare of the People), article 39(e) (health of workers, men, women and children must be protected against abuse), article 41 (right to Public assistance in certain cases including sickness

[163] (2002) 8 SCC 481

and disability) and article 48-A (the States duty to Protect the environment) of the Directive Principles.

The right to health has been perhaps the least difficult area for the court in terms of justiciability, but not in terms of enforceability. Article 47 of DPSP provides for the duty of the state to improve public health. However, the court has always recognized the right to health as being an integral part of the right to life.[164] In ***Paramananda Katara Vs. Union of India***[165], the professional obligation is casted upon all doctors whether private or Government to extend medical aid to the injured immediately to preserve life without waiting for legal formalities.

The principle got tested in the case of an agricultural laborer whose condition, after a fall from a running train, worsened considerably when as many as seven government hospitals in Calcutta refused to admit him as they did not have beds vacant. The Supreme Court did not stop at declaring the right to health to be a fundamental right and at enforcing that right of the laborer by asking the Government of West Bengal to pay him compensation for the loss suffered. It directed the government to formulate a blue print for primary health care with particular reference to treatment of patients during an emergency.[166] In ***Paschim Bang Khet Mazdoor Samit Vs. State of West Bengal***[167] denial of medical aid by government hospital to an injured person on the ground of non availability of beds amounted to violation of Art.21

In ***Consumer Education and Research center Vs. UOI***[168], Supreme Court held that *the right to health is an integral facet of a meaningful right to life. Reading article 21 with the relevant Directive Principles guaranteed in article 39(e) and 43* .The Supreme Court held that *the right to health and medical care is a Fundamental Right and it makes the life of Workmen meaningful*

164 .Parmanand Katara v. Union of India (1989) 4 SCC 286.
165 AIR 1989 SC 2039
166 . Paschim Banga Khet Majoor Samity v. State of West Bengal (1996) 4 SCC 37
167 (1996) 4 SCC 37
168 AIR 1995 SC 923

and purposeful with the dignity of person. In this case ,the court tackled the problem of the health of workers in the asbestos industry. Noticing that long years of exposure to the harmful chemical could result in debilitating asbestosis, the court mandated compulsory health insurance for every worker as enforcement of the worker's fundamental right to health

Further in ***Kirloskar Brothers Ltd. Vs. Employees State Insurance Corporation***[169] and in ***State of Punjab Vs. Mohinder Singh Chowla***[170], it was held that the right to health is a Fundamental Right of a workmen and 'the amount spent towards treatment has to be reimbursed'[171].

(iii) Right to Free Legal Aid

Article 39-A directs the State to ensure free legal aid to economically backward classes. Supreme Court in ***M.H. Hoskot Vs. State of Maharastra***[172], held that the *State in under a duty to provide lawyer to a poor person and it must pay to the lawyer his fee as fixed by the Court.*

Article 39-A has been read with article 21 and thus, free legal assistance at State cost has been raised to the status of Fundamental Rights of person, accused of an offence which may involve jeopardy to his life or personal liberty. The Court has also ruled that it would make a mockery of legal aid if it were to be left to a poor, ignorant and illiterate accused Person to ask for free legal aid. To implement article 39-A, the Supreme Court exhorted the Central and State Governments to introduce "Comprehensive legal service programme" in the country. SC has held that free legal aid has to be implemented by suitable legislation or by formulating schemes for free legal aid.

---

[169] (1996)2 SCC 682
[170] AIR 1997 SC 1225
[171] Ibid
[172] AIR 1978 SC 1548

(iv) Right to clean Environment

In ***M.C. Mehta(II) Vs. UOI***[173], the Supreme Court regard on article 48-A gave directions to the central and the State government and various local bodies and boards under various Statutes to take appropriate steps for the Protection and Control of Pollution of water.

(v) Right to livelihood

Right to livelihood is treated as Fundamental Right under article 21 and article 39(a). The Supreme Court has taken recourse to article 39(a) to interpret article 21 to include therein the right to livelihood. The Supreme Court has observed in ***Olga Tellis Vs. Bombay Municipal Corporation***[174] that:

"If there is an obligation upon the State to secure to the citizens an adequate means of livelihood and the right to work, it would be sheer pedantry to exclude the right to livelihood from the content of right to life. Any person who is deprived of his right to livelihood except according to just and fair procedure established by law, can challenge the deprivation as offending the right to life conferred by article 21."

(vi) Right to Equal Pay for Equal Work

---

[173] (1988) 1 SCC 471

[174] AIR 1986 SC 180

This Directive Principles is also declared as Fundamental Right in article 21. Art. 39(d) of Directive Principles provides that "the State has to ensure that there is equal pay for equal work for both men and women. Parliament has also enacted the Equal Remuneration Act, 1976 to implement article 39(d). The act provides for payment of equal remuneration to men and women workers for the same work or works of similar nature and for the Prevention of discrimination on ground of sex. Equal pay for equal work has been held to be a Fundamental Right in ***Randhir Singh Vs. Union of India***[175]. In this case Supreme Court held that, the Principles of 'equal pay for equal work' though not a Fundamental Rights is certainly a Constitutional goal and therefore, capable of enforcement through Constitutional remedies under article 32 of the Constitution.

In another case Supreme Court has Observed in ***Grih Kalyan Kendra Vs. Union of India***[176]:

"Equal pay for equal work is not expressively declared by the Constitution as Fundamental Right but in view of the Directive Principles as contained in article 39(d) of the Constitution. Equal Pay for equal work has assumed the status of Fundamental Right in service Jurisprudence having regard to the Constitutional mandate of equality in article 14 and 16 of the Constitution."

In a latest judgment, ***Union of India V. Dineshan K.K.***[177] the Supreme Court has extended the benefits of same rank and pay structure to a Radio Mechanic in Assam Rifle as was given to other Central Paramilitary Forces.

In ***State of Kerala Vs. B. Renjith Kumar & Others***[178], it was held that the claim of the Presiding Officers of the Industrial Tribunals' for equal scale of pay to that of the District Judges was upheld by considering the nature of functions or duties attached to those categories of posts.

---

[175] AIR 1982 SC 879
[176] AIR 1991 SC 1173
177 (2008) 1 SCC 586

(vii) Right to live with Human dignity

The Supreme Court in ***Bandhua Mukti Morcha Vs. Union of India***[179], that right to live with human dignity enshrined in article 21 derives it life breath from the Directive Principles and Particularly article 41 and 42.

In ***Francis Coralie Vs. union territory of India***[180] the court declared:

"*The right to life includes the right to live with human dignity and all that goes with it, namely, the bare necessaries of life such as adequate nutrition, clothing and shelter and facilities for reading, writing and expressing oneself in diverse forms, freely moving about and mixing and comingling with fellow human beings. The magnitude and components of this right would depend upon the extent of economic development of the country, but it must, in any view of the matter, include the bare necessities of life .*

In ***Vincent Parikurlangara Vs. Union of India***[181], the *Right to maintenance and improvement of Public Health is included in the right to live with human dignity.*

By the above decisions the directives under Arts. 39 (e), 42 & 47 were given the status of Fundamental Right under Art.21.

(viii) Right to Food

178 CDJ 2008 SC 1101

179 AIR 1984 SC 82

180 AIR 1978 SC 597)

181 [23] (1987) 2 SCC 165

Right to food is integral part of right to life. But in 1989 Supreme Court failed to recognise that the right to food is integral Part of life.[182] But in the case of ***Peoples Union for Civil liberty Vs. Union of India***[183], SC first time held that right to food is also a Fundamental Rights in article 21. in this case Justice B.N. Kirpal and K.G. Balakrishnan directed all state government to ensure that all public distribution shops are kept open with regular supplies and stated that it is the prime responsibility of Government to prevent hunger and starvation.

(B) Enforceability of Directives

The Directive Principle of the State outline fundamental guidelines for the state which it must strive to accomplish. There should not be any misunderstanding to think that they are the dead letter incorporated in the constitution, as perceived by the higher state machinery, because of their not having enforceable status in the court of law.[184] Dr. Ambedkar, Chairperson of the Constitution Drafting Committee, says that *whoever captures power will not be free to do that he likes with it in the exercise of it he will have to respect these instruments of instructions which are called Directive Principles. Emphasizing the obligatory nature of the Directive Principles, in his minority opinion delivered in the* ***Minerva Mills Ltd. v. Union of India***[185], *Justice P.N Bhagwati observed:*

"....merely because the Directive Principles are not enforceable in a court of law, it does not mean that they cannot create obligations or duties binding on the State.....In fact, non-

---

[182] Kishen Pattnayak Vs. State of Orrisa, 1989 Supp (1) SCC 258

[183] Jayana Kothari, "*Social rights and the Constitution* ", (2004) 6SCC (Jour) 1-23 at 7. www.Practical lawyer.ebc.India.com

[184] Kumar Regmi , The Directive principle: A misunderstanding constitution duty , (1999) 30/31 Essays on Constitutional Law , 61

[185] 16AIR 1980 SC 1789

compliance with the Directive Principles would be unconstitutional on the part of the State and it would not only constitute a breach of faith with the people who imposed this constitutional obligation on the state but it would also render a vital part of the Constitution meaningless and futile[186]*.* ''

Applying the doctrine of 'harmonious construction' the court has applied the Directives to adjust the ambit of Fundamental Rights to give a liberal interpretation to the ambit of a legislative entry so as to make it possible for the legislature to implement a Directive[187].

i) a favourable classification of an object, the promotion of which is encouraged by the directive principles, should be regarded as a reasonable classification.

ii) applying Art.39(d) it has been held that the right to "equal pay for equal work" as between the sexes or within the same age sex is a fundamental right included in Art 14. In determining whether the work done is similar, the court should take a broad view and also strike down any discrimination made on the ground of sex in view of Art.39 (a),(d)[188]

In Article 19:

i) Restrictions which are imposed on the exercise of Fundamental Rights for the purpose of securing the objectives enjoined by any of the Directives would be regarded as reasonable restriction when the meaning of cl (2) ofArt.19 because the Directive Principles embody the ideal of socio – economic justice as assured in the Preamble.

ii) Even though the implementation of a Directive Principles may cause hardship to a few individuals, it should be upheld in the larger interests of the community.

---

[186] Ibid. at p. 1849

[187] Jagannath L Vs. LRO Madurai AIR 1972 SC 425; Asstt. Commissioner Vs. B&C Co AIR 1970 SC 169

[188] Mackinon Mackenzie and Co. Ltd Vs. Andry D'costa AIR 1987 SC 1281

iii) In view of the absolute prohibition of consumption of liquor in Art.47, there cannot be any fundamental right to manufacture and sell intoxicating liquor.[189]

iv) Art.19(6) has been interpreted with the aid of Art. 46 and held that a ban imposed by the State of Kerala in fishing by mechanized nets and appliances is a reasonable restriction. The Supreme Court emphasized that the protection of the weaker sections is an obligation under Art. 46 and is also in the interests of general public under Art. 19(6).[190]

v) The prohibition of slaughter of any of the species of Cattle mentioned, irrespective of their utility from the stand point of agriculture or animal husbandry and such prohibitions cannot be held to be an unreasonable restriction upon the right conferred by art.19(1)(g) in view of the directive contained in the latter part of the article 48.[191]

Even though a contravention of Art.26 is not expressly shielded by Art.31-A, it has been held that Art.37 imposes an obligation upon the State to make laws to regulate the conduct of men and State affairs in order to secure social welfare, including secular activities of religious institutions,so long as the core of religion is not interfered with. There is no such interference, when the state undertakes legislation for agrarian reforms to prevent exploitation of tenants and cultivators or ownership of large areas of land exceeding the ceiling fixed by land even though the ownership of such estates belongs to religious institutions.[192]

Provisions in part IV have also been used as guide in matter of statutory construction[193] including subordinate legislation[194]

---

[189] Nashirwar Vs St of M.P AIR 1975 SC 360;
Razakbai Issukbai Mansuri Vs. State of Gujarat 19993 Supp (2) SCC 659

[190] State of Kerala Vs. Joseph Antony AIR 1994 SC 721

[191] Hanif Quareshi Mohd. Vs. State of Bihar AIR 1958 SC 731

[192] Narendra Prasadji Anand Prasadji Maharaj Vs. St of Gujarat AIR 1974 SC 2008

[193] UPSE Board Vs. Harishankar Jain AIR 1979 SC 65

[194] Ct Balwant Raj Vs U.O.I AIR 1968 ALL 14

1) Where two statutory constructions of a statute are available, the court should prefer that construction which is in conformity with the directives say Art.39 or 43[195].

Thus (i) a beneficial construction of Sec. 127(3) of Cr.P.C has been made with reference to Art. 41[196]

(ii) the scope of S.13B of the Industrial Employment Standing Orders, 1946 has been extended to employees of Statutory Corporations, in the light of Arts. 42- 43[197].

2) In view of Art.36,37& Art.41 is held to be a mandate both to legislature and the Courts, the Court should interpret a statute or sub ordinate legislation, if the language permits or will advance the objectives underlying Art.41.[198]

3) Art.46 has been relied upon in upholding a Service Rule which empowers the Government to exempt (for a specified period) members of S.Cs or S.Ts from the requirement to pass departmental tests for promotion[199].

4) The maternity leave entitled to women in regular employment under the provisions of the Maternity Benefit act, 1961 has been extended to the women engaged on casual basis or on muster roll basis on daily wages in view of Art. 38.[200]

---

[195] Mumbai Kamgar Sabha Vs. Abdul Bhai; AIR 1976 SC 1455, Ramesh Chandra Kaushal Capt Vs Veena Kaushal AIR 1978 SC 1807; N.T. Corpn. Vs Sitaram Mills Ltd AIR 1986 SC 1234

[196] Bai Tahisa Vs. Ali Hassein Fissali Chotia AIR 1979 SC 362

[197] UPSE Board Vs. Harishankar Jain AIR 1979 SC 65

[198] Daily Casual Labour Employees and P & T Dept., Vs. Union of India AIR 1987 SC 2342; Jacob Vs. Kerala Water Authority AIR 1990 SC 2228

[199] State of Kerala Vs. Thomas AIR 1976 SC 490

[200] Municipal Corporation of Delhi Vs. Female Workers (Muster Roll) AIR 2000 SC 1274

5) The Supreme Court further held that Courts should have regard to the Directive in Art.38 to promote welfare of the people and social justice so that where the municipality has failed to remove filthy conditions of drains etc., in slums. The Court should make a positive and mandatory order directing the municipality to remove the public nuisance within a given time irrespective of the financial sources of the municipality[201].

6) The Supreme Court deprecated the unfair labour practice of engaging contract labourers in public sector undertakings and made appropriate recommendations in ***Gujarat Electricity Board, Vs. Hind Mazdoor Sabha***[202].

7) The Supreme Court has held that the Tenants/ the tillers of soil have a fundamental right to economic empowerment under Art. 39 (b) and are entitled to ryotwari patta[203].

8) The nationalization of coal mines is upheld on the ground that it is a law for implementation of Art. 39(b)[204]

9) The children of prostitutes have right to equality of opportunity, dignity, care, protection and rehabilitation so as to be a part of the main stream of social life without any of the stigma attached to them in view of Clause (e-f) of Art.39.[205]

---

[201] Ratlam Municipal Counsil Vs. Vardhichand AIR 1980 SC 1622

[202] AIR 1995 SC 1893

[203] State of T.N. Vs Sri Ambalavana Pandara Samadhi Adheenakartha, (1997) 9 SCC 313

[204] Sanjeev Coke Manufacturing Co., Vs Bharat Coking Coal Ltd. AIR 1983 SC 239

[205] Gaurav Jain Vs. Union of India (1997) 8 SCC 114

10) In view of Art.41, the Court should not encourage a Transport corporation to indulge in false or technical pleas to defeat claims for compensation for injury caused by public carriers belonging to such Corporation leading to disablement and cases of undeserved want.

11) In view of directives under Art.41, the Supreme Court has held that the President cannot exercise his power under Rule 9 of the Civil Services Pension Rules 1972 to withhold Pension of a retired employee, even in part or for a temporary period in the absence of definite finding recorded in a departmental or judicial proceeding that the pensioner committed grave misconduct or negligence in the discharge of his duty while in office.[206]

12) In ***Tapan Kumar Sadhukhan Vs. Food Corporation of India***[207]. It was held that the Food Corporation of India, being an agency of the State must conform the letter and sprit of Art. 47 to improve public health and it should release sub standard rice to dealers only after upgrading it for human consumption and not otherwise.

13) The need for Uniform Civil Code was also emphasized by the Supreme Court in matters like divorce[208] or maintenance for divorced wife[209] which do not form the essence of any religion. The Supreme Court has observed that Art. 44 has so long remained a dead letter and recommended early legislation to implement it. Further in ***Sarla Mudgal Vs Union of India***[210], the Supreme Court expressed its views and requested the Government of India through Prime Minister to hove a fresh look at Art.44 and endeavor to secure for the citizens a uniform civil

[206] Kapoor Vs. Union of India AIR 1990 SC 1923
[207] (1996) 6 SC 101.
[208] Jordan Diengdeh Vs. Chopra SS AIR 1985 SC 935
[209] Ahmed Khan Mohd. Vs. Shah Banu Begum AIR 1985 SC 945
[210] AIR 1995 SC 1531 See also in Lilly Thomas Vs. Union of India AIR 2000 SC 1650

code throughout the territory of India. In the said Judgement the Supreme Court opined that there is no connection between religion and personal law in a civilized society.

14) In view of Art. 50, it was held that the Independence of judiciary is an essential attribute of Rule of Law which is a basic feature of the Constitution. Judiciary must be free not only from the executive pressure but also from other pressures. Independence of Judiciary is a wider concept which implies independence from any pressure or prejudice and fearlessness from any center of power.

15) In view of Art.51, the Supreme Court recognised the practice of interpreting the laws with the aid of International treaties/covenants, Further, in the absence of any contrary legislation, Municipal Courts in India would respect the rule of international law.

16) In ***Peoples Union for Civil Liberties Vs. Union of India*** it was held that the provisions of international conventions, covenants which elucidate and effectuate the Fundamental Rights can be relied upon the Courts in India as their facets and be enforced as such.

17) In ***Vishaka Vs. State of Rajasthan***[211]the Supreme Court laid down exhaustive guidelines to prevent sexual harassment of working women in places of their work until a legislation is enacted for its purpose taking the Convention on all forms of discrimination against Women (CEDAW) as its basis.

---

[211] AIR 1997 SC 3011

In appropriate cases, even though the Directives per se cannot be enforced by the Court nor can the Court compel the State to undertake legislation to implement a Directive, the Supreme Court has been issuing various direction to the Government and administrative authorities to take positive action to remove the grievances which have been caused by non implementation of the Directives.

The directives are thus enforced, indirectly, by the Courts by issuing such directions as follows:

1. To issue a notification under the minimum wages Act for the benefit of bonded and other exploited labourers.[212]

2. To set up a joint committee of the Union of India and a State Government concerned as a machinery to supervise and ensure that the poor and needy employees are not exploited by unscrupulous contractors in imposing terms violative of the Directives under Art 38, 41, 42, 43 and or the various provisions of the labour laws.[213]

3. To take various steps for extending the benefit of Art.39-A, to all under trial prisoners.[214]

4. To lay down procedural safeguards in the matter of adoption of Indian children by foreigners in view of Art.39(3)[215].

5. To lay down detailed guidelines for Speedy trial in order to render equal justice in view of Art.39A.[216]

6. To lay down guidelines for trial of rape cases[217]

[212] Mukesh Advani Vs. State of M.P. AIR 1985 SC 1363,
Bandhua Mukti Morcha Vs. Union of India. AIR 1984 SC 802
[213] Ibid
[214] Sheela Barse Vs. State of Maharashtra .AIR 1983 SC 378
[215] Laxmi Kant Panddy Vs. Union of India .AIR 1987 SC 232
[216] Abdul Rahman Antuley Vs. R.S. Nayak .AIR 1992 SC 1630
[217] Delhi Domestic Working Women's Forum Vs. Union of India (1995)1 SCC 14

7. To lay down exhaustive guidelines to prevent sexual harassment of working women in places of their work in view of Art.14 and Art.21 & 39 (e) to (f)[218]

8. To lay down guidelines to prevent air, water and environmental pollution[219]

9. To arrange free legal aid to the poor and needy[220]

10. To protection of monuments and places and objects of national importance[221]

11. To remove the impugned provisions of an act to restore independence of judiciary[222]

Further, two new Chapters i.e IX, IX-A, and two new Schedules Eleven and Twelve were added to the Constitution by 73rd & 74th Amendment in order to give effect to the Directives under Art. 40. Hence, it can be executed through Courts like any other constitutional rights though it is not a fundamental right.

Further, in view of the insertion of a New Art. 21-A, by the 93rdAmendment Act, providing free and compulsory education to all children of age 6 to 14 is declared as Fundamental Right in order to implement one of the directives under Art.45

The above study lead to the following findings that

1. Part IV of the Constitution which deals about Directive Principles of State Policy have imposed duty upon the legislature to implement the directives while making laws in order to

[218] Vishaka Vs. State of Rajasthan AIR1997 SC 3011
[219] M.C. Mehta Vs. Union of India (1986) 2 SCC 176; AIR 1997 SC 735
[220] Bajiban Salambhai Chauhan Vs. UPSRTC (1990) Supp SCC 769
[221] M.C. Mehta Vs. Union of India AIR 1997 SC 735
[222] Pareena Swarup Vs. Union of India 2009 AIR SCW 206

render social, economic and political justice to its citizen as declared in the preamble to the Constitution. The directives are declared as fundamental principles to be followed by the State in the governance of the Country.

2. At the same time, Part III of the Constitution guarantees Fundamental Rights to the citizens and the power of Judicial Review expressly made available with the higher judiciary to protect it from any infringement by State's action. In order to protect the sacrosanctity of the Fundamental Rights, all the Pre Constitutional laws that were inconsistent with the Fundamental Rights were declared void and the State is also further restrained from making any law infringing the fundamental right or taking away the fundamental rights.

3. In the said position, if the Parliament or State legislatures enacts any law inconsistent with the Fundamental Rights, the said law is liable to be declared as 'Unconstitutional' by the Courts even if the said Act was enacted with an intention to give effect to the directive principles since the Courts initially were of the view that the Fundamental Rights are so sacrosanct and the Directive Principles of State Policy have to conform and to run as subsidiary to the Fundamental rights.

4. Hence, the Parliament was left with no other option except to amend the Constitution in order to remove the difficulty in implementing the directive principles. When the said amendments were challenged before the Courts initially, the Courts held that the term 'law' in Art.13 did not include a law made by Parliament under Art.368 of the Constitution of India.

5. However, by the decision of the Supreme Court in Golaknath Vs. State of Punjab, the Amending Acts also met with the same fate of the ordinary legislation since the Supreme Court has given wide interpretation to the word 'law' in Art. 13, which include every branch of law either Statutory or Constitutional.

6. In order to remove the difficulty caused by the said decisions in implementing the Directive Principles, the Parliament enacted 24thAmendment Act and thereby made it clear that the word 'law' in Art.13 shall not include an amendment made to the Constitution under Art.368.

7. The said amendment was challenged before the Supreme Court in ***Kesavanada Bharti Case*** and for the first time the Court's responsibility in so interpreting the Constitution as to ensure implementation of the directives was recognized since the courts also form part of the State as defined under Art.36 r/w. Art.12. The Supreme Court further opines that Parliament is competent to amend the Constitution to over ride or abrogate any of the Fundamental Rights in order to enable the State to implement the Directives so long as the basic structure of the Constitution is not affected.

8. The Courts approach towards the Directive Principles has considerably changed after Kesavananda Bharati case and now the Courts are also bound to implement the directives in view of Art.36 read with Art.12.

9. The Court has given many of the Directives the status of Fundamental Right/ other Constitutional or Statutory rights, by giving wide possible interpretations to the Fundamental Rights or any other Constitutional or Statutory rights in the light of the Directive Principles.

10. The liberal attitude of the Courts in enforcing the Group/Class rights through 'Pro bono publico' proceedings also facilitates the above endeavour.

11. Furthermore, the Courts, in many occasions, in appropriate cases, issued many directions/guidelines and laid down policies to give effect to the directive principles either directly or indirectly in order to remove the grievances which have been caused by non implementation of the Directives.

12. The Amendments made to the Constitution in order to implement the Directive Principles also encourage the Courts to enforce those directives as any other Constitutional Rights though it is not a Fundamental Right.

It should be clear to everyone that the main objectives of the constitution declared under directive principle is to build a welfare society under an egalitarian social order with tranquility.

In view of the above discussions and findings, we can conclude that almost all the Directives have now become executable by the Courts except a few despite the express bar under Art.37. Let us hope for the implementation of the non - implemented directive principles also in the near future.

(C)Enforcement of Fundamental Duties[223]

1.1 *The Fundamental Rights in Part III, the Directive Principles of State Policy in Part IV and the Fundamental Duties in Part IVA form a compendium and have to be read together.*

[223] http://lawmin.nic.in/ncrwc/finalreport/v1ch3.htm

1.2 *It is true that there is no legal sanction provided for violation or non-performance of Fundamental Duties. There is neither specific provision for enforceability nor any specific prohibition. However, Fundamental Duties have an inherent element of compulsion regarding compliance.*

1.3 *Out of the ten clauses in article 51A, five are positive duties and the other five are negative duties. Clauses (b), (d), (f), (h) and (j) require the citizens to perform these Fundamental Duties actively.*

1.4 *It is said that by their nature, it is not practicable to enforce the Fundamental Duties and they must be left to the will and aspiration of the citizens. However, in the case of citizens holding public office, each and all Fundamental Duties can be enforced by suitable legislation and departmental rules of conduct. Appropriate sanctions can be provided for lapse in respect of each Fundamental Duty and it is quite practicable to enforce the sanction against every citizen holding a public office; for instance, departmental promotions can be deferred, increments can be withheld, etc. If an officer takes part in a strike or stalls the proceedings of his institution, he can be made to forgo the salary for that day.*

1.5 Likewise, sanctions can be provided for professional bodies such as the Bar Council of India, the Medical Council of India, the Institute of Chartered Accountants and the Institute of Engineers, etc.

1.6 It is no longer correct to say that Fundamental Duties enshrined in article 51A are not enforceable to ensure their implementation and are a mere reminder. Fundamental Duties have the element of compulsion regarding compliance. What is needed is to enact suitable legislation wherever necessary to require obedience of the duties by the citizens, with legal sanctions. There is need for comprehensive legislation in this area to ensure a faithful and effective implementation of the Fundamental Duties.

1.7 *A number of judicial decisions are available towards the enforcement of certain clauses under Article 51A. Comprehensive legislation is needed for clauses (a), (c), (e), (g) and (i). The remaining 5 clauses, which are exhortation of basic human values, have to be developed amongst citizens through the education system by creating proper and graded curricular input from primary level of education to the higher and professional levels.*

1. Statutory implementation of Fundamental Duties
2. Judicial implementation of Fundamental Duties

1. Statutory implementation of Fundamental Duties

1.1 The Verma Committee was conscious of the fact that any non-operationalization of Fundamental Duties might not necessarily be the lack of concern or non-availability of legal and other enforceable provisions; but it was more a case of lacuna in the strategy of implementation. It, therefore, thought it appropriate to list in brief some of the legal provisions already available in regard to enforcement of Fundamental Duties. A summary of such legal provisions is given below:

i. In order to ensure that no disrespect is shown to the National Flag, Constitution of India and the National anthem, the Prevention of Insults to National Honour Act, 1971 was enacted.

ii. The Emblems and Names (Prevention of Improper Use) Act 1950 was enacted soon after independence, inter alia, to prevent improper use of the National Flag and the National Anthem.

iii. In order to ensure that the correct usage regarding the display of the National Flag is well understood, the instructions issued from time to time on the subject have been embodied in Flag Code of India, which has been made available to all the State Governments, and Union territory Administration (UTs).

iv. There are a number of provisions in the existing criminal laws to ensure that the activities which encourage enmity between different groups of people on grounds of religion, race, place of birth, residence, language, etc. are adequately punished. Writings, speeches, gestures, activities, exercise, drills, etc. aimed at creating a feeling of insecurity or ill-will among the members of other communities, etc. have been prohibited under Section 153A of the Indian Penal Code (IPC).

v. Imputations and assertions prejudicial to the national integration constitute a punishable offence under Section 153 B of the IPC.

vi. A Communal organization can be declared unlawful association under the provisions of Unlawful Activities (Prevention) Act 1967.

vii. Offences related to religion are covered in Sections 295-298 of the IPC (Chapter XV).

viii.Provisions of the Protection of Civil Rights Act, 1955 (earlier the Untouchability (Offences) Act 1955)

ix. Sections 123(3) and 123(3A) of the Representation of People Act, 1951 declares that soliciting of vote on the ground of religion and the promotion or attempt to promote feelings of enmity or hatred between different classes of citizens of India on the grounds of religion, race, caste, community or language is a corrupt practice. A person indulging in a corrupt practice can be disqualified for being a Member of Parliament or a State Legislature under Section 8A of the Representation of People Act, 1951.

2. Judicial implementation of Fundamental Duties

2.1 In ***Chandra Bhavan Boarding and Lodging, Bangalore Vs. The State of Mysore and Anr.***[224], challenge was laid to a notification fixing minimum rates of wages, the problem posed before the court was to strike a balance between two propositions: one, should not a worker be paid, by way of minimum wages, an amount which would enable the two ends meet and to survive: and on the other hand, fixing of minimum wages may result in the industry or the unit being killed taking away its right to exist. The court held that freedom of trade does not mean freedom to exploit. Nor do the provisions of the Constitution are the barriers to progress. They provide a balance for orderly progress towards the social order contemplated by the Preamble of the Constitution. The court held:

"It is a fallacy to think that under our Constitution there are only rights and no duties. While rights conferred under Part-III are fundamental, the directives given under Part-IV are fundamental in the governance of the country. We see no conflict on the whole between the provisions contained in Part-III and Part-IV. They are complimentary and supplementary to each other. The provisions of Part-IV enable the legislatures and the Government to impose various duties on the citizens. The provisions therein are deliberately made elastic because the duties to be imposed on the citizens depend on the extent to which the Directive Principles are implemented. The mandate of the Constitution is to build a welfare society in which justice – social, economic and political, shall inform all institutions of our national life. The hopes and

[224] (1969) 3 SCC 84

aspirations aroused by the Constitution will be belied if the minimum needs of the lowest of our citizens are not met."

2.2 Officers in All-India Services (Administrative, Forest, Police, etc.) were not taking the training seriously resulting in deterioration of the services. Service Rules were amended so as to give weightage to the training and penalize the failure. On a challenge being laid to the constitutionality of the amendment in the Rules in ***Mohan Kumar Singhania & Ors. Vs. Union of India & Ors.***[225], in order to uphold the validity of the amendment, Ratnavel Pandian, J. drew strength from article 51A. Referring to clause (j), which commands every citizen of India to strive towards excellence in all spheres of individual and collective activity so that the nation constantly rises to higher levels of endeavour and achievement, it was held that the effort taken by the Government in giving utmost importance to the training programme of the selectees so that this higher civil service being the topmost service of the country is not wasted and does not become fruitless during the training period is in consonance with the provisions of article 51A (j). The constitutionality of the amendment was, thus, upheld.

2.3 In several cases, the Supreme Court has upheld the validity of laws relating to ecology and environment and has made directions binding the citizens and the State finding the source of power to do so in article 51A. In ***Rural Litigation and Entitlement Kendra & Ors. Vs. A State of Uttar Pradesh & Ors.,***[226] Ranganath Misra, J. held.

---

[225](1992) Supp.1 SCC 594

[226] (1986) Supp. SCC 517

"Preservation of the environment and keeping the ecological balance unaffected is task which not only governments but also every citizen must undertake. It is a social obligation and let us remind every Indian citizen that it is his Fundamental Duty as enshrined in Article 51A (g) of the Constitution."

2.4 In ***Rural Litigation and Entitlement Kendra, Dehradun & Ors. Vs. State of U.P.*** [227], in order to prevent imbalance to ecology and hazard of healthy environment being created due to working of lime-stone quarries, the Supreme Court directed the quarries lessees being cancelled and lime-stone quarries being closed down permanently. The directions were issued in face of fundamental right to trade and business and the right to earn livelihood. Assigning paramount significance to Fundamental Duties and rather placing the Fundamental Duties owing to people at large above the fundamental right of a few individuals the court held that such closure would undoubtedly cause hardship, "but it is a price that has to be paid for protecting and safeguarding the right of the people to live in healthy environment with minimum disturbance of ecological balance and without avoidable hazard to them and to their cattle, homes and agricultural land and undue affectation of air, water and environment".

2.5 In Sachidanand Pandey & Anr. Vs. State of West Bengal & Ors., (1987) 2 SCC 295, the court expressed in unmistakable terms that whenever a problem of ecology is brought before the court, the court is bound to bear in mind article 48A of the Constitution and article 51A (g) which proclaims the Fundamental Duty of every citizen of India to protect and improve the natural environment including forests, lakes, rivers and wild life, and to have compassion for living creatures. Policy decisions taken by State are not ordinarily to be interfered with by the

[227] AIR 1985 SC 652

courts. But if it is the question of giving effect to the Directive Principle and the Fundamental Duty, the court is not to shrug its shoulders and say that priorities are a matter of policy not to be touched by court, the court may always give necessary directions so as to secure implementation of Directive Principles and Fundamental Duties.

2.6 In ***State of Punjab & Ors. Vs. G.S.Gill and Anr.***[228], kindling the spirit of clauses (e) and (j) of article 51A and the Directive Principle contained in article 38 (1), the court reminded the administrators of the government that they too are primarily the citizens and, therefore, their vision should be of national interest. "The primary responsibility of an administrator is to perform his functions in the services of the nation as an enlightened citizen to strengthen a new democratic state. The public administrator should get rid of all mental reservations on narrow considerations of caste, religion, sectional or regional. He should have a wider concern for society as a whole. Otherwise he is not worthy to be an administrator or enlightened citizen to work for others. In public administration, responsibility is of highly personal and moral quality and is not necessarily related to formal status of power, although it is probably true that greater power brings greater responsibility." In short, the court held that the Fundamental Duties oblige the administrators of the government to be good administrators.

2.7 In ***M.C.Mehta (II) Vs. Union of India & Ors***.[229], article 51A containing Fundamental Duties of citizens was read casting duties on the government and for issuing certain directions consistently with article 51A. Directions were:-

[228] (1997) 6 SCC 129
[229] (1998) 1 SCC 471

(i) the Central Government shall direct to the educational institutions throughout India to teach at least for one hour in a week, lessons relating to protection and the improvement of the natural environment including forests, lakes, rivers and wild life in the first ten classes;

(ii) the Central Government shall get text books written for the said purpose and distribute them to the educational institutions free of cost;

(iii) the children shall be taught about the need for maintaining cleanliness and with the cleanliness of the house, both inside and outside and the street in which they live;

(iv) the Central Government shall consider training of teachers who teach this subject by the introduction of short-term courses for such training;

(v) the Central Government, the Government of the States and all the Union Territories shall consider desirability of organizing "Keep the city/town/village clean" week;

(vi) to create a national awareness of the problems faced by the people by the appalling all round deterioration of the environment.

2.8 In ***Vellore Citizens' Welfare Forum Vs. Union of India***[230], and ***Bandkhal and Surajkund Lakes matter,***[231], the Supreme Court recognized 'The Precautionary Principle' and the 'The Polluter pays' principle as essential features of 'Sustainable Development' and part of the environment law of the country. Article 21, Directive Principles and Fundamental Duty clause (g) of article 51A were relied on by the Supreme Court for spelling out a clear mandate to the State to protect and improve the environment and to safeguard the forests and wild life of the country. The court held it mandatory for the State Government to anticipate, prevent and attack the causes of environment degradation.

---

[230] (1996) 5 SCC 647

[231] (1997) 3 SCC 715

2.9 ***State of U.P. Vs. Yamuna Shanker Misra & Anr.***,[232] is an interesting case where the object of writing the confidential reports and making entries in the character rolls were read in the light of article 51(j) as giving an opportunity to a public servant to improve excellence. The net of this Fundamental Duty was spread so wide by the court as to spell out the eternal values of honesty, integrity, good conduct and efficiency getting improved in the performance of public duties and standard of excellence in services constantly rising to higher levels so as to be a successful tool to manage the services with officers of integrity, honesty, efficiency and devotion.

2.10 The State of A.P. appointed a person as Poet laureate in Telugu with an honorarium initially for five years and then for life accompanied by certain attractive perks. The successor government terminated the appointment. The learned poet challenged the termination. Though the High Court did not doubt the eminence and achievement of the petitioner, however, tracing the history of such appointments, the court found that it was not a recognition of merit but, in essence, a royal mirth-maker a reward for solemn flattery for the king. Referring to article 51A (j), Justice P.A.Chaudary said – "I have no hesitation in holding that the wild celestial fire that ever burns in the mortal frame of man should not be quenched either by indifference or mediocracy .... But when the State undertakes to promote excellence it can do so only through the methods which our Constitution permits it to adopt. Rewarding of sycophancy only helps to retard the growth of efficiency and excellence. Conferment of poet Laureateship which more of less looks life conferment of a title may be a constitutional anathema". [233]

[232] (1997) 4 SCC 7
[233] Dr. Dasarathi Vs. State of Andhra Pradesh AIR 1985 AP 136

2.11 Another interesting case is from Calcutta High Court. Syllabus was prescribed for readings in history in the State of West Bengal. West Bengal Head Masters' Association laid challenge to the syllabus as violative of inter-alia article 51A (b) of the Constitution inter alia. The grievance was that the syllabus lays emphasis on studying Bolshevik, Chinese and South-East Asia Revolutions but it does not specifically mention whatsoever on the social, literary, scientific, religious or political Indian Leaders, not the requisite emphasis on different phases of freedom movement in India. The association pleaded a fundamental right to read the Indian history. A Division Bench of the Calcutta High Court in ***West Bengal Head Masters' Association & Anr. Vs. Union of India & Ors.***[234], held that there was no such Fundamental Right,

"Article 51A(b) imposes a duty on every citizen of India to cherish and follow the noble ideals which inspired our national struggle for freedom. The performance of the duty is quite personal to every citizen of India. No duty has been imposed on the State, but on the citizens of India. There is much deference between right and duty. While a right can be claimed against another, duty has to be performed. It is not necessary for us to consider whether the duty imposed on every citizen of India under article 51A of the Constitution can enforced against a citizen or not. A citizen cannot claim that he must be properly equipped by the State so as to enable him to perform his duties under article 51A which does not confer rights but imposes certain duties. So a student cannot claim that he must be taught the Indian history in class VIII so that he can perform his duty under clause (b) of article 51A of the Constitution."

[234] AIR 1983 Calcutta 448

2.12 In ***Bijoe Emmanuel vs State of Kerala***[235]**,** it has been held that there is no provision of law which obliges anyone to sing the National Anthem nor is it disrespectful to the National Anthem if a person who stands up respectfully when the National Anthem is sung does not join the singing. It is true that article 51A (a) of the Constitution enjoins a duty on every citizen of India "to abide by the Constitution and respect its ideals and institutions, the National Flag and the National Anthem". Proper respect is shown to the National Anthem by standing up when the National Anthem is sung. It will not be right to say that disrespect is shown by not joining in the singing. It was observed that there was no law enacted by Parliament making it obligatory to comply with article 51A(a). The Supreme Court allowed the petition filed by the children and directed the authorities to re-admit the children into the school. The court ended their judgment by adding – "our tradition teaches tolerance; our philosophy preaches tolerance; our constitution practices tolerance; let us not dilute it." In another matter the correctness of this decision has been doubted. The matter has been referred to a Constitution Bench of the Supreme Court, which would examine correctness of the decision and also many a relation aspects.

2.13 The Supreme Court in ***Vishaka and others Vs. State of Rajasthan***[236] found it necessary for protection of working women from sexual harassment to lay and by this the classical exercise of the law making powers under article 141 of the Constitution laid:

[235] AIR 1987 SC 8 at pp.751, 752
[236] AIR 1997 SC 3011

"It is necessary and expedient for employers in work places as well as other responsible persons or institutions to observe certain guidelines to ensure the prevention of sexual harassment of women:

(1) The Duty of the Employer or other responsible persons in work places and other institutions:

It shall be the duty of the employer or other responsible persons in work places or other institutions to prevent or deter the commission of acts of sexual harassment and to provide the procedures for the resolution, settlement or prosecution of acts of sexual harassment by taking all steps required.

(2) Definition:

For this purpose, sexual harassment includes such unwelcome sexually determined behaviors (whether directly or by implication) as:

(a) physical contact and advances;

(b) a demand or request for sexual favours;

(c) sexually coloured remarks;

(d) showing pornography;

(e) any other unwelcome physical, verbal or non-verbal conduct of sexual nature.

Where any of these acts is committed in circumstances where under the victim of such conduct has a reasonable apprehension that in relation to the victim's employment or work whether she is drawing salary, or honorarium or voluntary, whether in Government, public or private enterprises such conduct can be humiliating and may constitute a health and safety problem. It is discriminatory for instance when the women has reasonable grounds to believe that her objection would disadvantage her in connection with her employment or work including recruiting or promotion or when it created a hostile work environment. Adverse consequences might be visited if the victim does not consent to the conduct in question or raises any objection thereto.

(3) Preventive Steps:

All employers or persons in charge of work place whether in the public or private sector should take appropriate steps to prevent sexual harassment. Without prejudice to the generality of this obligation they should take the following steps:

(a) Express prohibition of sexual harassment as defined above at the work place should be notified, published and circulated in appropriate ways.

(b) The rules/regulations of Government and Public Sector bodies relating to conduct and discipline should include rules/regulations prohibiting sexual harassment and provide for appropriate penalties in such rules against the offender.

(c) As regards private employers steps should be taken to include the aforesaid prohibitions in the standing orders under the Industrial Employment (Standing Orders) Act, 1946.

(d) Appropriate work conditions should be provided in respect of work, leisure, health and hygiene to further ensure that there is no hostile environment towards women at work places and no employee woman should have reasonable grounds to believe that she is disadvantaged in connection with her employment.

(4) Criminal Proceedings:

Where such conduct amounts to a specific offence under the Indian Penal Code or under any other law, the employer shall initiate appropriate action in accordance with law by making a complaint with the appropriate authority. In particular, it should ensure that victims, or witnesses are not victimized or discriminated against while dealing with complaints of sexual harassment. The victims of sexual harassment should have the option to seek transfer of the perpetrator or their own transfer.

(5) Disciplinary Action:

Where such conduct amounts to misconduct in employment as defined by the relevant service rules, the employer in accordance with those rules should initiate appropriate disciplinary action.

(6) Complaint Mechanism:

Whether or not such conduct constitutes an offence under law or a breach of the service rules, an appropriate complaint mechanism should be created in the employer's organization for redress of the complaint made by the victim. Such complaint mechanism should ensure time bound treatment of complaints.

(7) Complaints Committee:

The complaint mechanism, referred to in (6) above, should be adequate to provide, where necessary, a Complaints Committee, a special counsel or other support service, including the maintenance of confidentiality.

A woman should head the Complaints Committee and not less half of its member should be women. Further, to prevent the possibility of any undue pressure or influence from senior levels, such Complaints Committee should involve a third party, either NGO or other body who is familiar with the issue of sexual harassment.

The Complaints Committee must make an annual report to the Government department concerned of the complaints and action taken by them.

The employers and person on charge will also report on the compliance with the aforesaid guidelines including on the reports of the Complaints Committee to the Government department.

(8) Workers' Initiative:

Employees should be allowed to raise issues of sexual harassment at workers' meeting and in other appropriate forum and it should be affirmatively discussed in Employer-employee Meetings.

(9) Awareness:

Awareness of the rights of female employees in this regard should be created in particular by prominently notifying the guidelines (and appropriate legislation when enacted on the subject) in a suitable manner.

(10) Third Party Harassment:

Where sexual harassment occurs as a result of an act or omission by any third party or outsider, the employer and person in charge will take all steps necessary and reasonable to assist the affected person in terms of support and preventive action.

(11) The Central/State Governments are requested to consider adopting suitable measures including legislation to ensure that the guidelines laid down by this order are also observed by the employers in Private sector.

(12) These guidelines will not prejudice any rights available under the Protection of Human Rights Act, 1993.

Accordingly, we direct that the above guidelines and norms would be strictly observed in all work places for the preservation and enforcement of the right to gender equality of the working women. These directions would be binding and enforceable in law until suitable legislation is enacted to occupy the field. These Writ Petitions are disposed of accordingly."

2.14 It was also observed that these guidelines would not prejudice any rights available under the Protection of Human Right Act, 1993. These were the most effective measures for enforcement of the Fundamental Duties; in particular to renounce practices derogatory to the dignity of women – a Fundamental Duty enshrined in clause (e) of article 51A, in the effectuation of that duty.

Chapter VIII

Concluding Observation

The Constitution of India preamble with luscent Solemnity Pledged itself to secure socio-economic justice to all its citizens. The preambular promise of socio-economic justice was translated by the founding fathers in to the various provisions of Part III and IV dealing with Fundamental Rights and Directive Principles respectively. The incorporation of Fundamental Rights and Directive Principles in our Constitution was the result of our struggle for independence. In fact, the history of our country's struggle for independence was the story of a battle between the Forces of socio-economic exploitation and the deprived people of varying degrees.

With the advent of the British Raj, the Indian economy deteriorated day by day. At that time leaders demanded not only the political rights and civil liberties but also socio-economic rights also. At that time, no distinction between the two kinds of rights was made. The hopes aspirants, ideals and precepts of social policy precipitated first in the famous "Karachi Resolution" which was not only the declaration of rights but the first humanitarian manifesto of India.

Independence opened a new chapter in the history of India. The Constituent Assembly Separated the justiciable fundamental rights from the non justiciable Directive Principles and emphasised the significance of both. The Separation of was made because of the difficulty involved in enforcing the socio economic rights. On the other hand, fundamental rights of Part III were made enforceable so as to prevent the state from encroaching the individual liberties which were essential for the development with full human dignity. But in order to highlight importance of

Directive Principles of Part IV, they were made fundamental in the governance of the country" and it was further provided that it shall be the duty of the state to apply these principles in making laws. The state was required to achieve most of the directives in the shortest possible time and all the directives were to serve as goals for making laws.

The founding-fathers did not see any conflict between the justiciable fundamental rights and non justiciable directive principles. There were considered as complementary and supplementary to each other. There is no antithesis between them.

The nature and significance of the Directive Principles was also debated in the Assembly. They were rightly regarded as the germs of socialistic government and Part IV enshrining them was rightly considered as the most cardinal, important and creative part of the Constitution. These directives enjoins the character of obligations, rights, duties and principles. The term 'endeavour' used in various articles of Part IV is in the nature of command and the phrase 'Primary duty' as binding duty. Even the word strive has been expressed in the nature of binding character.

It is very easy to confine to Fundamental Rights only but the real liberty will have no meaning unless there is social and economic liberty. In fact the Directive Principles are more fundamental than Fundamental Rights. Because what is fundamental in the governance of the country can not be less fundamental to what is fundamental to an individual. Also the ideals enshrined in Directive Principles,that is justice, social, economic and political are loftier in conception and seek to secure to the individual tangible benefits of great significance than Fundamental Rights. Directive Principles represents the goals of an egalitarian social order which the state required to achieve. The Fundamental Rights will remain only as paper tigers for those, who do not have the bare necessities of life like food, clothes and shelter. The sole aim of Directive Principles is to provide socio-economic justice to all and create such conditions in which the enjoyment of Fundamental Rights can become a living reality for not only few but for all.

The non justiciable nature of the Directive Principles leads some people to think that they are having inferior status as compared to the Fundamental Rights. H.M. Seervai, a leading jurist of the country, said that *'the Directive Principles are not a part of the supreme law and hence they should be deleted from the Constitution'*. It is submitted, that, this view of Seervai is not tenable, because he has not viewed the Directive Principles in the historical context and the purpose for which they were enacted. The very fact that they were incorporated in the Constitution by founding fathers makes them a part of supreme law of the land. And if we apply only the test of enforcement as the test for determining the nature of Constitutional mandates, then we are left with too narrow a view of the Constitutional law whether or not a particular mandate of the Constitution is enforceable by court, has no bearing on the importance of that mandate. It would be wrong to say that the mandates of Part IV of lesser significance than the mandates under Part III of the Constitution. In fact both Part III and IV are fundamental and they fertilize each other.

Immediately after the commencement of the Constitution both the legislature and the judicature entered in the boxing ring and could not keep them out of the status controversy of Fundamental Rights and Directive Principles. During the first phase, the Supreme Court followed a purely technical and legislative approach. In *Champakam Dorairajan* [237], the Supreme Court subordinated the Directive Principles to Fundamental Rights. Thus it gave almost a death blow to the most dynamic Part of the Constitution. The parliament passed the most dynamic Part of the Constitution. The parliament passed the first amendment to undo *Champakam Dorairajan*. It also changes the dimension of Directive Principles. During the second phase there was change in

[237] State of Madras V. Champakam Dorairajan, AIR 1951 SC 226.

the judicial attitudc towards Directive Principles. *In M.H. Qureshi V. State of Bihar*[238] *and in re Kerla Education Bill*[239], the Supreme Court admitted the fact that although Directive Principles were non justiciable in character, the courts were to recognised their importance for the simple reason that they formed a vital Part of the Constitutional document. The Supreme Court Propounded the theory of harmonious construction of Part III and IV. The Supreme Court in *Golaknath V. State of Punjab*[240] again made Fundamental Right as transcendental, inalienable and 'Sacranct'. In this case, again Supreme Court followed technical and legislative approach towards Directive Principles.

Consequently, in the third phase the parliament enacted series of Constitutional amendments and established supremacy to the economic directives contained in article 39(b) and (c) by adding a new article 31-C into the Constitution. This was the first direct parliamentary attempt to give primary to certain directives over certain Fundamental Rights. In *Kesavanand Bharati,* Supreme Court first time expressly recognised the Supremacy of the socio economic directives over the Fundamental Rights.

In the fourth phase, the parliament passed forty second amendment to the Constitution and amended article 31-C thereby providing that if a law is made to give effect to "all or any of the directive principles", then that shall not be declared as unconstitutional on the grounds that if violated Fundamental Rights given in articles 14, 19 and 31. It is further submitted that in Part IV all the Directive Principles are of equal importance and if two of the directives could be given supremacy over certain Fundamental Rights, why the remaining directives can't be given the same status.

---

[238] M.H. Qureshi V. State of Bihar, AIR 1958 SC 731.
[239] AIR 1985 SC 956
[240] AIR 1967 SC 864

Now the situation has changed. Today legislative and Judicature is also in favour of enforcement of Directive Principles. In its recent judgments Court has declared many directives as Fundamental Rights and have enforced them. Today many directives, e.g. *Rights to Education*, *Right to Food, Right to Legal Aid, Right to Health* is recognised as Fundamental Rights under Article 21. Government also recognised Right to Education as Fundamental Right by inserting a new Article 21-A. This article is inserted by 86th Constitution Amendment Act, 2002. Equal pay for equal work is also recognised us Fundamental Rights by both legislature and judicature.

Suggestions:

On the 31st March 2002, *M.N. Venkatachaliah Committee*[241] suggested some directives as Fundamental Rights in Chapter III of the Indian Constitution. These directives are *Right to Work (article 21-C), Right to Justice and Legal Aid (article 30-B), Right to Education (article 30-C) and Right to Safe Drinking water, clean environment etc (Article 30-D) and Rights of children(Article* 24-A).

The committee recommended to add following Directive Principles as Fundamental Rights:

(i) Right to Work (Art. 21-C):

The commission recommends that a new article 21-C may be added to make *it obligatory on the state to bring suitable legislation for ensuring the right to rural wage employment for a minimum of eighty days in a year*[242].

---

[241] Report of the National Committee to Review the Working of Indian Constitution., Vol-I, Universal Publication.
[242] Supra Note 5 at 63

(ii)Right to Justice and legal aid (Art. 30-A, Art. 30-B)

The commission recommends that after art.30 the following art. should be added as Article 30-A. Article 30-A provides :

(a) *Everyone has a right to have any dispute that can be resolve by the application of law decided in a fair public hearing before an independent court or, where appropriate another independent and impartial tribunal or forum.*

(b) *The right to access to courts shall be deemed to include the right to reasonably speedy and effective justice in all matters before the courts, tribunals or other forum and the states shall take all reasonable stapes to achieve the said object.*[243]

Commission again said that legal aid is essential for effective implementation of the various rights included in Part III to help the needy and the indigent. The commission also recommends that article 39-A in part IV be shifted to part III as a new Article 30-B. Article 30-B provides equal justice and free legal aid. According to Venkatchaliah commission article 30-B provides that

"*the state shall secure that operation of the legal system promotes justice, on a basis of equal opportunity, and shall, in particular, provide free legal aid, by suitable legislation or schemes or in any other way, to ensure that opportunities for securing justice are not denied to any citizen by reason of economic or other disabilities.*[244]"

(iii) Right to Education (Art. 30-C):

[243] Ibid

[244] Supra Note 5 at 64

The commission recommends that a new article 30-C may be added for right to education. Article 30-C provides that *every child shall have the right to free education until he completes the age of fourteen years, and in the case of girls and members of the scheduled castes and scheduled tribes, until they complete the age of eighteen years*[245].

(iv)Right of Children (Art. 24-A):

The commission recommends that a new article 24-A may be added for rights of children. Article 24-A may be added for rights of children Article 24-A provides that *every child shall have the right to care and assistance in basic needs and protection from all forms of neglect, harm and exploitation*[246].

(v) Right to safe drinking water, clean environment (Art. 30-D):

The commission recommends that after the proposed article 30-C, the following article may be added as a article 30-D: *Every person shall have the right to safe drinking water and to an environment that is not harmful to one's health or well being*[247]. After this recommendation parliament inserted the right to education in new article 21-A.[248] Right to work is also implemented by stature, namely, National Rural Employment Guarantee Act. 2005.

Conclusions

---

[245] Ibid at 66
[246] Ibid
[247] Supra Note 5 at 67
[248] Article 21-A, Inserted by the Constitution (Eighty Sixth Amendments) Act, 2002

The constitution framers inserted Directive principles in the constitution so that the state should take endeavour towards making a welfare state. Though there has been a considerable improvement in understanding the importance of Directive principles but still there is a long way to go and it is the duty of judiciary to understand the essence of these principles and interpret them in such a way so as to make them at par with Fundamental rights. Though Directive principles cannot be claimed as a matter of right but state is under an obligation to provide its citizens with all those facilities like education, a descent livelihood, health, shelter and many other things which are essential to live a good life and all these issues are undoubtedly dealt in Directive principles and the only thing to be done is to realize their essence and implement them in a proper manner so as to achieve the goal of a welfare state and it calls for the efforts of all the three wings i.e. Parliament, Executive and Judiciary .All the three have to work together and transparently to promote the aim of constitution framers lying in Directive principles. Especially the Judiciary has to give a harmonious construction while deciding a case involving both fundamental rights and Directive principles so that the spirit of both is maintained and one is not overridden by other as was done in a very celebrated case of *Kesavananda Bharti v. State of kerala* wherein the court held that: *there are rights which are inherent in humans because they are human beings*. As the preamble says, it was to secure the basic human rights like equality and liberty that the people gave unto themselves the constitution which also aims at securing justice political, social and Economic. Hence the moral rights embodied in Part fourth of the constitution are equally essential, the only difference being that cannot be enforced in a court of law, but nevertheless they are essential for the proper governance of the country and all the organs including the Judiciary are bound to enforce Directive principles.

Bibliography

Document

All India Reporters

Constituent Assembly Debates, Vol. I to IX

The Constitution of India

Supreme Court Cases

Venkatchaliah Committee Report, 2002, Vol.1 & 2

Books

Austin, Granville : The Indian Constitution :Cornerstore of a Nation. Bombay, Oxford University Press, 1979.

Basu, D.D. : Commentary on the Constitution of India

Chander, Shailja : Justice V.R. Krishna Iyer on Fundamental Rights and Directive Principles. New Delhi, Deep and Deep Publications, 1998.

Chaudhari, A.S. : Constitutional Rights and Limitations. Allahabad, The law book Co. (Pvt.) Ltd., 1997.

Dubey, M.P. : Role of Supreme Court in Indian Constitution. New Delhi. Deep and Deep Publication, 1987.

Gledhill, Allan : Fundamental Rights in India. London, Stenvens and sons, 1956.

Gokulesh Sharma, Dr. : Indianization of Rights and Duties. New Delhi, Manas Publication, 2003.

Hasan, Shariful : Supreme Court: Fundamental Rights and Directive Principles New Delhi, Deep and Deep Publication, 1981.

Hegde, K.S. :The Directive Principles of State Policy in the Constitution of India. Delhi, 1972.

Hidaytullah,M. :Constitutional Law of India. Vol-I, S.K. Agrawal(ed.).New Delhi, Arnold Heinmann Publishers, 1984

Jain, M.P. : Indian Constitutional Law. Nagpur, wadhwa and co., 2005

Jaswal, Dr. P.S. : Directive Principles Jurisprudence and socio-economic justice in India. New Delhi, A.P.H. Publishing Corporation, 1996.

Kapur, A.C. : Constitutional History of India. New Delhi, S. Chand and Co. ltd., 1985.

Laskar, S.I. : Directive Principles of State Policy in Indian Constitution. New Delhi, Deep and Deep Publications, 1988.

Markandan, K.C. : Directive Principles of State Policy in the Indian Constitution. Jalandhar, A.B.S. Publishers, 1987.

Markandan, K.C. : Directive Principles in the Indian Constitution. New Delhi, Allied Publisher, 1966.

Mishra, Shashi, P. : Fundamental Rights and the Supreme Court : Reasonableness of Restrictions. New Delhi, Deep and Deep Publication, 1985.

Pandey, J.N. : Constitutional Law of India. Allahabad, Central Law Agency, 2006.

Paranjape, N.V. : Role of Directive Principles under Indian Constitution. Allahabad, Central Law Agency, 1975.

Pylee, M.V. : Constitutional Government in India. Bombay, Asia Publishing house, 1965.

Rao, B. Shiva : The framing of India's Constitution : Selected documents. Bombay, N.M. Tripathi Publication, 1968.

Rau, B.N. : India's Constitution in the making. Bombay, Allied Publishers, 1963.

Seervai, H.M. : Constitutional Law of India. Bombay, N.M. Tripathi Publication, 1981.

Verma, Manju : The Directive Principles of the Indian Constitution (with special preferences to Bihar). New Delhi, Janaki Publication, 1998.

Articles

Baxi, Upendr : Directive Principles and Sociology of Indian Law – A Reply to Dr. Jagat Narain, Vol. 11. 1969, J.I.L.L., P. 245.

HegdeK.S. : Directive Principles of State Policy in the Constitution of India. Vol.50, (1971)1 SCJ, P.12.

Jethmalani, Ram : Fundamental Rights versus Directive Principles, Vol. VIII (3) 1981, Journal of Bar Council of India, P.392.

Minattur, Joseph : Directive Principles: The Irish Example, vol. II, 1978, CULR, P.331.

Minattur, Joseph : The Unenforceable Directives.1973,KLT(J.L.),P. 104.

Narain, Jagat : Judicial Law making and the Place of Directive Principles in Indian Constitution,Vol.27,1985, JILI, P.198.

Ramachandran, V.G. : Significance of Directive Principles in the Indian Constitution, Vol. VII 1955, SCJ, P.233.

Rami Reddy, S. Sundara : Fundamentalness of Fundamental Rights and Directive Principles in the Indian Constitution, vol X, 1980,JILI, P.399.

Sharma, G.S : Concept of leadership implicit in the Directive Principles of State Policy in Indian Constitution, vol.7, 1965, P.173.

Tripathi, P.K : Directive Principles of State Policy : The Lawyer's Approach to them Hitherto Parochial Injurious & Unconstitutional, vol. XVII, 1957, S.C.J., P.7.

Newspaper

Dainik Jagaran, Varanasi

Hindustan Times, Lucknow

The Hindu, New Delhi

The Indian Express,New Delhi

The Times of India, New Delhi

Internet Materials

www. practical lawyer.com

www.indlaw.com

www.jstor.org

www.manupatra.com

www.supremecourtonline.com

www.wikipedia.org

http://lawmin.nic.in/ncrwc/finalreport/v1ch3.htm